A HISTORY OF
THE KING'S SERJEANTS AT LAW IN IRELAND:
HONOUR RATHER THAN ADVANTAGE?

IN THIS SERIES*

1 *Brehons, Serjeants and Attorneys: Studies in
the History of the Irish Legal Profession* (1990)

2 Colum Kenny, *King's Inns and the Kingdom
of Ireland: The Irish 'Inn of Court',
1541–1800* (1992)

3 Jon G. Crawford, *Anglicizing the
Government of Ireland: The Irish Privy
Council and the Expansion of Tudor Rule,
1556–1578* (1993)

4 *Explorations in Law and History: Irish Legal
History Society Discourses, 1988–1994* (1995)

5 W.N. Osborough, *Law and the Emergence of
Modern Dublin: A Litigation Topography for a
Capital City* (1996)

6 Colum Kenny, *Tristram Kennedy and the Revival
of Irish Legal Training, 1835–1885* (1996)

7 Brian Griffin, *The Bulkies: Police and Crime
in Belfast, 1800–1865* (1997)

8 Éanna Hickey, *Irish Law and Lawyers in
Modern Folk Tradition* (1999)

9 A.R. Hart, *A History of the King's Serjeants at Law
in Ireland: Honour rather than Advantage?* (2000)

ALSO AVAILABLE

The Irish Legal History Society (1989)

* Volumes 1–7 are published by Irish Academic Press.

A History of the King's Serjeants at Law in Ireland: Honour rather than Advantage?

A.R. HART

FOUR COURTS PRESS
in association with
THE IRISH LEGAL HISTORY SOCIETY

Typeset in 10.5 pt on 13 pt Plantin by
Carrigboy Typesetting Services, County Cork for
FOUR COURTS PRESS LTD
Fumbally Court, Fumbally Lane, Dublin 8, Ireland
e-mail: info@four-courts-press.ie
and in North America for
FOUR COURTS PRESS
c/o ISBS, 5804 N.E. Hassalo Street, Portland, OR 97213.

A catalogue record for this title is available
from the British Library.

ISBN 1–85182–528–2

Printed in Great Britain by
MPG Books, Bodmin, Cornwall

To Mary

Contents

List of illustrations

Illustrations appear between pp. 112 and 113.

CREDITS

No. 1: private collection; Nos. 2, 4, 5, 16: Courtesy of the National Gallery of Ireland; Nos. 3, 6–10: Courtesy of the National Library of Ireland; Nos. 11–13, 19, 21: Courtesy of the Executive Council of the Inn of Court of Northern Ireland; Nos. 14, 17, 18: Courtesy of the Honorable Society of King's Inns; No. 15: Courtesy of the National Portrait Gallery; Nos. 20, 22, 23: Courtesy of Mrs Laura Hely.

Abbreviations

Anal Hib	*Analecta Hibernica*
B	baron of the exchequer
Ball, *Judges*	F.E. Ball, *The judges in Ireland, 1221–1921*. 2 vols.
Baker, *Serjeants at law*	J.H. Baker, *The order of the serjeants at law*
Bradshaw, *The dissolution of the religious orders in Ireland*	Brendan Bradshaw, *The dissolution of the religious orders in Ireland under Henry VIII*
Brand, 'The judges of the lordship of Ireland'	Paul Brand, 'The birth of a colonial judiciary: the judges of the lordship of Ireland, 1210–1377', in W.N. Osborough (ed.), *Explorations in law and history: Irish Legal History Society discourses, 1988–1994*
Brand, 'The legal profession in the lordship of Ireland'	Paul Brand, 'The early history of the legal profession of the lordship of Ireland', in Daire Hogan and W.N. Osborough (ed.), *Brehons, serjeants and attorneys: studies in the history of the Irish legal profession*
BL, Add. MS	British Library, Additional manuscripts
Blackburne, *Life of Francis Blackburne*	Edward Blackburne, *Life of the rt. hon. Francis Blackburne*
BNL	*Belfast Newsletter*
Brehons, serjeants and attorneys	Daire Hogan and W.N. Osborough (ed.), *Brehons, serjeants and attorneys: studies in the history of the Irish legal profession*

Bolton, *The Irish Act of Union*	G.C. Bolton, *The passing of the Irish Act of Union: a study in parliamentary politics*
C	Conservative
Cal. Carew MSS.	*Calendar of the Carew manuscripts preserved in the archiepiscopal library at Lambeth.* 6 vols.
Cal. pat. rolls Ire.	*Calendar of the patent rolls of Ireland*
Cal. S. P. dom.	*Calendar of state papers, domestic series*
Cal. S. P. Ire.	*Calendar of the state papers relating to Ireland*
CB	chief baron of the exchequer
CCS	chief crown solicitor (NAI)
CJ	chief justice
Clarendon, *State letters*	*The state letters of Henry, earl of Clarendon.* 2 vols.
Commons' jn. Ire.	*Journals of the house of commons of the kingdom of Ireland* (1796 ed.)
CP	common pleas
DG	*Dublin Gazette*
DNB	*Dictionary of national biography*
EHR	*English Historical Review*
Ellis, *Tudor Ireland*	S.G. Ellis, *Tudor Ireland: crown, community and the conflict of culture, 1470–1603*
Explorations in law and history	W.N. Osborough (ed.), *Explorations in law and history: Irish Legal History Society discourses, 1988–1994*
Hand, *English law in Ireland*	G.J. Hand, *English law in Ireland, 1290–1324*
HMC, rep.	*Historical Manuscripts Commission, report*

Hughes, *Patentee officers*	*Patentee officers of Ireland, 1173–1826*, ed. J.L.J. Hughes
IHS	*Irish Historical Studies*
Ir L R	Irish Law Reports
ILT & SJ	*Irish Law Times and Solicitors' Journal*
J	justice
KB	king's bench
L	Liberal
L. & P. Hen. VIII	*Letters and papers, foreign and domestic, Henry VIII.* 21 vols.
Liber mun. pub. Hib.	Rowley Lascelles, *Liber munerum publicorum Hiberniae.* 2 vols.
LR Ch App	Law Reports Chancery Appeals
Lynch, *The legal institutions in reign of Henry II*	William Lynch, *A view of the legal institutions, honorary hereditary officers, and feudal baronies established in Ireland during the reign of Henry II*
Lords' jn. Ire.	*Journal of the house of lords of Ireland*
King, *The state of the protestants in Ireland*	William King, *The state of the protestants in Ireland under the late King James' government.* 3rd ed., 1692
NAI	National Archives of Ireland
NI	Northern Ireland Law Reports
NILQ	*Northern Ireland Legal Quarterly*
NLI	National Library of Ireland
OP	Official Papers (NAI)
Ormonde MSS.	*Calendar of the manuscripts of the marquess of Ormonde, preserved at Kilkenny Castle.* 11 vols.

Penal era and golden age	Thomas Bartlett and D.W. Hayton (ed.), *Penal era and golden age: essays in Irish history, 1690–1800*
PRONI T.	Public Record Office of Northern Ireland – Transcript
QB	queen's bench
RIA Proc	*Proceedings of the Royal Irish Academy*
Richardson & Sayles, *Admin. Ire.*	H.G. Richardson and G.O. Sayles, *The administration of Ireland, 1172–1377*
Rot.pat.Hib.	*Rotulorum patentium et clausorum cancellariae Hiberniae calendarium*, ed. E. Tresham
Sayles, *Select cases in the king's bench*	G.O. Sayles, *Select cases in the court of king's bench in the reign of Edward III*
Smyth, *Law officers*	C.J. Smyth, *Chronicle of the law officers of Ireland*
S.P. Hen. VIII	*State papers, Henry VIII.* 11 vols.
Strafford, *Letters and dispatches*	*The earl of Strafford's letters and dispatches*, ed. William Knowler
Stat. Ire., Hen. VI	*Statute rolls of the parliament of Ireland, reign of King Henry VI*, ed. H.F. Berry
Stat. Ire., 1–12 Ed. IV	*Statute rolls of the parliament of Ireland, 1–12 Edward IV*, ed. H.F. Berry
TCD	Trinity College, Dublin
U	Unionist

Preface

WHEN I STARTED work on the king's serjeants at law in Ireland in the autumn of 1987, I thought that I would be able to gather sufficient information for a brief essay in a relatively short period of time. Both assumptions proved to be hopelessly wrong, and as the years went by, there were times when I wondered if I would ever bring my researches to a conclusion.

I can only offer as a partial excuse for the prolonged gestation of this work that although the neglect of Irish public records prior to the nineteenth century, and the destruction of the Four Courts in 1922, meant that an immense quantity of legal records has not survived, nevertheless there is a huge amount of published material now available, as well as much unpublished material in various archives throughout the British Isles, all of which throw light on many aspects of Irish legal history. In 1960 in the introduction to his *Notes on Irish legal history* the late Professor Newark wrote that

... for the most part the original material for the history of the early legal system in Ireland was destroyed. In some cases gaps can be made good from records still preserved in England, and the task of reconstructing the story, though heavy, is not impossible.

Unfortunately, the task of reconstruction, although fascinating at times, can take a disproportionate amount of time for the amateur historian.

I am indebted to those who helped my researches in many ways: Jonathan Armstrong, librarian of King's Inns; Cregan Boyd; Miriam Dudley (then librarian to the Bar Library); Ivan Ewart of the Queen's University of Belfast Audio-Visual Unit; Brendan Garland; J.J.S. Grey; Jeffry Lefroy; J.I. McGuire; Dan MacLaughlin; and the staff of the many libraries and archives whose collections I consulted. In particular, I would like to thank the staff of the Irish Collection of the Linenhall Library and the staff of the Public Record Office of Northern Ireland. These institutions contain a great deal of published, original and transcribed material of great value to the legal historian.

I should also like to express my thanks to the following individuals and institutions who granted permission to quote from original documents in their possession: the Archivist (Modern Collections), Record Office, House of Lords; the Honorable Society of King's Inns; the Board of Trinity College, Dublin; the British Library; Council of Trustees, National Library of Ireland; the County and Diocesan Archivist, Derbyshire Record Office; Deputy Keeper of the Records, Public Record Office of Northern Ireland; Dublin Corporation; the earl of Donoughmore; Jeffry Lefroy, esq.; the marquess of Tavistock and the Trustees of the Bedford Estate; the National Archives of Ireland; the Trustees of the Chatsworth Settlement; the Trustees of the National Library of Scotland; the Surrey Record Office; the Syndics of the University of Cambridge Library; and the University of Nottingham Library.

I must also express my thanks to those who gave permission to reproduce various portraits and photographs. Mrs Laura Hely, the last surviving daughter of Serjeant Sullivan, kindly gave permission to reproduce the photograph of her father, the drawings of 'Johnny Moriarty' and 'The king's serjeants' which first appeared in Serjeant Sullivan's *Old Ireland: reminiscences of an Irish KC*. The National Gallery of Ireland, the National Library of Ireland, the National Portrait Gallery, the Honorable Society of King's Inns and the Executive Council of the Inn of Court of Northern Ireland all generously gave permission to reproduce items in their possession.

I owe a particular debt to several people whose comments helped to prevent me from making many mistakes and did much to improve the final text. His Honour Judge Martin QC and Daire Hogan each took the trouble to read much of the text and made many helpful comments. Dr Paul Brand FBA not only read the whole text and made many perceptive suggestions, but generously shared his enormous knowledge of the early common law in Ireland and pointed me to many references which had escaped my attention. Throughout my researches, Professor Nial Osborough drew my attention to several sources and possible lines of enquiry, before performing the invaluable role of editor with his customary erudition and tact, suggesting many improvements in the text. Any errors and imperfections which remain are solely my responsibility.

Finally, I would like to express my gratitude to my long-suffering wife and children. I suspect that they often wondered whether this project really existed, or was merely an excuse to spend week-ends and days on holiday avoiding them, on the pretext of going to yet another library to 'look something up'. My debt to their forbearance is incalculable and can never be repaid.

Introduction

DESPITE EXISTING FOR almost 700 years until its final extinction with the death of Serjeant A.M. Sullivan, QC in 1959, the office of the king's serjeant – or the king's serjeant at law in Ireland to give its full title – has received surprisingly little attention from writers on Irish legal history in recent years, even though the great majority of the 183 individuals known to have held office as king's serjeant later achieved high judicial office. Not only were the majority amongst some of the most distinguished members of the Irish bar, but many were also significant political figures, men as varied in character as Sir Maurice Eustace, prime serjeant and speaker of the Irish house of commons, a close confidant of Ormond, who was imprisoned during the Interregnum before becoming chancellor upon the restoration of Charles II; Alan Brodrick, solicitor general, attorney general, twice speaker of the Irish commons, chancellor, ultimately Viscount Midleton and the leading political figure in early eighteenth-century Ireland; John Hely-Hutchinson, prime serjeant for twelve years prior to his appointment as provost of Trinity College, Dublin in 1774; and John Scott, later earl of Clonmell, who, after his dismissal as attorney general in 1782, was content to return to office as prime serjeant for a few months before becoming chief justice of the king's bench in 1784.

The importance of the king's serjeants was recognized in the nineteenth century by Constantine Smyth, whose *Chronicle of the law officers of Ireland*[1] contained much useful information about the serjeants as well as valuable succession lists. In his classic study of the Irish judiciary, *The judges in Ireland, 1221–1921*,[2] published over eighty years later, Elrington Ball often referred to, and recognised, the professional and political standing of the serjeants (and the present study has drawn upon both works), but their effective disappearance from the Irish scene after 1922 and decline in status even before that have, no doubt, contributed to the serjeants being virtually ignored by more recent writers.

---

1   London, 1839.
2   2 vols., London, 1926.

This history was prompted by the tantalizing few references to the Irish serjeants in Professor Baker's *The order of the serjeants at law*,[3] the definitive study of the origin and history of the order of the serjeants at law in England. I have incorporated and revised material which initially appeared in 'The king's serjeants at law in Ireland: a short history'[4] and 'The king's serjeant at law in Tudor Ireland'[5] (which, with some slight alterations, is reproduced here as chapter 2). It soon became apparent that, despite the paucity of court and other records due to the destruction of Irish official records over the centuries, much material has survived which not only throws light upon the purely legal functions of the king's serjeants, but illustrates the way in which the legal and political functions of the office were inextricably intertwined. It is clear that, during the eighteenth century in particular, the prime serjeant was seen as a leading parliamentary figure and a prominent, though often unreliable, member of the Irish administration.

Recent studies[6] under the auspices of the Irish Legal History Society have examined the significance of events involving Irish lawyers and judges at various times during the nineteenth century. I have tried, therefore, to place the serjeants not just in the purely legal context, but to consider their significance in the wider political and historical context wherever possible, and so I have included some material of a general historical nature. In doing so, I gratefully acknowledge the work of those historians upon whose writings on Irish history I have drawn. In particular, like many others who have considered the early history of the common law in Ireland, my debt to the writings of the late H.G. Richardson and Professor G.O. Sayles is enormous, as it is to the work of Professor Geoffrey Hand and Dr Paul Brand on the same period.

The present work has been divided into three parts. Part One traces the king's serjeants from their origins in the second half of the

3   Selden Society, suppl. series 5 (London, 1984).
4   See W.N. Osborough (ed.), *Explorations in law and history: Irish Legal History Society discourses, 1988–1994* (Dublin, 1995).
5   Daire Hogan and W.N. Osborough (ed.), *Brehons, serjeants and attorneys: studies in the history of the Irish legal profession* (Dublin, 1990).
6   Jacqueline Hill, 'The legal profession and the defence of the *ancien régime* in Ireland, 1790–1840'; Daire Hogan, 'Vacancies for their friends: judicial appointments in Ireland, 1866–1867': both in *Brehons, serjeants and attorneys*; Colum Kenny, 'Irish ambition and English preference in chancery appointments, 1827–1841: the fate of William Conyngham Plunket', in *Explorations in law and history*.

thirteenth century and examines their professional, administrative, judicial and political roles in a broadly chronological fashion throughout the succeeding centuries. Part Two consists of a succession list showing the dates upon which all those who can be identified as king's serjeants were appointed and their terms of office, whilst Part Three contains brief biographical details of the professional and political careers of each serjeant.

PART ONE

CHAPTER ONE

The king's serjeant and the legal system of the medieval Irish lordship

THE ORIGIN OF THE office of the king's serjeant at law in Ireland can be traced directly to the appointment, between 1261 and 1265, of Roger Owen to represent the king's interests in the courts of the lordship of Ireland. In a petition which was probably sent to Edward I (who had been lord of Ireland at the time of Owen's appointment but was now king of England as well) early in 1275, Owen described himself as 'serviens domini regis' or king's serjeant, and asserted that he had never received the fee which he had been promised for his services, claiming that had he acted instead for Irish magnates, he would have been well rewarded.[1] Not only was Owen the first person known to be employed by the king for this purpose in Ireland, but he was one of the first to be so employed in England or Ireland. As such, his appointment is significant as evidence of the existence of an emerging legal profession within the English lordship of Ireland, itself in a process of expansion and development following the arrival of the Anglo-Norman invaders less than a century before.

Owen said that he was retained 'ad placita sua in Hibernia prosequenda et defendenda', that is to prosecute and defend the king's pleas in Ireland. To appreciate the implications of this phrase, it is necessary to view Owen's appointment in the context of the development of the common law and the legal profession in both England and Ireland during the thirteenth century.

---

1   H.G. Richardson and G.O. Sayles, *The administration of medieval Ireland 1172–1377* (Dublin, 1963), pp. 40 and 230. The petition which appears at p. 230 omits the phrase 'ubi dictus Rogerus magnum sallarium de magnatibus Hiberniae potuit recepisse': see G.J. Hand, *English law in Ireland 1290–1324* (Cambridge, 1967), p. 49 n. 2. However, Owen did act for other clients. He had a retainer of 40s. a year from 1275 from the chapter of St Patrick's cathedral, in both secular and spiritual matters, which indicates that he also acted as a canon lawyer. *Crede mihi: the most ancient register book of the archbishops of Dublin before the Reformation*, ed. J.T. Gilbert (Dublin, 1897), p. 113 no. cxxi. I owe this reference to Dr Brand.

7

If a litigant was not present in court on those occasions when his case was called, then, if he was the plaintiff, his case would be dismissed and his sureties amerced (fined) or, if he was the defendant, judgment would be given against him for that stage of the process. A litigant was permitted to appoint someone to appear on his behalf if he could not appear in person, and this person was referred to as his attorney. Whilst the attorney's function was initially confined to answering on behalf of the litigant, it became common for the attorney to take a number of procedural steps on behalf of his client. These included obtaining the correct writ to initiate the action, continuing the process by ensuring that the necessary entries were made in the court records to show that the plaintiff had been represented, as well as delivering the writ to the sheriff. The attorney was thus retained 'ad prosequendum et defendendum' and his appointment recorded in the plea rolls of the court. Although it was not necessary for an attorney to have any previous experience in that capacity, it was still common for an attorney to be recorded as acting as such on only a single occasion. By the middle of the thirteenth century in England, many attorneys can be identified as acting for a variety of clients, and, in doing so, must have acquired, and demonstrated knowledge of, and experience in, court procedures.[2]

Whilst the forensic process required the litigant to select the necessary writ and to be present at the various stages of the litigation, either in person or by his attorney, he was also required to pronounce a formal complaint (or 'count' in Norman French) or to make a formal defence to the complaint. This was a vital step, as a failure to use the correct formula could be fatal to the case. The litigant could therefore employ someone 'ad narrandum', that is, to recite the appropriate form of words. Such a person need not have acted in this manner before, but, as in the case of the attorneys, there were those who can be identified as acting in this capacity for several clients. At an early stage, the function of the pleader developed from that of simply pronouncing the appropriate formula to the more intricate process of advancing his client's case by seeking to formulate points of law, which would be decided by the judge, or to define issues of fact, which would

---

2   This topic is discussed in detail in Paul Brand, *The origins the English legal profession* (Oxford, 1992). In the Irish context, it is discussed by Brand in 'The early history of the legal profession of the lordship of Ireland, 1250–1350', in Hogan and Osborough (ed.), *Brehons, serjeants and attorneys*; Hand, *English law in Ireland*; and Richardson & Sayles, *Admin. Ire.*

then be answered by the jury. Whilst 'the distinction between the pleader and the attorney in its most basic form represents the difference between the intellectual or scientific function and the mechanical or ministerial function',[3] this distinction may not always have been strictly observed in practice. There were instances where, as we shall see, the same individual seems to have acted as an attorney and a pleader at different times, although the distinction between the two was well established by the beginning of the fourteenth century. The attorney's function was not confined exclusively to the mechanical processes of initiating and then continuing the suit, because he retained the important power to disavow or repudiate the arguments being advanced by the pleader on behalf of his client. In addition, it is likely that, in some cases at least, the attorney would advise the client as to who should be retained to plead on his behalf and inform the pleader what the facts of his client's case were.

Before we consider how the king's serjeants fit into this picture, it is convenient at this stage to consider the various terms used to describe the pleaders. As we have seen, Owen described himself as 'serviens' or serjeant, but a variety of terms were used, apparently interchangeably, for a century or so after his appointment, with 'narrator' being the term most frequently used. An example of the way in which these terms were used may be seen in the case of William of Bardfield, who acted on behalf of the king between 1297 and 1307 or 1308. In 1307, we find him referred to as 'alter narrator',[4] but in 1321, when he petitioned the king seeking compensation for losses he had suffered in the Bruce invasion, he described himself as having served 'in the office of serjeant',[5] thereby suggesting that the position was already a recognised office. In 1316, Nicholas of Snitterby was described as 'serviens narrator' or serjeant pleader.[6] Later still, John Gernoun, Simon Fitzrichard and John of Cardiff were described merely as 'narratores',[7] whereas Hugh Brown and William Petit reverted to the title of 'servientes narratores' in 1343.[8]

---

3   J.H. Baker, *The legal profession and the common law: historical essays* (London, 1986), p. 100.

4   G.O. Sayles, *Select cases in the court of king's bench in the reign of Edward III*, *vol. V* (Selden Society, 1957, vol. 76), p. xlv.

5   'en office de seriance': *Documents on the affairs of Ireland before the king's council*, ed. G.O. Sayles (Dublin, 1979), pp. 103–04.

6   Brand, 'The legal profession in the lordship of Ireland', p. 28.

7   Richardson & Sayles, *Admin. Ire.*, p. 176 n. 3.

8   C.J. Smyth, *Chronicle of the law officers of Ireland* (London, 1839), p. 182.

Whilst it would be perfectly correct to describe all 'servientes' and 'narratores' as 'serjeants', in England towards the end of the fourteenth century the suffix 'at law' came to be applied only to those serjeants who were entitled to practise in the common pleas,[9] who were, in turn, distinct from another group of pleaders called the apprentices of the law, from whom the modern barrister can be said to be descended. As we shall see, there is some evidence to suggest that in Ireland the term serjeant at laws (rather than serjeant at law) came to be applied only to the king's serjeant; so, to avoid any confusion between the king's serjeant and pleaders in general, those who were servientes or narratores will be described as pleaders and those pleaders retained by the king will be initially referred to as the king's serjeants.

The appointment of Roger Owen in the 1260s to represent the king's interests mirrored a similar development in England less than twenty years before, where Lawrence del Brok had been retained from 1247 onwards at an annual fee of £20 'for suing the king's affairs of his pleas'. Brok's main activities on behalf of the king were in the king's bench and the common bench,[10] but he also enquired into homicides. Professor Sayles described Brok as an attorney,[11] but Paul Brand has pointed out that the earliest known use of the term serjeant relates to a payment to Brok in 1252, when he was described as 'servienti nostro', and comments that this 'seems to refer to the position he held rather than to the function he performed'.[12] Brand has shown that whilst Brok is recorded as suing on behalf of the king in a manner that is suggestive of an attorney, he also received substantial retainers of a type which serjeants received, and concludes, 'It seems probable, however, that Laurence was more than just an attorney and also acted as the king's serjeant in those cases in which he represented the king'.[13]

If Brok combined the functions of an attorney and a pleader, then it would not be surprising were that precedent to be followed in Ireland when Owen was appointed some years later, in which case his reference to himself as a pleader would not necessarily mean that he did not act as an attorney at the same time, at least so far as the king's affairs were concerned. In the early part of the thirteenth

9 Baker, *Serjeants at law*, pp. 21–27.
10 Brand, *The origins of the English legal profession*, p. 64.
11 Sayles, *Select cases in the king's bench: vol. V*, p. xxxiii.
12 Brand, *The origins of the English legal profession*, p. 49.
13 Ibid., p. 64.

century in England, there were some examples of attorneys acting as pleaders later in their careers, or, in one case, acting as a pleader in or about the same time as he acted as an attorney;[14] and it might well be the case that, even towards the end of the thirteenth century, the distinction between attorney and pleader was not always recognised in Ireland. That there were individuals who acted as professional attorneys in Ireland seems clear, and Brand has identified ten individuals who acted in this capacity between 1290 and 1336, although it is not until 1313 that an attorney is known to have been appointed to act on behalf of the king.

Richard Manning, who appears as king's attorney in that year, and his successor, William of Woodworth, were attorneys, and are recorded as acting for other clients in that capacity in the early years of the century.[15] The absence of any reference to an attorney being retained on behalf of the king before 1313 is consistent with the king's serjeant acting as both pleader and attorney until then, although the paucity of references to both pleaders and attorneys is such that it has to be accepted that the absence of any reference to a king's attorney before 1313 may simply be due to the incomplete nature of the surviving records.

One of the pleaders who regularly acted on behalf of the king was William of Bardfield, to whom we have already referred. Of English origin, he acted as an attorney in the Westminster bench between 1279 and 1284, and by 1297 is to be found acting as the king's serjeant in Ireland, and continued to do so until appointed a justice of the bench in Ireland in 1308. Although retained by the king, Bardfield was clearly acting for other clients, and, given his previous history as an attorney, would have had the necessary experience to combine the roles of attorney and pleader,[16] as would John de Ponz who acted as a king's serjeant between 1292 and 1300. De Ponz acted as an attorney for Edward in 1269 and 1270, and, after Edward became king, then served Queen Eleanor in various capacities until her death. He may therefore have had the necessary experience to enable him to act as an attorney for the king at the same time as acting as one of his pleaders. De Ponz is unique because he appears to have acted solely for the king, and, because of this, received a fee of twenty marks a year when the other king's serjeants were only paid

---

14 Ibid., pp. 53, 56–57.
15 Brand, 'The legal profession in the lordship of Ireland', pp. 37–41.
16 Ibid., p. 29.

ten.[17] However, the evidence on this topic is so sparse that all one can say with any confidence is that, although the early king's serjeants in Ireland were pleaders, it is by no means improbable that they may have also acted as the king's attorney.

Not long after Owen's appointment, another king's serjeant was appointed, as Robert of St Edmund appears in that capacity in 1270 and is known to have served until 1285. Following Owen's death in 1280, John fitzWilliam was appointed in 1281, presumably to fill the vacancy caused by Owen's death, although there is no further reference to him.[18] The appointment of more than one pleader at a time to act as king's serjeant again reflected the contemporary English practice, because in the late 1260s and early 1270s a number of serjeants are known to have acted on behalf of the king, and by the end of the decade regular appointments are to be found of serjeants to represent the king's interests before the justices on the various eyre circuits: for example, William of Gisleham was retained at £10 per term on the southern circuit of the 1280s which covered Kent, Sussex, Surrey, Somerset, Hampshire, Wiltshire and Devon. Other serjeants were appointed to the other circuits, and, by 1286, all were receiving a standard fee of £10 per term, although on some occasions they were supplemented by ad hoc appointments, when this was required by the pressure of work.[19]

In Ireland there is a gap in the records between *c*.1285 and *c*.1292 when we find John de Ponz acting as king's serjeant, who was joined the following year by John de Neville. Although there are occasional gaps thereafter, as can be seen from the succession list in Part Two, for the next hundred years it was the practice for at least two, and sometimes three, pleaders to be appointed as king's serjeants at the same time. Again, there is a clear parallel with the English practice, because at Easter 1315 the king placed the previous arrangements upon a more regular and permanent basis by retaining four of the leading pleaders to act on his behalf at an annual salary of £20.[20]

In Ireland there were probably two reasons why there were at least two king's serjeants at a time, the first being that it appears to have been common for a client to retain at least two, if not more, pleaders,

---

17 Ibid., p. 28, where it is suggested that his name should be anglicized as John of Bridgewater. One mark = 13*s*. 4*d*.

18 Richardson & Sayles, *Admin. Ire.*, pp. 174–75.

19 Sayles, *Select cases in the king's bench*: *vol. V*, p. xli.

20 Ibid., p. xlvi.

in part to ensure that at least one was available when needed. Indeed, it was common for a litigant to have a minimum of two pleaders present on his behalf in court,[21] although a king's serjeant was obliged to give priority to the king over his other clients. Thus William of Bardfield agreed with Nicholas, son of John of Interberge, that his obligations to Nicholas were subject to his duty to the king ('salvo servicio regis') as well as to any client by whom he was already retained.[22] However, another, if not the principal, reason why there was more than one king's serjeant at a time must have been because it would have been very difficult indeed for a single individual to represent the king's interests effectively, particularly if, as has been conjectured earlier, the king's serjeant also performed those tasks normally discharged by an attorney in the period before 1313. By the end of the thirteenth century, it is possible to establish the structure of the various courts with some confidence, and whilst many details are obscure or unknown, it is clear that some were geographically dispersed or itinerant in nature.

The exchequer undoubtedly exercised some legal functions, although the exact nature of its jurisdiction is obscure. In theory, it was only concerned with those matters which involved the king or the ministers of the exchequer, but there were complaints in the 1280s that pleas which should have been heard in the Dublin bench or the county court were being dealt with by the exchequer,[23] which was normally based in Dublin. Also based in Dublin was the bench, which can be identified from at least 1248, although it was probably functioning before then. The judges of the Dublin bench also provided the judges who went on circuit as eyre justices, carrying out what were national visitations of the various counties in Ireland on a periodic basis. As it was not until the 1270s that distinct groups of judges sat in the bench and held the eyres, presumably the sittings of the bench were interrupted whilst the judges were on the eyre circuit, although towards the end of the thirteenth century the eyres appear to have gone into abeyance. They were suspended between 1279 and 1289, and again between 1292 and 1301, and after 1307 eyres were only held on two occasions, in Co. Dublin in 1310 and in Co. Meath in 1322.[24]

---

21 Brand, 'The legal profession in the lordship of Ireland', p. 17.
22 Ibid., pp. 20–21.
23 Hand, *English law in Ireland*, p. 11.
24 A.J. Otway-Ruthven, *A history of medieval Ireland*, 2nd ed. (London, 1980), pp. 158–60. Paul Brand, 'The birth of a colonial judiciary: the judges of the lordship of Ireland, 1210–1377', in W.N. Osborough (ed.), *Explorations in law*

Another court which was essentially peripatetic in nature was the justiciar's court. It appears to have had a regular existence from 1285, although there is evidence that it functioned earlier than that; certainly from 1285 a single judge was appointed to assist the justiciar. As the justiciar continued to sit in person, but was constantly on the move throughout the country, and had to hear pleas in such time as could be spared from the heavy administrative and military duties inevitably associated with his position as chief governor of the lordship, this naturally meant that on occasion the king's serjeants could be far from the Dublin courts.[25] By the death of Edward I in 1307 the lordship had reached its apogee with twelve shires: Dublin, Waterford, Cork, Kerry, Louth, Limerick, Tipperary, Connacht, Roscommon, Kildare, Meath and Carlow.[26] In addition, there were the liberties of Kilkenny, Wexford, Trim and Ulster where, although justice and courts were largely in the hands of the lord of the liberty, the four pleas of the crown (rape, arson, forestalling and treasure trove) were matters for the royal courts, as were matters relating to some of the church lands (or crosslands) situated within the liberties. The itinerant nature of the justiciar's court is graphically illustrated by the distribution of the locations at which sessions were held between September 1312 and August 1313. This resembles a crescent with its northern tip at Drogheda, then extending to the south with sittings at Dublin, Castledermot, Carlow, Kilkenny and Cashel, before reaching the south-western tip at Limerick, as well as sittings at Cork and Waterford.[27]

Whilst the evidence is sparse prior to 1313, we know that, apart from appearing in the justiciar's court as required, the king's serjeants represented the king in all courts in Ireland. In 1292, John de Ponz was appointed to represent the king before the common bench, the justices itinerant and the barons of the exchequer,[28] and, in 1295–96, John de Neville is recorded as being paid for acting as king's serjeant 'in all places of Ireland'. Thirteen hundred and one provides a rare glimpse of the extent of this obligation, with William of Bardfield pleading on behalf of the king in the eyres of counties Cork and Louth, and Richard le Blond, the other king's serjeant, appearing on behalf of the king at the Co. Louth eyre. Bardfield and

and history: Irish Legal History Society discourses, 1989–1994 (Dublin, 1995), pp. 8–10 and 12–13.

25 Brand, 'The judges of the lordship of Ireland', pp. 13–15.
26 Otway-Ruthven, *A history of medieval Ireland*, pp. 174–77.
27 This passage is based upon the map in Hand, *English law in Ireland*, p. 59.
28 PRO E 372/139, m.9. I owe this reference to Dr Brand.

le Blond both pleaded on the king's behalf in the Dublin bench, the exchequer and the justiciar's court during that year,[29] and Bardfield also appeared before the king's council, arguing that a fine made on eyre contravened the statute of Quia Emptores.[30]

With the appearance of Richard Manning as the king's attorney in 1313, it is possible to identify a distinction in succeeding years between those who acted as pleaders on behalf of the king, on the one hand, and as attorneys, on the other, although the distinction, so far as the terminology at least was concerned, was rather blurred at first. Manning and his successor, William of Woodworth, both acted as attorneys prior to being appointed king's attorney, and Manning continued to act in that capacity for others until 1327,[31] yet Manning, Woodworth and Thomas of Westham (who succeeded Woodworth in 1334) were variously described as king's serjeant or attorney, Manning being referred to as 'the king's serjeant' in 1318–19.[32] The distinction between the two offices was further blurred at the start because the king's attorney received the same fee of five marks a year as the king's serjeant until at least 1327, although the fee for the latter had been raised to five pounds a year by 1331. Despite the payment of the same fee, and the inconsistent terminology used to describe the king's attorney in the early years of that office, Richardson and Sayles established that the king's serjeants were always clearly marked off from the king's attorneys in the records of the time. That the king's serjeants were regarded as significantly superior in status to the king's attorneys may be deduced from the fact that none of the latter were raised to the bench between 1313 and 1377, whereas during that period six of the king's serjeants were appointed justices of the common bench, four becoming chief justice of that court, and a seventh became chief justice of the justiciar's bench.[33]

The beginnings of this close link between the bench and the senior branch of the legal profession can be identified by the closing years of the thirteenth century. From 1294 onwards John de Ponz, whilst king's serjeant, was regularly appointed a judge of assize in counties Louth, Tipperary, Cork and Limerick; was a judge of gaol delivery; and also acted as a judge of the Dublin bench in 1295, 1296

29 Brand, 'The legal profession in the lordship of Ireland', p. 42.
30 Hand, *English law in Ireland*, p. 162; *Cal. justic. rolls Ire., 1295–1303*, pp. 383–85.
31 Brand, 'The legal profession in the lordship of Ireland', pp. 40–41.
32 Richardson & Sayles, *Admin. Ire*, p. 41 n. 6.
33 Ibid., pp. 41–42.

and possibly in 1299/1300,[34] before becoming a permanent justice of the Dublin bench in 1301. De Ponz may have been called upon to an exceptional extent because he was solely employed by the king, but he was not unique in becoming a judge. Other king's serjeants of this period to become judges were William of Bardfield, a justice of the Dublin bench from 1308 to 1312 and from 1316 to 1319, and Richard le Blond, a justice of the Dublin bench between 1322 and 1325. Although the ranks of the royal justices at this time were not filled exclusively by the king's serjeants, or even from the ranks of the pleaders, because many of the judges do not appear to have had legal experience before their appointment, it was soon clear that to be made a king's serjeant was a strong indication that the individual would ultimately become a judge, a pattern which we shall see running consistently and strongly through the history of the king's serjeants.

Apart from their services as pleaders, another reason why the king's serjeants were promoted with such frequency in the thirteenth and fourteenth centuries was, no doubt, because at a very early stage they came to be regarded not just as advocates, but as amongst those from whose ranks the king's advisers were usually selected. A similar development was evident in England as early as 1318 when the four king's serjeants who had been placed on a permanent footing in 1315 were summoned to parliament.[35] The absence of records means that it cannot be established when a similar practice was instituted in Ireland, but it appears to have existed by 1348 as Edmund of Barford and William Petit were paid for their services in attending a parliament or great council held at Kilkenny in May of that year.[36] Writs which have survived from the 1370s and 1380s show that on a number of occasions some (though not all) of the king's serjeants were summoned to attend parliament. For example, we find Richard Plunkett and John Tyrell present in 1375; they were summoned to a great council held at Castledermot, Co. Kildare in 1378; to a parliament in 1380, and to a tractatus (or council) in

---

34 Hand, *English law in Ireland*, p. 11; *Chartularies of St Mary's abbey, Dublin, with the register of its house at Dunbrody, and annals of Ireland*, ed. J.T. Gilbert (Rolls series, 1884), i, 295; *Irish cartularies of Llanthony Prima and Secunda*, ed. E. St J. Brooks (Dublin, 1955), pp. 88, 89, 110–11, 120–22; and *Cal. justic. rolls Ire., 1295–1303*, p. 318. I owe the latter references to John's services in the Dublin bench to Dr Brand.

35 Sayles, *Select cases in the king's bench: vol. V*, p. xlvi.

36 H.G. Richardson and G.O. Sayles, *Parliaments and councils of medieval Ireland* (Dublin, 1947), p. xi.

1382.[37] It seems probable that they were summoned, not just because they were king's serjeants, but because they were the permanent king's serjeants and, as such, members of the king's council.[38] Plunkett was also summoned to attend the council at Dublin in 1372, and in 1384 was paid for his attendance at parliaments, councils and discussions for five years.[39] We know that not all the king's serjeants were summoned because Walter Coterell was not summoned in 1375, despite being a king's serjeant, even though John Mitchel, the king's attorney, was. As we shall see, Coterell was appointed on a local and supernumerary basis, and one may therefore deduce that, despite the inferior professional standing of the king's attorney, Mitchel was summoned because, unlike Coterell, his office was considered to be part of the administration.[40]

It would seem that the permanent king's serjeants (as opposed to ad hoc appointments) were ranked amongst the king's advisers from the 1340s. There is evidence that, in addition to their parliamentary duties, they were amongst those who were regularly summoned to the king's council (or privy council, to use the later term). Richardson and Sayles pointed to an instance in 1342 when two serjeants at law were amongst those present when a keeper was sworn in, and they were of the opinion that the inclusion of the law officers amongst the list of those ministers who were summoned to parliament indicated that the king's serjeants were amongst the normal members of the privy council.[41]

One may reasonably infer that the admittedly slight evidence from the 1340s and 1370s represents early instances of what was to become the invariable practice by the fifteenth century, namely, that the king's serjeant at law (as he was by then called) attended parliament in his official capacity, and was the junior member of the inner circle of ministers who were the advisers of the chief governor of the day.

---

37 William Lynch, *A view of the legal institutions, honorary hereditary offices, and feudal baronies established in Ireland during the reign of Henry II* (London, 1830), pp. 325–28. *Rot. pat. Hib.*, p. 119, no. 126. I owe the latter reference to Dr Brand. For the distinctions between parliaments, great councils and councils, see H.G. Richardson and G.O. Sayles, *The Irish parliament in the middle ages* (Philadelphia, 1952), ch. 7, passim.

38 Richardson & Sayles, *Ir. parl. in middle ages*, pp. 32–33.

39 *Rot. pat. Hib.*, p. 84b, no. 137 and p. 122b, no. 18. I owe these references to Dr Brand.

40 Lynch, *The legal institutions in Ireland during the reign of Henry II*, p. 324, and Richardson & Sayles, *Ir. parl. in middle ages*, p. 135.

41 Richardson & Sayles, *Ir. parl. in middle ages*, pp. 32–33.

However, this is to anticipate matters somewhat, and we must now examine the activities of the king's serjeants in the latter half of the fourteenth century. If the lordship of Ireland achieved its greatest extent and prosperity by the death of Edward I in 1307, half a century later the situation had markedly deteriorated, and the sphere of direct or effective control by the Dublin government had been greatly reduced. Connacht appears to have been effectively beyond its sphere of influence, and Ulster beyond the Bann, and Thomond in the south-west, were irretrievably lost. Although the government was active in Desmond, much land on the fringes of Westmeath was lost, with the Irish dominant north of Nenagh and in what amounted to an almost continuous state of insurrection in the mountainous areas of south Co. Dublin, Co. Wexford, and the modern Co. Wicklow.[42] The lordship was on the defensive, and this state of affairs had repercussions for the king's serjeants, just as it undoubtedly affected others involved with the legal system.

One of the obvious consequences of the weakened state of the lordship, so far as the legal profession was concerned, was the transfer of the exchequer to Carlow in 1361, followed some years later by the common bench. It had originally been intended to transfer the common bench to Carlow in 1363, but this was postponed, and the exchequer temporarily moved back to Dublin in Michaelmas term of that year, because the town had been burnt several times by the Irish and there was no suitable accommodation for the courts. However, by 1371 the common bench was established in Carlow, although the chancery and the lieutenant continued to be based in Dublin.[43] This change was made for strategic reasons, since Carlow was used as a centre from which the southern fringes of the lordship could be more readily defended. The itinerant nature of much of the legal system and the difficulties and dangers which travellers and royal officials faced at this time are shown by the travels of the king's lieutenant, Lionel of Clarence, in 1365, a year in which the king described Ireland 'as sunk in the greatest wretchedness through the poverty and feebleness of his people there because of the destruction and hostile attacks often made by his Irish enemies'. In the spring, Lionel went to Carlow and then to Cork; by August he was at Kilmallock; in October at Carlow, Castledermot and Trim; and by

42 Otway-Ruthven, *A history of medieval Ireland*, pp. 270–71.
43 Ibid., p. 287. *Calendar of Ormond deeds*, ed. Edmund Curtis, 6 vols. (Dublin, 1932–43), ii, 120–21, no. 166. I owe this reference to Dr Brand.

early December at Drogheda. In February 1366, he held a parliament at Kilkenny which produced the famous Statutes of Kilkenny.[44] Journeys of this sort must have had implications for the king's serjeants, because one would assume that it was essential that the king have a representative available to appear before the justiciar's court, and, with some of the courts remaining in Dublin, it might well be the case that there would be occasions when a clash of business, or travel difficulties, rendered it essential to have more than one king's serjeant.

That the king's serjeants were called upon to represent the king throughout the length and breadth of the lordship during the latter part of the fourteenth century can be seen from the activities of Robert de Preston and Walter Coterell. In 1357, Preston, as one of the king's serjeants (serviens domini regis), was directed 'to accompany the lord justice towards the parts of Leinster and Munster, to plead and defend the pleas of the crown, and should receive 4s. a day wages for himself and a man and horse at arms'. That this could be an onerous task, and one which could seriously interfere with the serjeant's private practice, is clear because Preston was engaged on these duties for 149 days from 19 February to 17 July, for which he was paid the substantial sum of £29 10s.10d.[45]

Walter Coterell was frequently employed as a king's serjeant between 1372 and 1388. Initially, he appears to have acted within the counties of Wexford and Waterford, and in June 1374 he was paid ten marks, having spent four weeks 'holding sessions in those parts with eight horses'. His duties seem to have extended beyond holding sessions, because he was also required to arrest and make stay of ships and to take inquisitions. He also spent fourteen days with John Keppok, chief justice of the justiciar's court, and William de Karlell, a baron of the exchequer, making enquiries about hidden treasure in Co. Wexford. That Coterell did not receive any fee for the latter task might suggest that such duties were considered to be within the ordinary scope of his retainer. The local nature of his appointment, and the dangers created by the continuing warfare, are evident from a reference to him being appointed in 1380 to act in Munster and the counties of Kilkenny and Wexford, 'by reason that John Tyrell could not attend his duty in these parts, on account of the dangers of

44 Otway-Ruthven, *A history of medieval Ireland*, p. 291.
45 Smyth, *Law officers*, pp. 182–83.

the roads etc'.[46] Coterell's supernumerary status is confirmed by his description as 'serviens ad leges deputatos' in 1388.[47]

Coterell's appointment as a king's serjeant for a limited area was not unique, as can be seen from the terms of the appointment in 1388 of John Bermingham 'within the counties of Dublin, Meath, Kildare, Uriel (Louth) and Cathirlagh (Carlow)'.[48] The reference to Coterell in 1388 is also of importance as the first known instance of the use of the title 'serjeant at laws' (serviens ad leges) in Ireland. The suffix 'at law' (ad legem) was rarely found in England before the 1370s, and was associated with those pleaders who were in the process of becoming a closed order enjoying the exclusive right of audience in the common pleas, membership of which was conferred by a royal writ directing the recipient to receive the degree of serjeant at law.[49] There are several instances of the suffix 'at laws' being used in Ireland at this time. It was also applied to John Bermingham when he was sworn in as 'serviens regis ad leges' in September 1388,[50] and in 1392 John Haire was described in the response to a petition before the justiciar and council as 'serjeant at laws of our lord the king in his common place of Ireland'.[51]

Tempting as it would be to see this reference to a serjeant at law functioning only, it would seem, in the court of common pleas as evidence of the existence of a group of serjeants with exclusive rights of audience before the common bench (as the common pleas was then called) in Ireland, as had evolved in England, such a conclusion would be quite unjustified. There is no evidence whatever of such a development in Ireland, and Haire's appointment to represent the king before the common pleas is entirely consistent with the pattern of limited or local appointments, such as those of Coterell and Bermingham, particularly as the entire lordship was in a very disturbed state indeed at the time. It was impossible to get to Youghal, Cork or Limerick without an armed escort, and Carlow, seat of the exchequer since 1361, 'had been burnt and the country had gone up in flames'.[52] In such

---

46 Ibid., pp. 183–84.
47 *Rot. pat. Hib.*, p. 141b, no. 200. I owe this reference to Dr Brand.
48 Smyth, *Law officers*, p. 184.
49 Baker, *Serjeants at law*, pp. 21–27.
50 *Rot. pat. Hib.*, p. 139, no. 63. I owe this reference to Dr Brand.
51 'Sergeant des Leys notre Seignour le Roy en son Commun Place Dirland': *A roll of the proceedings of the king's council in Ireland 1392–93*, ed. James Graves (Rolls series, 1877), p. 51.
52 Otway-Ruthven, *A history of medieval Ireland*, pp. 324–25.

circumstances, there would have been great difficulty in a single king's serjeant representing the king throughout the lordship. In all probability, therefore, Haire was either an ad hoc appointment in the common bench, or a second and permanent king's serjeant. The latter possibility cannot be excluded because, although we do not have any record of John Bermingham still serving as king's serjeant in November 1392 when Haire appears, Bermingham was king's serjeant until October of that year, and, as he is found acting in that capacity again between 1400 and 1403, it may well be that he continued to act after October 1392.

Although only a handful of references to the king's serjeant have survived from the three-quarters of a century following the description of Haire as the king's serjeant at law, the suffix at law (or laws) is always used, and it would seem that in Ireland, unlike England, the title serjeant at law came to be exclusively applied to the king's serjeants, because such references to other pleaders as have survived describe them solely as pleaders, generally using the French word countor. In 1455, we find Thomas Snetterby described as 'serjeant at laws of our said sovereign lord the king in his whole land of Ireland', followed by a reference to Esmond Bryne as 'countor',[53] and in 1467 Thomas Dowedall is described as pleader and as holding the office of serjeant.[54]

Although there would seem to be no doubt that during the fifteenth century the king's serjeants at law were drawn from the ranks of the pleaders, the distinction between the king's serjeant and the king's attorney was again becoming blurred. It is perhaps significant that by the middle of the fifteenth century the king's serjeant and the king's attorney received the same remuneration. In 1440, Edward Somerton's fees as king's serjeant were said not to exceed £9 a year, and, because this was insufficient to cover his expenses in attending parliaments and councils, he was granted 100s. a year in addition for his life.[55] By 1450, his successor Thomas Snetterby was receiving the same additional fee of 100s., as was the king's attorney, Robert Fitz Rery, whose annual fees also amounted to £9,[56] although neither received these amounts regularly. Indeed, they had to be given power to distrain

53 *Stat. Ire., Hen. VI*, p. 383.
54 *Stat. Ire., 1–12 Edw. IV*, p. 549.
55 Smyth, *Law officers*, p. 185.
56 *Stat. Ire., Hen. VI*, pp. 275–77.

for them in 1453,[57] despite which it was admitted in 1455 that 'they are oftentimes very badly paid'.[58]

We also find that although Thomas Dowedall was the king's serjeant in 1462, he appears to have become king's attorney in 1463. By 1467, he had, apparently, reverted to being the king's serjeant as he was confirmed in that office. By September 1471 he was described as a 'countor' when granted the office of keeper of the rolls at £20 a year.[59] If typical, Dowedall's career would suggest that by the 1460s the office of king's attorney could be held by a pleader, who presumably discharged the functions hitherto carried out by an attorney on the king's behalf. Whilst Dowedall's holding the office of king's attorney as a pleader may simply be unique to him, it may also be seen as an early example of a development which did not become a fixed practice for another forty years or so. As we shall see in the next chapter, there were a number of instances early in the sixteenth century where the king's attorney was promoted to be the king's serjeant.

What we know of the king's serjeants during the fifteenth century is almost entirely confined to their ministerial functions. The obligation to attend parliaments and councils which we considered in the latter part of the fourteenth century continued during the fifteenth century. We have already seen how the burdensome nature of this obligation led to Somerton's fee being augmented in 1440, which followed a similar increase in Christopher Barnewall's annual fee in 1432.[60]

Throughout the fifteenth century the king's serjeant remained the principal Irish law officer of the crown, to use the modern term, and, as such, was always the junior member of the inner council of seven ministers who were the advisers of the chief governor of the day. Although his role as a law officer was clearly superior to that of the king's attorney, who was not a member of this inner council, the importance of the king's serjeant was overshadowed to a considerable extent by the chancellor, the chief justices of the two benches and the chief baron of the exchequer, all of whom were also members of the council.[61]

By then there was only one king's serjeant at a time, probably because of a diminution in the volume of business with which the

57 Ibid., p. 296.
58 Ibid., p. 349.
59 *Cal. pat. rolls, 1461–67*, p. 184; *Stat. Ire., 1–12 Edw. IV*, pp. 111, 549 and 735–57, no. 13. I owe these references to Dr Brand.
60 Smyth, *Law officers*, pp. 184–85.
61 Richardson & Sayles, *Ir. parl. in middle ages*, pp. 164–65.

king's serjeant might be expected to deal. The area of effective royal jurisdiction had been drastically reduced until it was confined to the Pale and outlying areas such as the ports of Wexford, Youghal, Cork, Kinsale, Limerick and Galway. Outside these areas lay the earldoms of Kildare, Butler and Desmond, covering in effect the rest of Leinster and Munster where the earls administered justice within their possessions. Nevertheless, as Dr Ellis has demonstrated, there was still a considerable degree of royal involvement in the administration of justice in the form of periodic commissions outside the Pale.[62] For example, in May and June 1438 the second justice of the king's bench and the king's serjeant went on commission through Kerry, Kilkenny, Limerick, Tipperary, Waterford and Wexford.[63]

It is convenient to bring this chapter to a close in 1485 at the end of the Yorkist era. By this time, the office of the king's serjeant at law had existed for over two centuries, during which it evolved from his being a pleader retained solely to act on the king's behalf in his courts to being one of the leading officers of state in the Irish administration, being summoned to parliament and serving as one of the inner circle of advisers of the chief governor. The king's serjeant continued his original function of prosecuting and defending the king's pleas by representing the king before the courts, the council and parliament, as well as exercising judicial or quasi-judicial functions from time to time. This status as one of the king's principal servants meant that from an early stage the king's serjeant could expect judicial preferment, and although the distinction between the king's attorney and the king's serjeant may not always have been clearly defined, nevertheless the latter was the senior and more important of the two offices. Combining ministerial (and hence political) and legal functions whilst continuing to represent private clients in the courts, the king's serjeant had evolved into an office which was to remain essentially unchanged for several centuries, and is recognisable as the precursor in Ireland of the modern law officer, although, historically, the attorney general traces his descent directly from the king's attorney. Nevertheless, as we shall see in the succeeding chapters, it was to be some time before the junior office became more important in practice, and indeed it was not until the early years of the nineteenth century that this was formally recognised.

62 S.G. Ellis, *Reform and revival: English government in Ireland, 1470–1534*, Royal Historical Society studies in history, 47 (London, 1986), pp. 136–42.
63 Ibid., p. 137; *Rot. pat. Hib*, p. 262, no. 24, and p. 263, no. 24.

CHAPTER TWO

The king's serjeants in Tudor
Ireland, 1485–1603

THE EARLIER PART of the period covered in this chapter, between
1485 and 1532, is characterised by a scarcity of references to the
king's serjeant in such contemporary documents as have survived,
and, as a result, little is known of his precise functions at that time;
indeed, it has not been possible to identify all of the holders of the
office between 1487 and 1532. It is not until a later period that a
more detailed, though still incomplete, picture of the functions of the
king's serjeant can be constructed. Yet, despite these difficulties, we
would probably be justified in assuming that during this period the
role of the king's serjeant was much as it had been before, and as we
know it to be in later years.

At the beginning of the reign of Henry VII in 1485, the Irish
council and the administration of the medieval lordship were
dominated by the justiciar, Gerald, eighth earl of Kildare, who had
first been elected in 1478 by the seven members of the council
following the unexpected death of his father, and who remained
chief governor for most of the period from 1479. The king's serjeant
at that time was John Estrete who, together with the other six
ministerial members of the council, had been assured tenure of his
office for life by virtue of an act confirming the statute of Henry
FitzEmpress passed by the Irish parliament at Kildare's instigation in
1485 to ensure that, in the event of a change of dynasty, Kildare,
through the council, could ensure the continuity of his power.[1]
Estrete, who had a common law background and who is to be found
acting as a lawyer in 1477 and 1478,[2] was clearly a trusted adherent
of Kildare, who dispatched him to London in 1486 to negotiate
confirmation of Kildare's authority to govern Ireland on behalf of

1   10 Hen VII, c.2. Richardson & Sayles, *Ir. parl. in middle ages*, pp. 169, 330–31.
2   'Cal. Christ Church deeds', *P.R.I. rep. D.K. 20*, pp. 92, no. 308 and 93,
     no. 314. I owe this reference to Dr Brand.

Henry VII.[3] Estrete appears to have remained king's serjeant until about March 1487, when he was granted the office of master of the coinage in Ireland at an annual salary of £20. Such was his standing that he was sworn as a councillor in England about this time before being appointed chief baron of the exchequer in 1487.[4] The next known appointment as king's serjeant is that of Thomas Kent in 1497. The parliament summoned by Sir Edward Poynings between December 1494 and April 1495 passed an act that the seven chief officers of state should no longer hold office for life but at pleasure, so we may assume that Kent was appointed upon that basis. A native of Drogheda, Kent had held the minor office of escheator of the exchequer since November 1495, and became chief baron in 1504.[5] Kent's appointment marked the reversal of Poynings's policy of appointing English-born officials. Kildare was by now lord deputy again, and had obtained from Henry VII the right to make all appointments except that of chancellor, a right generally reserved by the king in order to place a check on the power of the chief governor of the day.[6] Kent's background as a lawyer of Irish birth and his previous service in a lesser post before his elevation were typical of the serjeants throughout this period.

One of the most striking features in any study of the leading figures in Ireland during the Tudor period is the frequency with which the same Old English families appear as holders of legal or judicial office. John Barnewall, Kent's succcessor, exemplifies this tradition of involvement in public affairs and royal service in the lordship. The great-grandson of Christopher Barnewall who was the king's serjeant at law in 1423, John Barnewall was the son of Robert Barnewall, Lord Trimleston. A pleader at the Irish bar when he was appointed king's attorney in 1504, he became king's serjeant at law and solicitor general later that year. In the course of a long public career, he was to become second justice of the king's bench, deputy treasurer, treasurer and, in 1534, chancellor, in which year his nephew, Patrick Barnewall, became king's serjeant and solicitor general.[7]

3   Richardson & Sayles, *Ir. parl. in middle ages*, p. 328.
4   *Cal. pat. rolls, 1485–94*, pp. 158 and 169 (where he is described as the 'king's servant and councillor'); PRO E 101/248/12; Ball, *Judges*, i, 187.
5   Ball, *Judges*, i, 191.
6   S.G. Ellis, *Tudor Ireland: crown, community and the conflict of culture, 1470–1603* (London, 1985), p. 78.
7   Ball, *Judges*, i, 193 and 204.

John Barnewall's tenure as king's serjeant was brief, being succeeded in the office by Clement Fitzleones in 1505, and Barnewall does not appear to have held further office until he became a justice of the king's bench in 1514. Fitzleones had acted as deputy chief baron in 1493 and as king's attorney in 1502.[8] It is not known whether Fitzleones continued to act as king's serjeant until 1509 when Patrick Finglas was appointed, nor whether Finglas in turn continued as serjeant until the appointment of Thomas Rochfort as king's serjeant and solicitor in 1511.[9] Finglas, like Barnewall, was to fill many judicial offices until his death in 1537. In common with many of the serjeants, Finglas was appointed soon after he embarked upon a legal career, having entered Lincoln's Inn in 1503.[10]

Thomas Rochfort's appointment was unique during this period: he was a cleric, having become precentor of St Patrick's cathedral in 1502 and dean in 1505. His clerical background merits some notice: although it was still common for the chancellor to be a cleric, it was by now unusual to find a cleric acting in the common law courts, something later evidence confirms that the king's serjeant was required to do. Rochfort continued to be active in ecclesiastical matters and remained dean until his death in June 1522, but his clerical background was not a handicap because he served in various legal capacities during that time. He is also to be found as a clerk in chancery in 1515, by which time he had previously ceased to be the king's serjeant. He also appears as keeper of the rolls in December 1520.[11] However, it is not known how many of the serjeants received their training in the common law during the early Tudor period. Of the six serjeants who can be named between 1485 and 1513, Estrete,[12] Barnewall and Finglas have identifiable common law backgrounds before their appointment, Barnewall as a narrator and Finglas at Lincoln's Inn.

---

8 Ibid., p. 188.

9 Ibid., p. 192.

10 Ibid., pp. 193–94.

11 Ellis, *Reform and revival*, p. 170 states that he ceased to be king's serjeant in 1513, and was keeper of the rolls 1513–21, but gives no source. In his Ph.D. thesis, he relies on Ball, *Judges*, i, 192. However, W.M. Mason, *Historical annals of the collegiate and cathedral church of St Patrick, near Dublin, from its foundation in 1190, to the year 1819* (Dublin, 1820), pp. 142–44 gives more detail, and says that Rochfort did not appear as keeper of the rolls until Dec. 1520.

12 Colum Kenny, *King's Inns and the kingdom of Ireland: the Irish 'inn of court', 1541–1800* (Dublin, 1992), pp. 21–22. I owe this reference to Professor Osborough.

Sparse though the detail is for the period between 1485 and 1532, we catch occasional glimpses of the serjeant's activities in the courts. In 1506, John Barnewall laid an information that one Thomas Ryan of Dunboyne, Co. Meath, was an 'hibernicus' and, as such, in possession of land without the king's permission, but the jury accepted Ryan's plea that he was 'anglicus'.[13] This was an example of the serjeant's function to lay informations in the exchequer on behalf of the king. In 1510, we find Patrick Finglas seeking the forfeiture of recognizances entered into by Plunkett of Balrath to keep the peace. Only one of the three sureties appeared and denied his liability, 'which plea is denied by Patrick Finglas, who sues for the king', and judgment was given against the defendants for the amount of their recognizances.[14] Another example of an information that has survived dates from 1517, when Thomas Fitzsimon laid an information that Edward Becke of Manchester exported two horses from Dalkey without a licence.[15] However, the serjeant was not the only person who laid informations on behalf of the king, as accountants and the attorney general did so as well; indeed, the surviving records show that the attorney general laid eight out of 17.[16]

As in previous centuries, the serjeant's activities on behalf of the king were not confined to the courts, and use was made of him in other, quasi-judicial, capacities. In 1532, we find the serjeant heading a commission which was enquiring into the king's feudal rights at Trim, Co. Meath.[17] Although this is an isolated example from this period, similar functions had been carried out by the serjeants in earlier centuries, and we will see a number of similar examples during the reigns of Elizabeth and James I.

It was, perhaps, a sign of the continuing superiority of the king's serjeant over the attorney general that when we find the first reference to the king's solicitor in Ireland in 1504, the post is annexed to that of the king's serjeant. When the office first appeared in England in 1461, it was both junior, and auxiliary, to that of the king's attorney.[18] That was not to be the case in Ireland for a lengthy

---

13 10 May, 21 Hen. VII: NAI, Ferguson MS, iv, ff. 9–10.
14 1 Hen. VIII, Hilary term: NAI, Ferguson MS, iv, f. 8.
15 12 May 1516: NAI, Ferguson MS, iv, f. 39.
16 Ellis, *Reform and revival*, p. 125.
17 Ibid., p. 199.
18 T.W. Moody, F.X. Martin and F.J. Byrne (ed.), *A new history of Ireland*, ix (Oxford, 1984), p. 517.

period of time, where the post was annexed to that of king's serjeant, although, as we shall see, a new post of principal, or chief, solicitor was created in 1537. For some time the principal solicitor was a distinct office from that of the solicitor general, until the two posts were effectively unified from 1574 onwards.

From 1485 until 1532, such evidence as there is suggests that the king's serjeant was still the principal law officer, and so one of the leading members of the council which ruled the lordship under the chief governor of the day. The appointment of Luttrell as king's serjeant at law and solicitor general in 1532 provides a convenient starting-point for the next part of this chapter. Not only is it possible to identify all of the king's (or queen's) serjeants from that date onwards, but there is also a markedly greater volume of contemporary documentary evidence about the various functions which the king's serjeant performed. This is especially so in the period from 1532 to 1554 when there were three king's serjeants and one of the three, Patrick Barnewall, was, albeit briefly, a highly significant figure in one of the most important episodes in the Tudor period. As a result, a picture emerges which, although necessarily shadowy in some areas, is considerably more detailed than at any time since the fourteenth century.

Luttrell's appointment in September 1532 was directly due to the influence of Thomas Cromwell who marked him out for advancement. In October 1534 Luttrell became chief justice of the common pleas (then still called the common bench or common place), replacing Richard Delahide, who was a Geraldine supporter. However, during his period of office, which largely coincided with the final term of office as deputy of Gerald, ninth earl of Kildare, Luttrell was not a member of the council. This represented a major departure from the practice which had continued for over one hundred and fifty years.[19] We do not know why this occurred, but it may be that it was symptomatic of a focusing of attention upon the major offices, as happened in 1529 and 1530 when a secret council of three was entrusted with the powers of deputy in the absence of the lieutenant, the infant duke of Richmond who was the king's illegitimate son.[20]

---

19 D.B. Quinn in Art Cosgrove (ed.), *A new history of Ireland, ii* (Oxford, 1987), p. 682.
20 Ellis, *Tudor Ireland*, p. 119.

Cromwell's close and continuing interest in Irish affairs resulted in his advancing to high legal office those whom he believed would further the policy of reform in Ireland, upon which he had embarked. As part of this policy, he appointed Luttrell's brother-in-law, Patrick Barnewall, king's serjeant and solicitor general in 1534.

Barnewall, the nephew of John Barnewall, a former king's serjeant who was now chancellor, had entered Gray's Inn in 1527.[21] When appointed, he was a pleader in the courts and, like other lawyers who reached high office at this time, his legal activities involved him with the affairs of leading magnates and monastic institutions. Together with his uncle, Barnewall was steward of seven estates in north Co. Dublin held by the English abbey of Keynsham,[22] and, in addition, he was the agent for the Irish estates of Sir Thomas Boleyn, earl of Wiltshire and father of the queen. That this involved him in a significant conflict of interest can be seen by his interceding with Wiltshire in April 1535, saying that many of Wiltshire's tenants alleged that they had supported Silken Thomas in the recent rebellion in order to protect their lives.[23] Although one might have expected a prominent royal official to be unsympathetic to those who had lent aid and comfort to a rebellious subject, Barnewall's action illustrated the dilemma all too frequently faced by royal officials in Ireland. They had to combine loyalty to the king's policies, which were formulated in England, with their anxiety to alleviate the plight of their neighbours and those with whom they had business links. It may also be seen as a forerunner of his position in 1536 and 1537 during the so-called Reformation Parliament. Barnewall also acted on behalf of a number of monastic houses, and in later years was granted several annuities secured on their revenues by these houses. Some of these grants were clearly made in anticipation of their foundations being suppressed, but some may have been made in recognition of past services: for example, in October 1537, the abbot of the Cistercian house of St Mary's, Dublin granted him an annuity secured on its revenues.[24] Barnewall was not alone in combining such activities as a steward or agent with

21 Ball, *Judges*, i, 204.
22 Brendan Bradshaw, *The dissolution of the religious orders in Ireland under Henry VIII* (Cambridge, 1974), p. 53.
23 R.D. Edwards, 'The Irish Reformation Parliament of Henry VIII', *Historical Studies:VI*, ed. T.W. Moody (London, 1968), p. 62.
24 Bradshaw, *The dissolution of the religious orders in Ireland*, p. 88.

his other duties; so did Thomas Luttrell and Robert Dillon, king's attorney between 1534 and 1555.[25]

As we have already seen, the first pleader retained by the king in the reign of Edward I was retained to 'prosecute and defend the king's pleas in Ireland', and this appears to have continued to have been the role of the king's serjeant thereafter, judging by a letter which Barnewall wrote to Cromwell in April 1538. Between July 1537 and April 1538, four commissioners, led by Sir Anthony St Leger, represented the king in Ireland, and were engaged in a thorough investigation into all aspects of the Irish administration. The commissioners appear to have considered increasing the role of the king's attorney (or attorney general as he became known) at the expense of the king's serjeant, prompting Barnewall to write in the following terms:

Part of the commissioners was minded, amongst other things, to order that the king's attorney should maintain and confess pleas for the king; where that the king's serjeant, for the time being, has always used to maintain pleas, and confess the same, for the king's highness, as the case did require; as by the records thereof plainly may appear, for this two hundred years and more.[26]

Since the king's attorney had also maintained and defended the king's pleas since the first such appointments early in the fourteenth century,[27] it would seem that the commissioners may have contemplated the abolition of the office of the king's serjeant, perhaps to save money, or because the post appeared to be an anomaly, or both. In any event, the details of this proposal are unknown, and as the office of king's serjeant survived, Barnewall's plea appears to have been successful.

However, Barnewall had been less successful in defending his position in 1536 and 1537 when he was challenged in several ways by Robert and Walter Cowley. Robert Cowley, aptly described as an 'ambitious mischief-making adherent of the Butlers',[28] and his son Walter had long been intimate with the earl of Ormond. They were amongst Cromwell's most indefatigable Irish correspondents and

---

25 Ibid., p. 53. Robert Dillon was attorney general 1534–55, second justice of the king's bench 1555–59, and chief justice of the common pleas 1559–80: Ball, *Judges*, i, 206.

26 *S.P. Hen. VIII*, ii, 570.

27 Richardson & Sayles, *Admin. Ire.*, p. 41.

28 Edwards, 'The Irish Reformation Parliament of Henry VIII', p. 70.

were constantly intriguing in order to advance their fortunes, often at Barnewall's expense. In June 1535, Barnewall added the post of customer of customs for Dublin and Drogheda to his responsibilities, but this no doubt lucrative post was quickly removed from him, Robert Cowley becoming customer of Dublin, and Walter of Drogheda, in December of the same year.[29] By August 1536 Barnewall clearly felt that his hold on the office of king's serjeant and solicitor general was threatened, to judge by the abject terms in which he wrote to Cromwell:

Till I may know your lordship's further pleasure I shall be contented that Master Cowley enjoy my office, and for no right he hath to the same, but only during your pleasure, which without fail I shall accomplish in everything, to my power, during my life. If it shall be your pleasure that I may appoint such a person for the exercising of my office, as shall be well known here to be of more better learning and experience than I am, so that I may have licence to repair to my learning, I trust in God to do the king, in my office, the better service.[30]

Nothing came of this move then, although, as we shall see, a new post was created for Walter Cowley in 1537, and Barnewall remained king's serjeant and solicitor general. That Barnewall had to appeal to his patron illustrates the manner in which Cromwell and Henry VIII were now directly making and changing appointments in Ireland, whereas in the early years of Henry's reign, under the Kildare domination, such interest was spasmodic. The letter also shows that the king's serjeant's activities were not necessarily confined to the courts or the council chamber, because Barnewall wrote from Limerick where he was in attendance upon Lord Deputy Grey, who was campaigning at the time against the O'Briens and their supporters.

Barnewall was soon to emerge for a short time as a significant political figure, in part because he was the king's serjeant, playing a pivotal role in the activities of the parliament, which sat intermittently from May 1536 until December 1537, and during which highly contentious legislation was brought before the Irish parliament to reform the customs, raise taxes and suppress the monasteries. The royal proposals received a severe set-back at the hands of determined

---

29 *Patentee officers in Ireland, 1173–1826*, ed. J.L.J. Hughes (Dublin,1960), pp. 7 and 33; Bradshaw, *The dissolution of the religious orders in Ireland*, p. 88.
30 *S.P. Hen. VIII*, ii, 360.

opponents, and Barnewall was alleged to be the leading spirit amongst the opposition. It is beyond the scope of this work to examine the history of this parliament in detail and the wider significance of Barnewall's actions. These have been fully considered elsewhere, notably by Dr Bradshaw in *The Irish constitutional revolution of the sixteenth century* and *The dissolution of the religious orders in Ireland under Henry VIII*, but no survey of Barnewall's career as king's serjeant would be complete without some reference being made to these events.

We have already seen that Barnewall was closely involved with the financial affairs of Irish monastic institutions, links which would be threatened by the proposal to suppress the monasteries and take their possessions into royal hands. By the early sixteenth century the monasteries in Ireland, and, in particular, those within the Pale and the lordships of Kildare and Ormond, had, in general, fallen victim to a secular malaise. This resulted in the communities dwindling in size to a point where they often consisted of less than half a dozen members, if not completely derelict, and with little evidence of spiritual intensity. In addition, they possessed much more landed wealth than they were able to cope with, a great deal of which had passed into the hands of the laity by various means such as alienations and leases.[31] The royal proposals thus threatened the interests of the Old English lawyers of the Pale who were intimately involved, both professionally and personally, in the existing state of affairs. Barnewall's position as serjeant and a leading representative of this class was clearly a difficult one, since his private interests and connections were at variance with his role as a prominent royal official. Certainly by October 1536 he and Robert Dillon, the king's attorney, had been selected by the Irish commons to go to London to place their objections to the royal proposals before the king. In doing so, Barnewall and Dillon were in a difficult, not to say dangerous, position at a time when opposition to the king's wishes might result in the opponent's death if pressed too far, particularly if Henry considered that his vital interests were being threatened. We are solely dependent for a description of Barnewall's views at this moment upon a long letter written to Cromwell early in October 1536 by Robert Cowley, in which he characteristically sought to portray his rival's actions in the most unfavourable light. After

---

31 Bradshaw, *The dissolution of the religious orders in Ireland*, pp. 33–39.

referring to the opposition in the commons to the bills and the decision to send Barnewall and Dillon to England, he contended that they were

> to persuade, and if they could, inveigle the king's council to defeat and reject the king's advantage and profit by feigned suggestions. Of which two, Patrick Barnewall, the king's serjeant, is one principal champion; who, and in effect all his lineage of the Barnewalls, have been great doers and adherents, privy counsellors to the late earl of Kildare.[32]

Given that later in the letter Cowley asked that he might be granted the manor of Holmpatrick at a yearly fee if it were suppressed, a monastic property in north Co. Dublin where the Barnewalls' estates were particularly concentrated, and the rivalry concerning Patrick Barnewall's offices, it may be justifiable to treat Cowley's suggestions with some reserve, particularly the allegation that Barnewall was an intimate supporter of the Kildares. As we have already seen, both Patrick Barnewall and his uncle, the chancellor, had been advanced by Cromwell to their present offices in 1534, and although the chancellor's long official career started under the lord deputyship of the eighth earl, and the ninth earl appointed him treasurer in September 1524 shortly after the ninth earl was reappointed lord deputy, a contemporary chronicler suggested that their relations were poor in 1520 to 1522.[33] However, Cromwell was prepared to rely upon the chancellor, who survived an allegation that during Silken Thomas's siege of Dublin in September 1534 he had tried to bribe the constable of Dublin Castle to surrender the city to the rebels,[34] and in 1536 he did much to prove his loyalty when, with Brabazon, the under-treasurer, he led an expedition which expelled the O'Connor from Offaly where he had been attacking Anglo-Irish settlements;[35] and, as we have already seen, in August of the same year Patrick Barnewall was with Lord Deputy Grey at Limerick when O'Brien's bridge was destroyed.

Nevertheless, in setting out on his journey to England at the end of 1536, Patrick Barnewall was embarking upon a very important, delicate and possibly dangerous mission as he might be seen not

32 *S.P. Hen. VIII*, ii, 370.
33 *Cal. Carew MSS, 1515–74*, p. 191.
34 Ellis, *Tudor Ireland*, p. 127.
35 See entry in *DNB*.

merely as an emissary, but as a leading opponent of the king whose servant he was. Cowley, in the letter quoted earlier, told Cromwell:

the said Patrick Barnewall, serjeant, who now repaireth thither, said openly in the commons house, that he would not grant that the king, as head of the church, had so large power as the bishop of Rome; and that the king's jurisdiction therein was but a spiritual power, to reform or amend the enormities and defaults in religious houses, but not to execute men's laws, nor to dissolve abbeys, or to alter the foundation of them to any temporal use.[36]

Whilst one might question whether he expressed his views quite so plainly, nevertheless Barnewall's appointment as one of the two emissaries is indicative of his sympathy, if not his support, for the opposition to these contentious measures. He and Dillon remained in England until well into 1537, and they succeeded in persuading Henry to abandon the plan to extract additional revenue. They also persuaded him to grant a general pardon to those involved in the revolt of Silken Thomas. Their success may be seen from the grant (rarely given) of permission to purchase a grant of inheritance in monastic properties, which they had leased at a discount of five years upon the price of twenty years purchase.[37]

However, despite the success of his mission to London, and the high regard in which he was held in Dublin (the under-treasurer, Brabazon, writing to Cromwell 'that such an earnest officer cannot here be spared'),[38] Barnewall's career received a set-back when he failed to become chief baron upon the death of Chief Baron Finglas, despite a recommendation to that effect by the lord deputy and council in August 1537, the post going instead to Richard Delahide, who had been removed as chief justice of the common pleas in 1534.[39] In September 1537, his position as king's serjeant and solicitor general was altered to some extent (though not to his financial disadvantage), with the appointment for the first time of a separate principal or chief solicitor in the person of Walter Cowley. Upon his appointment as king's serjeant, Barnewall, as had John Barnewall, Rochfort and Luttrell before him, also became solicitor general. Appointment to both offices was made by the same letters

36   *S.P. Hen. VIII*, ii, 372.
37   *S.P. Hen. VIII*, iii, 298.
38   *L. & P. Hen. VIII*, xii (1), 470.
39   Bradshaw, *The dissolution of the religious orders in Ireland*, p. 185.

patent which provided that the holder was to receive a single annual fee. Thus, on Luttrell's appointment, he received a salary of twenty marks a year, to be paid equally by the treasury and the sheriff of Drogheda, illustrating the perennial difficulty which the administration faced in securing funds, even to pay such a senior official.[40] Although Cowley is generally referred to by writers on this period as being the solicitor general, it is clear that the existing title of solicitor general continued to be enjoyed by the king's serjeant. Cowley was described as the principal or chief solicitor, being appointed by a patent dated 7 September 1537 at an annual fee of £10.[41] As the existing administration in Dublin was dependent upon a small number of officials at this time, the creation of a separate post of principal solicitor no doubt served the dual purpose of rewarding Cowley and enabling the considerable administrative burden involved in the projected dissolution of the monasteries to be shared more widely. Despite the creation of the new post, Barnewall not only continued to be described in official documents as 'king's serjeant and solicitor general' until his appointment as master of the rolls, but he also continued to be paid for the office, probably in addition to his annual fee of twenty marks, since in 1542 a payment is noted to 'Patrick Barnewall, the other solicitor, for his reward 4*l*'.[42]

Although he had been instrumental in persuading the king to modify his plans to raise additional revenue etc., Barnewall did not continue his opposition to the proposed suppression of the monasteries, opposition which was ultimately confined to the spiritual lords in the upper house and the clerical proctors who still had a place in the house of commons. However, in September and October 1537, even this opposition collapsed and the proctors were henceforth excluded from parliament.[43] By this time the writing was clearly on the wall for the monasteries, the more far-sighted of which were doing what they could to ensure their future by rewarding those who had been linked to them in the past and who might be of assistance in the days to come, Barnewall himself being the recipient of an annuity in October, granted by the Cistercian abbot of St Mary's, Dublin.[44]

---

40 *Cal. pat. rolls Ire., Hen. VIII– Eliz.*, p. 5. 20 marks = £13 6*s*. 8*d*.; one mark = 13*s*. 4*d*. The attorney general received £12 p. a.: ibid.
41 Smyth, *Law officers*, p. 172.
42 *Cal. S.P. Ire., 1509–73*, p. 62.
43 Bradshaw, *The dissolution of the religious orders in Ireland*, p. 64.
44 Ibid., p. 89.

Apart from the grant of a licence to himself and Dillon to purchase grants of inheritance in the monastic lands which they had leased, and obtaining annuities, Barnewall did not, contrary to what is generally inferred, immediately profit to any significant extent from the dissolution of the monasteries during the first phase of their suppression in 1537 and 1538.[45] Indeed, although he and another lawyer, Thomas Houth, had taken a lease for thirty-five years from the king of lands which had formerly belonged to the English priory of Cartmel in Lancashire, it was declared void, prompting Barnewall to write to Cromwell in April 1538 asking that the lease be confirmed.[46]

Fifteen thirty-nine to 1541 saw Barnewall playing a prominent part in the final phase of the suppression of the monasteries. The machinery created to carry out this policy involved the appointment of commissioners, who visited each institution in turn and received a formal surrender of the abbey, priory or convent from its members, together with all of its estates and possessions. The commissioners were accompanied by assessors who witnessed the surrenders and, presumably, ensured that the necessary legal formalities were complied with. Robert Cowley, by now master of the rolls, and Barnewall are frequently found acting as assessors, and in July 1539 Barnewall was present at the surrender of the Augustinian convent of St Brigid of Odder, Co. Meath, on the 16th; on the 25th at the much wealthier St Thomas Court near Dublin, and on the 26th at the surrender of the Augustinian foundation of St John the Baptist at Naas, Co. Kildare.[47] Between October 1540 and January 1541, he is recorded as acting as assessor in surveys of various monastic properties,[48] and, ultimately in July 1541, he purchased the nunnery of Gracedieu, Co. Dublin. As can be seen from the details enrolled in the patent and close rolls, the properties held by the nunnery were scattered through six parishes in north Co. Dublin, and included mills at Portmarnock.[49]

---

45 His name is not to be found in the list of beneficiaries of the distribution of properties set out in Bradshaw, *The dissolution of the religious orders in Ireland*, at p. 233. In this respect, Barnewall is to be distinguished from several other officials of the period.

46 *S.P. Hen. VIII*, ii, 571; *L. &. P. Hen. VIII*, xiii (1), 259; *Cal. S.P. Ire., 1509–73*, p. 39.

47 *Cal. pat. rolls Ire., Hen. VIII–Eliz.*, pp. 134–35.

48 *Extents of Irish monastic possessions, 1540–1541*, ed. N.B. White (Dublin, 1943), pp. 177 and 183.

49 *Cal. pat. rolls Ire., Hen. VIII–Eliz.*, pp. 73–74.

Undoubtedly, Barnewall did very well out of his part in the dissolution of the monasteries, but, as can be seen from the details in appendix I of Bradshaw's *The dissolution of the religious orders in Ireland under Henry VIII*, so did other leading royal officials of the time: magnates such as the earls of Desmond and Thomond, merchants and gentry. Indeed, others such as his brother-in-law, Thomas Luttrell, chief justice of the common pleas, and Thomas Cusack, master of the rolls, did as well, if not better, in obtaining leases and grants of valuable properties. Whilst Barnewall in due course shared in the spoils, he did so primarily in 1541, and not as an immediate consequence of his mission to London in 1536–37.

Barnewall's prominence in the Reformation Parliament of 1536–37 gives a false impression of the importance of the office of king's serjeant at law at this time. There can be little doubt that his emergence as a spokesman for the opposition to the initial royal proposals was due to his position as a leading royal official and to his legal expertise. Nevertheless, Barnewall's political prominence was short-lived and, with his return to Ireland in 1537, the office of king's serjeant resumed its accustomed place in the Irish official hierarchy of the time: of lesser importance than the chancellor, the chief justices and chief baron, or even of the vice-treasurer and the master of the rolls, though clearly ranking above the other law officers of the day, and so continuing to play a significant role in both legal and political affairs. Unfortunately, the comparative wealth of contemporary material relating to Barnewall's activities as a royal official in the political and in the administrative or quasi-legal sphere is in sharp contrast to the scarcity of material which throws some light on the functions of the king's serjeant in the purely legal sphere, a scarcity which only allows glimpses of his role in the law courts of the Pale.

In 1538 Barnewall had asserted that it had been the function of the king's serjeant to maintain and confess the king's pleas, thereby inferring perhaps that this was solely the responsibility of the king's serjeant, no doubt mainly before the king's bench. If the king's serjeant was unavailable, presumably the king's attorney would act in his place, since the latter had also prosecuted and defended the king's pleas from the creation of that office.[50] A letter to Cromwell of November 1537 from one John Bolter, a goldsmith, suggests that Barnewall was also engaged in cases before the chancellor, though

50 Richardson & Sayles, *Admin. Ire.*, p. 41.

whether in his official capacity as king's serjeant or as a pleader or as a litigant, is unknown. Bolter complained that he could have 'no furtherance in his causes before the lord chancellor, but is driven from term to term by the importunity of Patrick Barnewall, the king's serjeant'. Given Barnewall's involvement in affairs of state at this time, it is hardly surprising that he was unable to attend to his cases before the chancellor, although his 'consanguinity with the judges', as Bolter alleged, may well have helped him to have his cases delayed.[51]

Barnewall's long tenure of the office of serjeant came to an end when he was appointed master of the rolls in 1550 in place of Sir Thomas Cusack who became chancellor. Barnewall's successor was John Bathe, who was called to the bar at Lincoln's Inn in 1539 and had been the principal solicitor since 1546. From Co. Meath, he was related to James Bathe, chief baron, and was at one time recorder of Drogheda.[52] The importance attached by the king and his advisers to the major legal offices in Ireland may be gathered from the fact that these appointments were all communicated to the lord deputy and council by a letter from Edward VI, the terms of which make it clear that whilst the lord deputy had advised the appointments, the final say rested with the king in London. As we have seen in the case of Patrick Barnewall in 1537, the recommendations from Dublin were not always followed. Bathe was duly appointed serjeant at law and solicitor general, but by separate patents dated 16 October, and whilst Barnewall had held both offices for life, Bathe's patents appointed him as serjeant at law for life but as solicitor general during pleasure.[53] This distinction between the terms upon which the two offices were held no doubt envisaged that they might be held by different individuals in future, a possibility foreshadowed by the appointment of a principal solicitor in 1537. At first sight, it seems that this separation did occur in 1553 when Richard Finglas (who had been principal solicitor since 1550) became solicitor general, because an undated patent appointing him solicitor general is included amongst the calendar of patent and close rolls for that year. However, Smyth in his *Chronicle of the law officers of Ireland* records that Bathe was continued in office as solicitor general by Mary by a patent dated 12 February 1554, Finglas also being continued as principal solicitor by a patent of the same date. From this it would

51 *Cal. S.P. Ire., 1509–73*, p. 34.
52 Ball, *Judges*, i, 206; *Cal. pat. rolls Ire., Hen. VIII-Eliz.*, pp. 166–67.
53 *Cal. pat. rolls Ire., Hen. VIII-Eliz.*, p. 209.

appear that the undated patent has been incorrectly attributed, and that Bathe did in fact continue to enjoy both offices until his appointment as chief justice of the common pleas later in 1554.[54] It would seem that Richard Finglas, Bathe's successor, also continued to hold the offices of serjeant and solicitor general until his death in 1574, having received a fresh patent as solicitor general in 1566 from Elizabeth,[55] although in contemporary documents it was customary to refer to him as simply the serjeant, and to the principal solicitor of the day as the solicitor or solicitor general.

During his tenure as serjeant, Bathe continued to act as his predecessors had done by appearing occasionally as a member of various judicial commissions. Thus he served as a commissioner of gaol delivery and was named in the commission of the peace for Dublin. He appears to have impressed by his legal knowledge as well as by his diligence, discretion and loyalty. Bathe's successor as serjeant and solicitor general, as previously noted, was Richard Finglas who had been principal solicitor since 1550 and who was destined to hold both offices until his death in 1574. Unlike Bathe, Finglas was appointed serjeant during good behaviour, a highly unusual stipulation at a time when even judges were appointed at pleasure, and one which was not to be repeated until the reign of Charles II. This was almost certainly the reason why his patent was not renewed upon Elizabeth's accession, it being the custom to issue fresh patents by a new sovereign to all such office holders.

In 1574, Finglas was succeeded by Fitzsimon (or Fitzsymon) who had been attorney general since 1570 and was to equal his predecessor's tenure of office, remaining as serjeant until his death in 1594. A native of Dublin, he entered the Inner Temple in 1555 and became justice of the liberty of Wexford in 1563.[56] As his predecessors had done, he too acted on occasion in a quasi-judicial or inquisitorial role. An instance of this occurred in 1584, when he was one of a number of commissioners inquiring as to all persons attainted in Dublin, Kildare, Meath, Westmeath, Louth, Waterford and Carlow, and all their possessions. Similarly, in 1588, he was one of several commissioners sitting at Sligo to ascertain what lands O'Connor Sligo held of the queen.[57] In

---

54 Ibid., p. 313; Smyth, *Law officers*, p. 173.
55 Hughes, *Patentee officers*, p. 49; but see *A new history of Ireland, ix*, pp. 518 and 520, n.11.
56 Ball, *Judges*, i, 219.
57 *Cal. pat. rolls Ire., Eliz.*, pp. 71 and 145.

1578, Fitzsimon was appointed to act as master of the rolls in place of Nicholas White. This is one of the few occasions at this time when the serjeant was called upon to perform a judicial office, although, as we have seen, this was common from the early days of the office, and was to remain so until the twentieth century.

Apart from his functions in the courts of law, it is clear that the king's serjeant was constantly called upon, as were the king's attorney and the principal solicitor, to assist in the resolution of matters which came before the king's council in its judicial role. As Richardson and Sayles have shown, in the fourteenth and fifteenth centuries the medieval Irish parliament constantly acted as a judicial forum for the resolution of disputes, the parties to which either could not, or were unwilling to, litigate through the courts of law.[58] During the Tudor period when parliaments were summoned at infrequent intervals, the council assumed the judicial role formerly performed by parliament. The common procedure was for the council to appoint a number of commissioners who would investigate the matter, hear the parties, and then report their conclusions to the council which would act accordingly. The general pattern was that two or three commissioners would be appointed, of whom at least one would be a judge of the common law courts and another would be one of the law officers. The law officer was usually the king's serjeant, though occasionally the attorney or solicitor would be included. Two examples illustrate the type of dispute which came before the council at this time. In 1547 Lord Protector Somerset directed Sir Thomas Luttrell, chief justice of the common pleas, Walter Kerdiff, justice of the common pleas, and Barnewall to investigate a petition in which the widow of the earl of Clanrickard claimed a third of his estate. The commissioners were appointed under the great seal and required 'to hear and examine the petition of Piers Marten and wife, to call witnesses before them, and to determine some better decision than heretofore has been pronounced', as the matter had already been referred to the lord deputy and council and the complainant 'could obtain no final order from them'.

The commissioners duly reported that, as the earl's first wife was still alive when he married the petitioner, the later marriage was void, and so she was not entitled to one third of his estate. However, she was entitled to £300, being the amount of a bond entered into as part of

---

58 Richardson & Sayles, *Ir. parl. in middle ages*, pp. 216–17.

the marriage settlement, together with various items of plate. That this decision took the form of a binding judgment may be inferred from its being enrolled as a decree. The commissioners also provided that the widow was to be at liberty to seek to have the earl's first marriage annulled, in which case she should be entitled to one third of the earl's possessions and lands.[59] A similar form had been adopted in 1545 when it was decreed by Gerald Aylmer, chief justice of the king's bench, Thomas Houth and Walter Kerdiff, justices, and Barnewall in a suit between the portrieve and commons of Cashel 'that the corporation, their successors and assigns, should have and possess "the commons" and every part thereof, without let or interruption'.[60]

By the reign of Mary, the need to diligently attend to royal business, that is to plead and defend the queen's pleas before the queen's bench and common pleas, was such that a blistering rebuke was administered to the Irish judges and law officers in 1556 by the queen herself. The language used described the financial benefits which were expected to accrue to the crown from the administration of justice, as well as the failure of those addressed to administer justice impartially:

And where in times past, justice being ministered and executed, much profit, besides the common quiet of our realm, hath been made to the use of the crown by the seals and process of those courts, we now understand that of all escheats by forfeiture of recognizance, attainders, escapes, breach of peace, riots, unlawful assemblies, false verdicts, forfeitures upon penal statutes, false recoveries, fines, amerciaments, and such like, little profit or none hath accrued and been answered to us, the default whereof is to be chiefly ascribed to negligence of officers; our pleasure therefore is, that our said deputy and council shall command and diligently call upon our judges of either bench, our serjeant, attorney, solicitor, and other officers from henceforth to use good diligence in their several offices, not only in ministering justice to all men without respect indifferently, the lack whereof hath caused many mischiefs and disorders in that realm, but that also they shall most diligently see to our profit, and that we lose no duties, as we specially trust them; requiring our said deputy to declare unto them and every of them that we are not now ignorant of the ill husbandry in past times used in those courts, which we trust shall from henceforward be amended.[61]

---

59 *Cal. pat. rolls Ire., Hen. VIII–Eliz.*, pp. 170–71.
60 Ibid., p. 112.
61 *Cal. Carew MSS, 1515–74*, p. 254.

That these defects were not confined to the queen's bench and common pleas was emphasized in the letter, equally trenchant criticism being directed at the failure of the exchequer to ensure that royal rents and revenues were collected. Indeed, at frequent intervals throughout Elizabeth's reign complaints were made, often in the most forceful terms, about the inability of the Irish judges and law officers to perform their duties, and requests were frequently made that they be replaced by English lawyers. Such an example occurs in 1597, when, upon the death of Serjeant Corye, a request was made to Sir Robert Cecil that he

might consider some fit man from England to supply his place. This may greatly advantage the revenues and exchequer causes, which for want of good assistance, have hitherto grown to no small disorder and prejudice through her officers, among whom the solicitor only hath taken more care and pains than all the rest.[62]

Although these calls were not always heeded, on occasion law officers were appointed from England. One was Thomas Snagge who became attorney general in 1578,

her majesty observing that the public service had not been a little hindered through the default and insufficiency of the officers in the law previously appointed; for redress whereof her majesty thought that a person well-chosen in England might be sent over to exercise the office of attorney general.[63]

Given the importance which the Tudors attached to the law, and the constant warfare associated with the efforts made throughout Elizabeth's reign to extend effective royal control over the whole of Ireland, one might have expected that the law officers, and the serjeant in particular, would feature more prominently in official records as representing the royal interest, but that is not always the case. The explanation probably lies in a combination of several factors. In part, it is consistent with the reliance which was prin-cipally placed upon the judges to protect the royal interest in the manner that Mary clearly expected in 1556. It may also reflect the destruction of so many legal records, which inevitably leads to a reliance upon contemporary documents which survived, either

---

62 *Cal. S.P. Ire., 1596–97*, pp. 390–91.
63 *Cal. pat. rolls Ire., Eliz.*, p. 11.

because they were removed from Ireland by holders of high office upon their return to England, or were correspondence with officials in London when legal matters would not constantly require explanation or attention, and which may not, therefore, contain more than occasional references to the law and the law officers in action. Another factor may be that, as the Tudor era progressed, detailed control of Irish affairs was increasingly exercised directly from London, thereby reducing the importance of Irish officials other than the major officers of state.

One important occasion where we catch a glimpse of the serjeant in action occurred in 1577, during Sir Henry Sidney's second term as lord deputy. This was in the course of the controversy over cess, when a petition or bill was brought before the lord deputy and council challenging the legality of impositions placed upon the inhabitants of the Pale, whereby they were required to provide and transport supplies for the soldiers at prices fixed by the government, which were well below the market price. A substantial number of landowners complained, and, as they were not prepared to accept the lord deputy's views, they petitioned to be allowed to go to London to press their case. But before they did so, Sidney referred the matter to the chancellor, Gerrard, who conducted a hearing at which the petitioners were represented by counsel. After they had been heard, because it was 'the queen's cause he called her majesty's serjeant [Fitzsimon] and attorney and willed them to consider of it, and the morrow after to say in maintenance of her majesty's prerogative what they could'.[64]

Few examples have survived of the serjeant acting as a general legal adviser to the crown in the manner of law officers in later times, but there is no reason to believe that he did not perform this function regularly. One that has survived involved Fitzsimon who, a few months after his appointment, was asked to give his opinion as to the adequacy of a commission concerning reformation of the customs at Chester, presumably because of the importance of the port for trade to and from Ireland. However, he declined to do so because the bearer would not leave the commission until the next day and Fitzsimon could not give his opinion in such a short time.[65]

64 *Anal Hib*, no. 2 (1931), p. 132; Ellis, *Tudor Ireland*, pp. 272–73; N.P. Canny, *From reformation to restoration: Ireland, 1534–1600* (Dublin, 1987), pp. 94–97; J.G. Crawford, *Anglicizing the government of Ireland: the Irish privy council and the expansion of Tudor rule, 1556–1578* (Dublin, 1993), pp. 392–407.
65 *Cal. S.P. Ire., 1574–85*, p. 76.

As we have seen in the case of Patrick Barnewall, the office of serjeant was one which enabled its holder to accumulate considerable wealth, and there is some evidence to suggest that other serjeants were also men of substance, if the position of Christopher Fitzsimon was representative. The son of Serjeant Fitzsimon and a student at the Middle Temple, in December 1575 he wrote to Burghley asking that a warrant for £100 which had been sent to him by his father be paid,[66] although, as Fitzsimon had only become serjeant that year, he had presumably acquired such means earlier in his career. Christopher Fitzsimon again appears in 1581 as a recusant, writing to his father that he had temporarily withdrawn from his studies in the Temple because

by virtue of a commission not only sent thither but also to all other houses of court and chancery for the trying and finding out of those that would not go to church and [receive communion] I separated myself from them, lest being unknown, by being called before them in examination I should be known.[67]

Like many other students from Old English Pale families in London at this time, the serjeant's son was obviously a conscientious roman catholic and, understandably in the climate of the time, anxious that his religious beliefs should not be discovered.

The financial rewards available to the serjeant by virtue of his office were ostensibly modest. First of all, there was an annual fee. In 1606, Serjeant Kerdiff's fee was £27 6s. 8d., whereas Sir Charles Calthorpe, the attorney general, and Sir John Davies, the solicitor general, each received £159 6s. 8d., compared with a salary of £133 6s. 8d. received by the puisne judges of the king's bench and common pleas and the barons of the exchequer.[68] Kerdiff's fee was greater than the fee of £13 6s. 8d. received by Thomas Luttrell in 1532, but in 1627 the serjeant's fee was still only £27.[69] As the attorney general received a fee of £10 in 1532, the increase for him by 1606 had been very much greater. That such salaries had been paid to the attorney general and solicitor general for some years is

---

66   Ibid., p. 87.
67   Ibid., p. 286.
68   *Cal. S.P. Ire., 1603–06*, pp. 429–30.
69   *Cal. S.P. Ire., 1647–60 and addenda, 1625–1660*, p. 345. This gives a breakdown of the amount as the serjeant's 'ancient fee' of £17 6s. 8d. and £10 'for his attendance at Star (i.e. Castle) Chamber'.

apparent from a request in 1601 by Saxey, chief justice of Munster, that he might have the same fee as the attorney and solicitor, who each received a yearly fee of £200 as well as what they might make in practice.[70] However, this disparity in salaries must be considered in the context of other income available to the serjeant. Thus Serjeant Finglas was granted an annuity of £10 Irish 'in recompense of his labour, diligence, and attendance had and to be had in the castle chamber before the privy council, from time to time, as often as should be requisite and fit'.[71] As this payment was expressed to be at pleasure, it was presumably an additional payment over and above the normal emoluments which the serjeant could expect to receive. As well as such ad hoc payments, the serjeant was also entitled to 'the accustomed fees and perquisites', which cannot now be completely identified.[72] It would appear that the 'accustomed fees' included the right to charge fees on the making of grants in the exchequer, as a complaint was recorded in 1597 against the solicitor general, Sir Roger Wilbraham, that 'he takes the making of all grants, both from the serjeant, attorney and remembrancer, who ought to have the making of them all'.[73] Fees upon the granting of pardons were probably also payable to the king's serjeant at this time, because in 1690 it was alleged that Serjeant Osborne was motivated in part in his desire to have all protestants who acted in any civil employment under King James II declared guilty of high treason by the prospect of the fees he would receive for passing the fiants necessary to enable such individuals to obtain pardons.[74] It would seem very unlikely that this was an innovation at that time and therefore such fees were, no doubt, payable during the sixteenth century. As fees were the recognised method of remunerating judges and officials, we may be justified in assuming that the serjeant could

---

70 Ibid., p. 301.
71 Smyth, *Law officers*, pp. 185–86.
72 *Cal. pat. rolls Ire., Eliz.*, p. 466: the patent of Serjeant Loftus in 1597. In 1608 the judges and the serjeant each received £17 15s. 6^{1}/2d. for their robes: *Cal. S.P. Ire., 1608–10*, p. 77. This was not an isolated instance of such a payment, as the civil list for 1666/1667 contains an entry for robes for 'the three king's counsel' (the prime serjeant, attorney general and solicitor general) at £13 6s. 8d. each: *Cal. S.P. Ire., 1666–69*, p. 75. It is probable that these payments existed in the sixteenth century as well.
73 *Cal. S.P. Ire., 1596–97*, p. 497.
74 Archbishop King's letters, 1690–1715 (NLI, MS 2055). William King (later Archbishop King) wrote that Osborne would get 'some thousands' in fees.

receive substantial amounts from this source. Another profitable area was wardship of minors: in 1538, Serjeant Barnewall mentioned in a letter to Thomas Cromwell that he had purchased a king's ward for £200, although as the ward turned out to have only £18 in possession, it was not as profitable as he had anticipated.[75]

The end of the Tudor era is a convenient point at which to evaluate the position of the serjeant before the considerable changes which occurred in the Irish legal world in the years immediately following the death of Elizabeth in 1603. As we have seen, the serjeant continued to act on behalf of the sovereign in all the common law courts, defending or prosecuting cases involving the royal interest as required, as well as playing a leading part in the judicial role of the privy council, and generally acting as a law officer of the crown. It is plain that the serjeant was the senior Irish law officer throughout the Tudor period. In the early years he was a member of the council whilst the attorney was not, and in mid-Tudor times his annual fee was greater. In addition, where both are named in the same document, the serjeant is almost invariably named first. This pattern is so consistent that it clearly establishes that the serjeant was viewed as the senior office. This is underlined by three serjeants in this period serving as attorney immediately before they became serjeant (John Barnewall, Fitzleones and Fitzsimon), whereas no serjeant subsequently served as attorney. In the early Tudor period, to be serjeant was usually a stepping-stone to the bench, as was to be the case in later times. However, in the half-century from the appointment of Serjeant Finglas in 1554 to the accession of James I in 1603, no serjeant was promoted to permanent judicial office. Whilst this might suggest a decline in the importance of the serjeant, there are two other factors which explain this development. First of all, some judges showed considerable longevity and so there were not a great many vacancies to be filled. Secondly, when vacancies did occur, as we have seen, Elizabeth's dissatisfaction with the quality of the Irish bench and law officers led her to appoint English judges or lawyers on a number of occasions. This policy was naturally a source of grievance in Ireland, and it is interesting to note that the earl of Tyrone included in the articles submitted to the English government as peace terms in 1599 a demand that, amongst others, 'the justices of the laws, queen's

75 *S.P. Hen. VIII*, ii, 571.

attorney, queen's serjeant and all other officers appertaining to the council and laws of Ireland be Irishmen'. This was not something that the English government was prepared to countenance, Sir Robert Cecil tersely endorsing the proposal 'Utopia'.[76]

As we shall see in the next chapter, the status and, to some extent the function, of the serjeant was to change considerably in the next century. Although he retained formal precedence ahead of both the attorney general and solicitor general until the office of prime serjeant (as it became known later) was abolished in 1805, there was an unmistakable and significant sign at the end of the sixteenth century that, in reality, the serjeant was no longer the most important law officer in Ireland when the attorney general and solicitor general received the much more substantial fees that have already been described. This disparity is striking, and cannot be interpreted in any fashion other than as an indication that these offices were more important than that of the serjeant at law, which office therefore had its status and prestige significantly eroded, an erosion which became more obvious in the seventeenth century.

76 *Cal. S.P. Ire., 1599–1600*, pp. 279–80.

CHAPTER THREE

The serjeants in the Stuart era, 1603–1690

THE EARLY YEARS of the seventeenth century were years of profound change in the Irish legal system. The surrender by Tyrone to Lord Deputy Mountjoy in 1603 marked the end of resistance to the Tudor conquest and enabled the English government to exercise effective control throughout the whole of Ireland for the first time. A crucial ingredient in the consolidation and exercise of this control was the extension of the common law and its enforcement through the courts. An incidental result of this process was the further diminution of the role of the king's serjeant in the Irish governmental and legal hierarchy.

The leading figure in the extension and enforcement of the common law was the remarkable Sir John Davies, who became solicitor general in 1603 and was attorney general from 1606 until 1619. As attorney general, 'the weight of Davies's intellect and driving power were given full rein'.[1] During his tenure of office he dominated the Irish legal system, organising commissions of assize so that the judges could go on circuit throughout the whole island, as well as providing the intellectual and philosophical basis for the extension and supremacy of the common law at the expense of Irish customary law by his arguments in, and reports of, a number of highly significant cases.

Davies's domination of the Irish legal world as attorney general was due to several factors, the most important being that he enjoyed the confidence and backing of the English government. Another was that in England the posts of attorney general and solicitor general were overtaking the king's serjeant in importance.[2] This trend had already been apparent in Ireland, and as many of the leading offices in Ireland were now occupied by men who were familiar with this development because of their professional and public lives in England,

---

1   Ball, *Judges*, i, 232.
2   J.L.J. Edwards, *The law officers of the crown* (London, 1964), p. 30.

it was natural that there was a similar change in Ireland at approximately the same time. Finally, there were the personal factors of Davies's intellect, legal knowledge and experience, coupled with his enormous energy. Aged thirty-four when he arrived in Ireland in 1603, Davies had already established a reputation as a poet. Although his legal career had suffered a severe setback when he was expelled from the Middle Temple in February 1598 for a gross breach of discipline, he had been re-admitted in 1601, the same year as he was returned to parliament as member for Corfe Castle. It is clear from the range and depth of learning which he displayed in his law reports that Davies was a person of exceptional ability.[3] Against such a combination of factors the king's serjeants of the time were unable to maintain their previous pre-eminence, particularly as the holders of the office during this period were young and inexperienced.

Serjeant Loftus, the second son of Archbishop Loftus who had been chancellor for many years, might have been in a stronger position than his successor Nicholas Kerdiff to assert the pre-eminence of the king's serjeant, had Loftus not been killed at the siege of Kinsale in May 1601.[4] A native of Co. Dublin, Kerdiff had been called to the bar by the Middle Temple in February 1600 and although he held office until 1609, given his youth and lack of experience, it is hardly surprising that he was completely overshadowed by Davies. Nevertheless, the serjeants continued to play an important role as royal law officers.

The expansion of the assize system so that it covered the entire island created a need for more judges to go on the circuits. The demand for judges could not be met by the existing judges of the king's bench, common pleas and exchequer alone. The administration was forced to look elsewhere, and amongst those called upon were the king's serjeants.[5] Kerdiff went on circuit seven times between 1603 and 1609, and John Beere, his successor, went nine times between 1610 and 1615.

---

3   See *DNB* and H.S. Pawlisch, *Sir John Davies and the conquest of Ireland: a study in legal imperialism* (Cambridge, 1985).

4   John Lodge, *The peerage of Ireland*, ed. Mervyn Archdall, 7 vols. (Dublin, 1789), vii, 251.

5   Others who were called upon at this time included the master of the rolls; Richard Bolton, recorder of Dublin; and Henry Dillon, attorney general of Ulster. John McCavitt, ' "Good planets in their several spheares" – the establishment of the assize circuits in early seventeenth-century Ireland', *Ir Jur*, xxiv (1989), 248.

Service as an assize judge was an onerous duty and could occupy a substantial period of time. In the summer of 1613, Beere spent sixty-eight days, starting on 14 July, on circuit in the counties of Waterford, Tipperary, Limerick, Clare, Kerry and Cork, as well as the Cross of Tipperary and the cities of Limerick and Cork.[6] However, the rewards were not insubstantial. Between 1607 and 1609, Kerdiff received allowances of £37, £47, £29 and £20 for his services, together with payments of £17 15s. 6½d. and £13 6s. 8d. for his judicial robes.[7]

As in earlier centuries, the serjeants were also called upon to act in a quasi-judicial or inquisitorial capacity. In 1605, Kerdiff was one of several commissioners who carried out inquisitions in Co. Dublin relating to forfeitures arising out of the rebellion against Elizabeth.[8] In June 1611, Beere was appointed as one of the commissioners to enquire into the king's title to lands comprised in the plantation of Wexford.[9] In 1615, having already spent 50 days on assize earlier in the year, Beere spent a further 42 days, beginning on 11 July, with Lord Deputy Chichester in 'Longford, Leitrim and other counties'.[10] They were enquiring into crown titles to land in these counties, and Chichester obviously felt that Beere's services were worthy of reward as Beere was knighted on 19 August.[11]

It was natural that the serjeants were called upon to perform such quasi-judicial and judicial functions. As we have seen, this had frequently been the case from the late thirteenth century, and a practice was now evolving whereby the serjeants, together with the attorney general and solicitor general, were repeatedly called upon to serve as assize judges. By 1637 this practice was firmly established. In April of that year Serjeant Catelyn died whilst on circuit with Baron Lowther. Chancellor Loftus suggested to the lord deputy that Jerome Alexander be sent to complete the circuit, 'all the other judges and the king's counsel being otherwise employed by your lordship's commandment'. A sharp reply from Wentworth insisted that Eustace, as the king's serjeant, should replace Catelyn. The chancellor argued that Alexander was the older man, to which

6 Ibid., 276.
7 *Cal. S.P. Ire., 1608–10*, pp. 72–81 and 232–33.
8 *Pat. rolls Ire., Jas. I*, ed. Erck, p.142.
9 *Cal. S.P. Ire., 1611–14*, p. 450.
10 McCavitt, ' "Good planets in their several spheares" ', 278.
11 *Cal. Carew MSS, 1603–24*, p. 385.

Wentworth replied, 'I know the one is the king's serjeant and the other is not, which enables him, or at least qualifies him, to be trusted as a judge of assize before the other', remarking that Eustace was held 'as able in his own profession', and well provided 'with learning and integrity'.[12] Thereafter, it was unusual for counsel who were not law officers to be called upon to serve as assize judges, although it was not completely unknown. In the summer of 1661 John Povey, ultimately chief justice of the king's bench, and Oliver Jones, later a justice of the common pleas and then of the king's bench, acted as assize judges.[13]

Throughout the seventeenth century the state papers and private correspondence of the chief governors contain many references to instructions being given to the judges to emphasize the government's views on current issues of importance in their charges to grand juries, as well as to the desirability of giving decisions in favour of the crown.[14] The importance of sending as assize judges lawyers who were not only competent but compliant was not overlooked, and, as royal law officers, the serjeants could be expected to display at least one, if not both, of these qualities.

During the latter part of the seventeenth century, we find that the chief governors refer more and more to the attorney general and the solicitor general, both for legal advice and as the officers entrusted with the responsibility of instituting and pursuing proceedings on behalf of the crown. This was particularly the case after the restoration of Charles II. Thereafter, it is unusual to find references to advice being sought from the king's serjeants. As we shall see, part of the explanation for this may be that the then prime serjeant, Sir Audley Mervyn, was suspected of disloyalty to the crown. Another factor was that Sir William Domville, attorney general from 1660 until 1686, and Sir John Temple, solicitor general from 1660 until 1689, enjoyed the confidence of successive chief governors during their exceptionally long periods of office.[15] Nevertheless, quite apart

12 *The earl of Strafford's letters and dispatches*, ed. William Knowler, 2 vols. (London, 1739) i, 67–69. I owe this reference to Professor Osborough. In 1660, after the restoration of Charles II, Alexander became a judge of the common pleas.
13 H.M.C., *Ormond MSS (n.s.)*, iii, 378 and 395.
14 For example, *Cal. S.P. dom., 1690*, p. 204.
15 In 1675, the lord lieutenant, the earl of Essex, recommended that Temple should be given lands worth £500 p.a. because Domville enjoyed lands worth £800 p.a.: *Letters of the earl of Essex, lord lieutenant of Ireland, 1675* (London, 1770), p. 97.

from the influence of individual office holders, it is clear that by this time the attorney general had finally supplanted the prime serjeant as the senior law officer of the crown in Ireland in fact, if not in terms of formal precedence, as can be illustrated by a number of examples.

In 1633, Wentworth was incensed to learn that witnesses in proceedings before the court of castle chamber argued that their testimony should be regarded as being true, not because it was given on oath before the court, but because they had sworn in church that it was true. It was to the attorney general that Wentworth gave instructions to file an information against the priest and parties concerned.[16] In 1687, when the government dissolved protestant corporations in order to issue fresh charters with catholic majorities, the machinery used was to issue writs of quo warranto at the suit of the attorney general.[17] Finally, in times of great political tension, the power of the attorney general to initiate prosecutions and to stop cases in which the king was involved by way of entering a nolle prosequi was of great importance, notably during the reign of James II.[18]

Although the Stuart era saw the prime serjeant permanently eclipsed by the attorney general, this eclipse was gradual and far from total, and the prime serjeant was to retain his precedence over both the attorney general and solicitor general until 1805. This was a valuable privilege because cases were heard in order of the seniority of counsel, and, as the prime serjeant had precedence over every other member of the bar, this naturally enhanced his attractiveness to potential clients, as well as his professional standing. Apart from continuing to act as assize judges, the serjeants were also employed on royal business in the ordinary courts and elsewhere. In particular, their talents were heavily relied upon in parliament. The post still enjoyed considerable prestige, and the gradual eclipse of the serjeants' position was neither constant nor obvious. Indeed, in 1627 a new post of second serjeant was created with the appointment of Nathaniel Catelyn to the position. Why this post was created is not clear, the king's letter appointing Catelyn merely stating

16 Strafford, *Letters and dispatches*, i, 203–04.
17 *Calendar of the Orrery papers*, ed. E. MacLysaght (Dublin,1941), pp. 326–27, and William King, *The state of the protestants in Ireland under the late King James' government*, 3rd. ed. (London, 1682), p. 89.
18 King, *The state of the protestants in Ireland*, p. 73.

we understand that it is expedient for our services that we should have another serjeant at law in that our kingdom, of whose diligence use may be made in such causes as concern us and the rights of our Crown.[19]

This could mean that there was an identifiable need at the time for the services of another royal counsel. It has been pointed out that in the 1630s there was a considerable expansion in the business coming before the common pleas, the court of chancery and the equity side of the exchequer,[20] and it may be that there was a corresponding need to employ additional counsel to deal with an increase in business affecting the crown as early as 1627. On the other hand, in 1666, the then viceroy, the duke of Ormond, stated that the position had been 'introduced by favour to some lawyer'. He pointed out that the position was supernumerary, as it did not appear upon the Irish civil establishment of the time, which would suggest that the post was not regarded as a permanent one. Ormond continued: 'it is wholly useless to the king and little profitable to anybody'.[21] Ormond's great experience of the Irish administration, stretching back to the parliament of 1634, means that his opinion of the origin and utility of the office of second serjeant must command respect, although it may be that he was influenced in his assessment by the need for economy to which he referred when he suggested that the office need not be filled.

Whatever may be the reason for the creation of the office of second serjeant, the terms governing the first such appointment are of interest. Catelyn was formally appointed by letters patent but, as the king's letter setting out the terms upon which he was to be appointed made no reference to the question of his precedence relative to the other law officers, this question was referred to the king. It was then directed that Catelyn was to have

precedence in our courts of judicature and castle chamber, and in all subscriptions and meetings of our learned counsel, in the quality of our learned counsel there, above our attorney and solicitor general, as our other serjeant there hath, as is used here in England.[22]

19 *Cal. pat. rolls Ire., Chas. I*, p. 211.
20 Raymond Gillespie, 'The end of an era: Ulster and the outbreak of the 1641 rising', in Ciaran Brady and Raymond Gillespie (ed.), *Natives and newcomers: the making of Irish colonial society, 1534–1641* (Dublin, 1986).
21 *Cal. S.P. Ire., 1666–69*, p. 230. The post had become vacant upon the death of Serjeant Griffith.
22 *Cal. pat. rolls Ire., Chas. I*, p. 278.

The reference to 'as is used here in England' is significant, because in England at this time there were usually between two and four king's serjeants drawn from the ranks of the serjeants at law. The increased importance of the positions of attorney general and solicitor general in England had been recognized by a royal warrant of 1623 which gave them precedence before all of the serjeants, save the two 'ancientest' king's serjeants.[23] It would seem probable that, in granting Catelyn precedence in this way, the recent English precedent was being followed, rather than recognising his personal standing in Ireland. His appointment also emphasized a distinction between the king's serjeants in England and Ireland, which was to last until the offices became extinct in both countries, because Catelyn was appointed to an office by letters patent. In England, apart from occasional appointments in the eighteenth century, the king's serjeants did not occupy an office. This grant of precedence to the second serjeant proved to be a short-lived arrangement as the order of precedence for the law officers at the opening of the parliament of 1634 ranked 'the king's puisne serjeant at law' (the second serjeant) after the attorney general, the solicitor general and the masters in chancery, who in turn ranked after 'the king's ancientest serjeant at law'.[24] The title 'prime serjeant' does not appear to have been used to describe the king's or first serjeant until after the restoration, Sir Audley Mervyn being variously described as 'principal serjeant at law', and 'prime serjeant at law', the latter title being commonly used thereafter.[25]

At the time of his appointment as second serjeant, Catelyn was recorder of Dublin, and provision was made in the patent that

the said Nathaniel Catelyn, to hold still his place as recorder of the city of Dublin, and that he may have liberty, in all causes and matters, concerning the city, to be on their side and stand for them, although the same do concern us or our own causes.[26]

This provision recognised that a recorder was expected to act as counsel for, as well as the judge of, a borough, and was nearly to prove Catelyn's undoing. In 1628, the government sought to

---

23 Baker, *Serjeants at law*, pp. 60 and 112.
24 *Cal. S.P. Ire., 1637–47*, p. 59.
25 Ibid.; Baker, *Serjeants at law*, p. 61.
26 *Cal. pat. rolls Ire., Chas. I*, p. 211.

suppress the open observance of the mass in Dublin, and on St Stephen's day the lords justices sent troops into the city to prevent this. A serious riot followed, a mob estimated at 3,000 stoned the protestant archbishop and mayor, and forced them to seek refuge in nearby houses. Troops sent to the city to restore order were refused admittance by the corporation, and, as recorder, Catelyn argued on the corporation's behalf that its refusal was justified by its charter. As a result, on 7 January 1629, the king drafted a letter directing the lords justices and council 'to remove the man Catelyn, who was a ringleader, from our (counsel), as it is not meet to pay people to plead against our prerogative'.[27] Catelyn was duly removed from office on 3 February, but Lord Deputy Falkland intervened on his behalf, with Catelyn putting up a spirited defence of his conduct:

The lord mayor assured the [lords] justices that I had said nothing except what I had been directed to say by the city. His lordship [Wilmot[28]] said I could not serve two masters, and be (counsel) both to the king and the city, but I answered that this was often done in London. I refused the chancellor's request that I should confess that I was in error.

Catelyn went on to allege that although the chancellor, the two lords justices and the earl of Cork accepted that he had not done anything wrong, he been unable to practise for a week.[29]

Perhaps because the terms of his patent expressly permitted him to continue to represent the city as recorder, Catelyn managed to weather the storm, and his removal from office was obviously revoked, because he continued to enjoy the confidence of the administration. In 1632, he was commended to the English privy council by the lords justices,[30] and was later knighted by Wentworth. Somewhat surprisingly in view of Catelyn's experience in 1629, when he was succeeded by William Sambach as second serjeant in 1637, Sambach was permitted to continue as recorder of, and counsel for, Carrickfergus.[31] Such permission was unusual, and it may be that both Catelyn and

27 *Cal. S.P. Ire., 1625–32*, p.504.
28 Charles Wilmot, 1st Viscount Wilmot of Athlone, was lord president of Connacht 1616–30, and (with Lord Ranelagh) 1630–44, and a leading member of the Irish administration for many years.
29 *Cal. S.P. Ire., 1625–32*, p. 520.
30 Ibid., p. 659.
31 Smyth, *Law officers*, p. 194.

Sambach believed that they might lose financially by accepting the post of second serjeant, and persuaded the Irish administration to agree to their holding both posts, despite the obvious risk of a conflict of loyalties which this created. Permission may have been granted more readily if the administration recognised that the post was 'little profitable to anybody', in Ormond's words.

In 1635, we have a rare glimpse of one of the serjeants acting in a forensic capacity, albeit in a highly political matter. Determined to establish royal title to lands in Connacht and Co. Clare so that they could be planted, Wentworth summoned juries and conducted inquisitions as to the king's titles in several counties. At the first of these in Co. Roscommon in July 1635, Catelyn opened the case for the king and received the lord deputy's approval.[32] In Galway matters did not go so smoothly, and the desired verdicts for the king were only returned after Wentworth exerted enormous pressure, including the imposition of heavy fines upon the recalcitrant jurors.

Although only five parliaments were held in Ireland between 1618 and 1689, when they were summoned the administration was always alert to the need to keep them in check, and relied upon the abilities of the law officers to achieve this, one of whom became speaker of the commons in every parliament. Catelyn was the first serjeant to hold the position, and the circumstances surrounding his election as speaker in 1634 graphically illustrate the skill, energy and ruthlessness which made Wentworth such a formidable servant of the Crown.

Wentworth's strategy was to conciliate catholic opinion by granting their desire that a parliament should be summoned, a parliament which he decided would sit in two sessions. In the first, short, session Wentworth intended to take advantage of the goodwill created by calling the parliament to obtain a grant of vital subsidies and taxes. Once this objective had been achieved, in the second session the crown would be in a position to stand upon the defensive against the claims which he anticipated would be made by the catholics for increased religious tolerance. The successful implementation of this strategy clearly depended upon as many 'quiet and governable men'[33] being returned to the commons as possible, and, to achieve this, over a hundred letters were sent out recommending individuals of whom Wentworth approved.

32 Strafford, *Letters and dispatches*, i, 442–44.
33 Ibid., 259.

He decided to make Catelyn speaker, 'being a very able man for that purpose, and one I assure myself will in all things apply himself to his majesty's service'. As he was to demonstrate in Galway in 1635, Wentworth was never reluctant to use whatever means were necessary to achieve the desired result. In order to secure Catelyn's election in Dublin, the lord deputy brought a sheriff who had the temerity to defy his wishes before the court of castle chamber. The court fined the sheriff £700, and disqualified him from office for life. In the face of such action, it is hardly surprising that Catelyn was duly returned. When the commons assembled to elect their speaker, Wentworth dispatched the chancellor to inform them that they should not elect a speaker of whom the king disapproved, because such a nominee would be rejected by the lord deputy.[34] This produced the desired result, and Catelyn's election as speaker demonstrates that it is upon the parliamentary, and not the legal, stage that we see the serjeants playing their most important role before and after the civil war; and this was to be the case for the rest of the seventeenth, and throughout the eighteenth century. The speaker of the next parliament, that summoned in 1640, was Sir Maurice Eustace, who had been appointed principal serjeant in 1634. In 1661, his successor as principal serjeant, Sir Audley Mervyn, successfully claimed the speakership, although his election was at the expense of the crown's nominee.

Eustace had been identified as a lawyer of considerable promise as early as 1623. Having distinguished himself at Trinity College, Dublin, he became a student of Lincoln's Inn where he was granted an allowance by the king upon the recommendation of the privy council.[35] Thereafter his advancement was rapid. In 1627 he was granted lands in Co. Kildare, and in 1629 the king sent a letter to the lords justices appointing him king's (that is, principal) serjeant in place of the recently deceased Serjeant Brereton. Unfortunately for Eustace, the lord deputy had already promised the post to James Barry.[36] Nevertheless, the Irish administration retained a high opinion of Eustace's ability, the chancellor urging that he be appointed a serjeant because 'his majesty's present serjeant is young and incompetent. If there is a parliament in Ireland we shall want able men in parts like this'.[37] As we have seen,

34 Ibid., 270 and 277.
35 *Cal. S.P. Ire., 1615–25*, p. 424.
36 *Cal. S.P. Ire., 1625–32*, pp. 239 and 493.
37 Ibid., p. 540.

Wentworth's choice for the speakership in 1634 fell upon Serjeant Catelyn, although Eustace was MP for Athy in that parliament. However, when the next parliament was summoned in March 1640, Eustace was elected speaker.

Sixteen forty and 1641 were turbulent years during which much attention focused upon the Irish parliament. Wentworth was re-called to England in November 1639 and created earl of Strafford in January 1640. In his absence, the Irish administration proved unequal to the task of controlling the various factions, and a struggle for power took place in Ireland, a struggle which was closely connected with Strafford's progress to the scaffold in England. Highly contentious issues, involving the grant of subsidies, the powers of prerogative courts, such as the court of castle chamber, and, in 1641, the impeachment of four of Strafford's principal lieutenants in Ireland, dominated the proceedings of the Irish parliament. Although contemporary records do not refer to Eustace in his role as speaker, it is reasonable to suppose that, as a leading royal servant, he was expected to do what he could to uphold the royal position. That this was expected of the law officers, but not always achieved, may be illustrated by Serjeant Sambach, MP for Carrickfergus and second serjeant, who found himself the sole supporter of the king on a commons committee appointed to vindicate the commons' position on the issue of the assessment of subsidies.[38]

Despite the failure of the Irish administration to control the Irish commons,[39] Eustace's services as speaker were appreciated, the king agreeing in 1641 that he be paid £1,000 as compensation for his loss of practice whilst speaker, following the precedent of a grant of £1,600 to Serjeant Catelyn in 1634. Eustace did not actually receive this amount, which was redeemed in 1644 by a grant of lands of the abbey of Cong, Co. Galway and lands at Athy, Co. Kildare.[40]

Following the outbreak of rebellion in Ulster in October 1641, civil war spread throughout Ireland and, although it remained in being, the Irish parliament was an impotent body. Eustace was there-

---

38 Wandesworth to Wentworth during the session of 11–17 June 1640: Hugh Kearney, *Strafford in Ireland 1633–1641: a study in absolutism* (Manchester, 1961), p. 190.

39 See the writer's 'Sir Audley Mervyn, lawyer or politician?' in Osborough, (ed.), *Explorations in law and history*, for a description of the role of Mervyn and others as opponents of the administration at this time.

40 *Cal. S.P. Ire.,1633–47*, pp. 268 and 400.

after one of Ormond's closest confidants and advisers. In September 1642, when Ormond was ill, he appointed Eustace one of his executors, and in 1643 he was one of the commissioners appointed by the king to treat with the Confederation of Kilkenny. Remaining as speaker until 1647, Eustace was then imprisoned in Chester between 1648 and 1655.

The early years of the Cromwellian period in Ireland were marked by ambitious plans to radically reform the structure of the courts,[41] in striking contrast to England where existing judicial and legal offices continued in being, with minimal alterations in both titles and functions. When Serjeant Sambach was appointed solicitor general in 1640, it appears that no one was appointed to succeed him as second serjeant, the post remaining vacant until 1661. Nor was any effort made to replace Eustace as a serjeant after his arrest in 1648. Although Cromwell reserved the appointment of the Irish serjeants at law to himself in 1654, the serjeants were simply ignored in Ireland during the Cromwellian era. In England, the position was quite different, with the appointments of Sir Thomas Widdrington and John Greene as 'Serjeants of the Commonwealth of England' in 1650. In 1654, 1657 and 1658, further appointments were made as 'His Highness's Serjeants at Law', in keeping with the increasingly regal style of government adopted by Cromwell as lord protector.[42]

Towards the end of the Cromwellian era in Ireland, under the more benign rule of Henry Cromwell as lord deputy, Eustace's talents were increasingly recognized, although he came under suspicion shortly after his release.[43] In 1658, the lord deputy recommended a grant of lands to him as having been 'in many cases very friendly', and went on to say that he was beholden to Eustace.[44] The extent to which Eustace was favourably regarded at this time is illustrated by his membership of a committee considering proposals to establish a second college within the University of Dublin, another member

41 See T.C. Barnard, *Cromwellian Ireland* (Oxford, 1975), ch. 9.
42 'Instructions for the Lord Deputy and Irish Council', *Thurloe state papers*, 7 vols. (London, 1742), ii, 508–09. I owe this reference to Professor Osborough. Baker, *Serjeants at law*, p. 59 n. 1.
43 An order was granted in Oct. 1656 to secure Eustace's papers and letters in Dublin: *Ireland under the Commonwealth: being a selection of documents relating to the Irish rebellion from 1651 to 1659,* ed. R. Dunlop, 2 vols. (Manchester, 1913), ii, 629.
44 *Anal Hib*, no. 1 (1930), 28.

being William Basil, attorney general since the execution of Charles I in 1649, and later chief justice of the upper bench.[45]

The restoration of Charles II in 1660 was followed by the re-establishment of all judicial and legal posts as they existed before the interregnum. Eustace's services to the crown were recognized by his appointment as chancellor, and his successor as principal serjeant was Sir Audley Mervyn. In 1641, Mervyn had been one of the most prominent opposition figures in the commons, although he fought on the royalist side for most of the 1640s. Despite demonstrating considerable legal knowledge in 1641, he did not acquire a formal legal qualification until he was admitted to King's Inns in Trinity term 1658. Having played an active part in the proceedings of the convention in 1660, he was one of the twelve commissioners sent to London to represent the protestant interest, when decisions were made about the form of the post-restoration settlement in Ireland.[46] Mervyn was knighted on 19 July 1660, and on 20 September was appointed principal serjeant under the privy seal, an appointment which must have been entirely due to his political standing, as he had only been in practice for two years.

Another unusual feature of his appointment was that Mervyn, the attorney general and the solicitor general were each appointed to hold office 'during good behaviour' and not 'during pleasure', as was customary. During pleasure meant that the office holder concerned could be dismissed at will by the sovereign, or in Ireland by the chief governor of the day as the sovereign's representative. As we shall see, there were numerous examples during the next 160 years of serjeants being dismissed. Given that even the judges were not to receive the security conferred by appointment during good behaviour for more than a century, it is a mystery why there was such a departure from the usual practice in 1660, although this was not the only occasion when this was done in the reign of Charles II. When Sir William Davys succeeded Mervyn as prime serjeant in 1675, he was also appointed during good behaviour, as was John Osborne when he was appointed prime serjeant in reversion to Davys in 1676, a unique

---

45 William Urwick, *The early history of Trinity College Dublin, 1591–1660* (Dublin, 1892), pp. 63–68.

46 J.I. McGuire, 'The Dublin convention, the protestant community and the emergence of an ecclesiastical settlement in 1660', in *Parliament and community, Historical Studies: XIV*, ed. Art Cosgrove and J.I. McGuire (Belfast, 1983), p. 145.

occurrence in the history of the serjeants.[47] However, when, as was customary, Osborne was issued a fresh patent upon the accession of James II, this was during pleasure. Robert Griffiths was appointed second serjeant in 1661 during pleasure, as were his successors as second serjeant. Ultimately, the third serjeants were appointed during pleasure as well, so during this period the three senior law officers enjoyed an exceptionally privileged position. Whatever was the reason for this development, it proved shortlived, as the practice was discontinued upon the accession of James II.

In May 1661, Mervyn was elected speaker of the commons, thereby ostensibly following the precedents of Serjeants Catelyn and Eustace. Unlike them, he was not the royal nominee, despite his position as prime serjeant, because Charles intended that Domville, the attorney general, would be put forward. When the king learnt that Mervyn wanted the post, he left the choice to the commons. Deprived of active royal support, Domville's position was greatly weakened and Mervyn was elected, thereby becoming for a time one of the most powerful figures in Ireland. He combined the post of speaker, which was extremely influential in managing parliament and the passage of legislation, with that of prime serjeant, which enjoyed considerable prestige as well as playing an active part in any court proceedings in which the crown was involved.

Before Mervyn could take up the position of speaker, he had to divest himself of one of the traditional obligations of the prime serjeant, namely to attend the proceedings of the house of lords whilst parliament was sitting. It was the custom for all the judges, king's counsel (as the attorney general, solicitor general and serjeants were commonly collectively described) and the masters in chancery to receive writs of summons at the commencement of each parliament, requiring their attendance to assist the lords. Although both Eustace and Catelyn sat in the commons in 1634, and Eustace and Sambach in the commons in 1640, the requirement that the serjeants attend the lords was still recognized in 1661, when Mervyn's election as speaker of the commons led the lords to convene a committee of privileges to decide whether his 'attendance upon the lords as prime serjeant could be dispensed with. The matter does not appear to have been regarded as a mere formality, although Mervyn and the solicitor general, who was in the same

47 Smyth, *Law officers*, p. 187.

position, were excused attendance upon the lords and took their seats in the commons.[48] However, the *Commons' journals* for 1661 record many instances of Serjeant Griffiths and the judges acting as messengers on behalf of the lords to the commons, although only the judges were called upon to advise the lords. This was a long-established custom which had been recorded in Ireland in 1569, and was to continue until well into the eighteenth century, Serjeant Purdon being recorded as a messenger to the commons in 1733.[49] So far as law officers who had seats in the commons were concerned, the practice of their attending upon the lords fell into disuse because the lords' journals do not record their being summoned as assistants in either 1692 or 1695. This was undoubtedly because of the importance of the law officers to the administration in the commons.

Mervyn's election as speaker meant that for a considerable period he had little time to spare for his duties as prime serjeant. He spent nine months in England in connection with the Act of Settlement, returning to Dublin in the spring of 1662. Upon his return, Mervyn combined his duties as speaker, where he was regarded as having great influence over the passage of legislation, with appearing on behalf of the crown before the court of claims. The court had been set up after the restoration of Charles II by the Act of Settlement to decide claims to confiscated lands, and Mervyn's alleged partiality and corruption, as well as his domination of the court, led to complaints of injustice.[50]

In 1663 Mervyn's influence declined rapidly. As speaker, he made a speech suggesting that changes were necessary in the procedures of the court of claims so as to secure the protestant interest. This led to an angry and public rebuke from Ormond, who regarded this as inopportune, since it rendered the already difficult political situation more unsettled, as well as being personally offensive.[51] That year was also marked by a number of abortive plots, and Mervyn came under suspicion of being at least sympathetic to, if not actually involved with, those of republican views.[52] Although he was to remain speaker

48 *Lords' jn. Ire.*, i, pp. 3 and 7, and 231–33.
49 *Commons' jn. Ire.*, i, pp. 499, 511, 528. In 1569, law officers and judges were in attendance: *Irish historical documents, 1172–1922*, ed. T.C. Curtis and R.B. McDowell (Dublin, 1943), p. 92. *Commons' jn. Ire.*, iv, p. 99.
50 Thomas Carte, *A history of the life of James, duke of Ormonde from his birth in 1610 to his death in 1688*, 3 vols. (London, 1735–36), i, 365.
51 Ibid., pp. 264–65 and appendix, letter xl, for a letter of 9 Mar. 1663.
52 *Cal. S.P. Ire., 1663–65*, pp. 121 and 157. In June 1663, Secretary Bennet,

until parliament was dissolved in 1666, and prime serjeant until his death in 1675, Mervyn's influence was never the same after these events.[53] After 1663, the state papers contain few references to his advice being sought on legal matters, Ormond preferring to rely upon the attorney general, Sir William Domville. It seems likely that Ormond did all he could to reduce Mervyn's influence, the events of 1663 reviving or strengthening doubts about Mervyn's loyalty stretching back to the civil war.

Although Mervyn's eclipse undoubtedly emphasised the continuing decline in the importance of the prime serjeant's position, the office was still sought after, despite being described by Archbishop Boyle, the chancellor, as 'of honour rather than advantage' in 1675.[54] Despite this, the following year saw a unique event in the seven centuries of the history of the serjeants at law in Ireland when John Osborne, then second serjeant, was appointed prime serjeant in reversion to Sir William Davys, who was to hold the post until he became chief justice of the king's bench in 1680. Osborne's appointment occurred because of a dispute between himself and Davys as to their respective precedence.[55] Osborne had been second serjeant since May 1674 and, according to the lord lieutenant, was an eminent lawyer. Osborne felt aggrieved at being passed over in favour of Davys, although, as recorder of Dublin, Davys occupied a post of considerable importance. That such an arrangement was made for no other reason than to soothe an individual's feelings might not appear particularly significant, but it proved to be a forerunner of the events which culminated in the creation of the position of third serjeant in 1682, purely as a consolation prize for John Lyndon when he was passed over for a vacant judgeship in the common pleas. The circumstances surrounding his appointment are of interest because they illustrate the way in which prominent office holders intrigued to secure advancement for their protégés, as well as the attitude of Ormond and others to the serjeants.

later earl of Arlington, wrote to Ormond that Mervyn was one of those viewed by the king as the 'extreme faction'.

53 Although voted £6,000 as compensation for his loss of practice whilst speaker, this was not paid, his heirs petitioning parliament for payment in 1697. *Commons'jn. Ire.*, ii, pp. 81, 98 and 185.

54 BL, Stowe MSS, f. 364.

55 Smyth, *Law officers*, p.187, and Ball, 'Some notes on the Irish judiciary in the reign of Charles II, 1660–85,' *Journal of the Cork Historical and Archeological Society, 2nd series,* ix (1903), 85.

In December 1681, the earl of Arran, Ormond's son and lord deputy, recommended to Ormond that Lyndon succeed Mr Justice Cusack, who was believed not to have long to live. However, Archbishop Boyle supported the claim of William Beckett to the post. As Boyle and Arran were Ormond's principal lieutenants in Ireland, this placed him in a quandary, from which he escaped by appointing Arthur Turner, the attorney to the duke of York, to the post.[56] In 1682, the question of the preferment of Lyndon or Beckett again arose when Ormond considered the dismissal of Sir Richard Stephens, the second serjeant, because he was believed to be linked to the 'fanatic party' (the dissenters) and was unable to satisfy Ormond (a staunch anglican) of his loyalty to the established church.[57]

With Stephens's dismissal imminent, in June Boyle urged that Beckett succeed Stephens as second serjeant or, failing this, as third serjeant.[58] This is the first reference to a third serjeant, but it proved to be Lyndon who was appointed, and not Beckett, no doubt to console the former for his disappointment earlier that year. As happened on a number of occasions with other serjeants, the king issued his privy seal and some time later the letters patent were forthcoming in Dublin.[59] Strictly speaking, letters patent were necessary before a serjeant could be said to have taken up his office, but, as a substantial period could elapse before this was done, the earlier date is in reality the date of appointment.

Following Stephens's dismissal in September, Boyle wrote to Ormond thanking him for the promise of the second serjeant's post to Beckett. What had hitherto been a conventional intrigue now took on an air of farce. A few days later, there came an angry intervention by the recorder of Dublin, Sir Richard Ryves, claiming the post as the longest serving of the king's counsel. This failed to prevent Beckett becoming second serjeant on 11 November, but Lyndon now protested furiously that Beckett had now been placed above him. Ormond admitted to Arran that, when recommending Beckett as second serjeant, he had forgotten that Lyndon had already been made a serjeant! From London Ormond wrote that, as it was doubtful

---

56 H.M.C., *Ormond MSS (n.s.)*, vi, 252 and 291.
57 Ibid., pp. 32 and 452.
58 Ibid., p. 389.
59 The king issued his privy seal at Windsor on 24 July 1682: *Cal. S.P. dom., 1682*, p. 311. Smyth, *Law officers*, p. 225 and H.M.C., *Ormond MSS (n.s.)*, vi, 194.

whether Beckett would forego his advantage, amends would be made to both. Arran was able to resolve this imbroglio by negotiation with Boyle. It was agreed that when an anticipated vacancy in the common pleas occurred, in return for Lyndon waiving his claim to be second serjeant, he would have the next vacant judgeship before Beckett.[60]

In January 1683, the expected vacancy did occur, and Lyndon became a judge with Ryves succeeding him as third serjeant.[61] Beckett's death in July led to a flurry of letters to Ormond in England about who should succeed him. In the space of a few days, Lord Chief Justice Keatinge, Arran and the solicitor general, Sir John Temple, each wrote pressing the claims of their respective candidates. Temple reminded Ormond that he had put forward Henry Echlin when Lyndon was raised to the bench. Temple's comments on Echlin and another candidate are revealing:

[Echlin] hath been seven or eight years at the bar, and very studious and industrious in his profession, though I cannot say that either he or Mr. Sprigg are yet in any great practice, wherein there is no great difference between them.

Despite being only thirty-one and six years at the bar, Echlin was made third serjeant, with Ryves being promoted second. Echlin had been proposed as third serjeant by Arran the previous December, when the lord deputy wearily urged, 'when this is granted I desire that the number of serjeants may not be increased further'. No doubt somewhat wary of a further battle when the vacancy created by Beckett's death came to be filled, Arran left the matter to Ormond, 'only desiring that whoever you pitch upon may not come over Sir Richard Ryves, who is now second serjeant'.[62]

Several lessons can be drawn from these events. Firstly, despite the prime serjeancy being described as a post 'of honour rather than advantage', even the lesser posts of second and third serjeant were very definitely seen as being of advantage; hence the intense manoeuvring that went on when a vacancy occurred or was anticipated. Secondly, whilst there was never to be an inflexible tradition that an existing serjeant would be promoted to a more senior serjeant's post when a vacancy occurred, nevertheless the expectation that this would be

60 H.M.C., *Ormond MSS (n.s.)*, vi, 467, 477 and 483.
61 Smyth, *Law officers*, p. 195.
62 H.M.C., *Ormond MSS (n.s.)*, vii, 69–72, 83 and 91.

the case was being established. Thirdly, the post of third serjeant was created to gratify a desire for office and not to meet a need for another royal law officer. This was not as surprising as it might seem, given that the office of king's counsel had its origin in the desire of Roger Bacon for a sign of royal favour that would confer professional precedence. Fourthly, to become a serjeant meant that a step had been taken which would normally result in elevation to the bench. Fifthly, the serjeants were seen by chief governors as persons who could and should be appointed or dismissed because of their political position rather than their professional competence. The next one hundred and twenty years were to see numerous occasions when the serjeants, and the prime serjeant in particular, were highly political figures, who were appointed or dismissed solely because of political considerations.

Ormond's dismissal of Stephens in 1682 created a precedent which was to be followed on a larger scale when James II embarked upon a policy of replacing protestant civil and military office holders with catholics. As is well known, legal posts were included in this process. In February 1687, Prime Serjeant Osborne was replaced by Garrett Dillon, and Sir Richard Ryves and Echlin were later dismissed as second and third serjeants. Smyth says that Sir John Barnewall became third serjeant on 6 May, which implies that Echlin was dismissed on or before that date. However, no record can be found of an appointment to replace Ryves as second serjeant. In 1689 Barnewall became a baron of the exchequer, and was followed as third serjeant by Sir Toby Butler, who held that office until he became solicitor general in July. It would seem that nobody was appointed to succeed Butler, but this is hardly surprising, as civil war had broken out by then. However, despite the doubtful need for a second or third serjeant, there is no obvious reason why a successor to Ryves as second serjeant was not appointed in 1687, even though a third serjeant was appointed, and it may be that someone was made second serjeant, but details of his appointment have not survived.

Thus, by the last years of the reign of James II, the principal features of the serjeancy, as the three posts were to become collectively known, had become established. All three posts, and that of prime serjeant in particular, were regarded as highly political, and the occupants were often dismissed for political reasons. However, it would be wrong to assume that the serjeants were purely political figures devoid of any professional ability or standing, although this was so in some cases. Many were chosen precisely because they had impressed as lawyers, as in the case of the young Maurice Eustace. Just as Osborne was described as an eminent lawyer, so the earl of Clarendon when lord lieutenant described Dillon as 'in very great practice, he is a very honest gentleman', when appointing him prime serjeant in 1687,[63] and Sir Toby Butler also had a very high reputation. Throughout the seventeenth and eighteenth centuries lawyers were amongst the most vigorous and able opponents of the administration in parliament, and it was essential for the crown to enlist the services of those who would prove able defenders of its policies in parliament as well as in the courts. The serjeancy provided an ideal method of recruiting such men by conferring upon them posts which carried prestige, some profit and, most important of all, a clear expectation of further promotion to the bench. As we shall see in the next chapter, these characteristics were to manifest themselves on a regular, and sometimes dramatic basis, throughout the eighteenth century.

63 *State letters of Henry, earl of Clarendon*, 2 vols. (Oxford, 1765), ii, 136.

CHAPTER FOUR

From the Boyne to the Union: the serjeants in eighteenth-century Ireland

IN THIS CHAPTER, we shall first of all examine the manner in which the serjeants carried out their functions as royal law officers in the eighteenth century, and then consider their sources of income and professional standing in general. The remainder of the chapter will be devoted to a detailed examination of the political role of the serjeants, and of the prime serjeant in particular.

Then, as now, the duties of a law officer involved giving advice to the government on various matters as well as appearing in court. Although such references to the advisory role of the serjeants as have survived are scattered and fragmentary, nevertheless they are sufficient to allow it to be said with some confidence that it was the practice for the Irish government to make use of the prime serjeant's services, both for advice and, more frequently, to represent it in court. When advice was sought, this was often done by referring the matter in question to the prime serjeant, attorney general and solicitor general for their joint opinion. One such instance was the trial of Lord Santry for murder, when he claimed the right to be tried by his peers. This was so rare that the lords justices had to ask these three law officers whether Santry was entitled to such a trial, and in November 1739 they gave their joint opinion that he was.[1] Not all advice would be given in writing, and in the following month the same law officers are recorded as attending a meeting to discuss the alleged export of wool from Ireland, a matter of great commercial importance.[2] Such examples as have survived do not suggest that it was the invariable practice to refer matters to the three senior law officers for their joint advice, and clearly there would be occasions when this would not be possible, particularly when the matter was urgent. One such occasion occurred in June 1693 when Viscount Sidney, the lord lieutenant, dissolved parliament and wrote: 'I ordered [Prime] Serjeant Donnellan (the solicitor not being in town) to draw

1 PRONI, Wilmot papers, T.3019, pp. 186–87.
2 This meeting was on 16 Dec. 1739: ibid., p. 210.

a proclamation for that purpose, which is accordingly done and published'.[3]

No doubt there were occasions when the opinion of only one of the senior law officers was sought at first. One such instance that has survived occurred in January 1748 when Anthony Malone, then prime serjeant, was asked for his opinion as to the rights of the crown relating to the appointment of deans in the Church of Ireland. His advice was not palatable, and the matter was then referred to the solicitor general who gave a contrary opinion, whereupon the attorney general drew up a case signed by all three law officers which was submitted to the attorney general and solicitor general in London for their opinion.[4] Whilst it was the invariable practice for the English law officers to settle parliamentary bills submitted by the Irish privy council for approval in accordance with Poynings's Act, we do not know how often the Irish administration either by-passed its own law officers completely, or how often those law officers differed amongst themselves and the matter was then referred to London.

It was much less common for advice to be sought from the second and third serjeants. Indeed, I have been unable to trace any instance where this was done, although no doubt there may have been some instances, details of which have not survived. Certainly, there is some contemporary evidence to suggest that the third serjeant at least was almost completely redundant in this respect. Following his dismissal as third serjeant at the end of 1692, in the spring of 1693 Alan Brodrick wrote a lengthy letter to his brother St John (himself a barrister in London, who was to become a serjeant at law in England in 1705), explaining the events leading up to his dismissal, and commenting upon the almost total absence of any duties attached to his post:

altho I had been near two years one of their Majesties Serjeants, yet I had not (that I remember) been advised with more than once, nor had I ever had any opportunity to act in any of their Majesties concerns, save once that by order from the lords justices I had a letter wrote to me by Mr Secretary Davies to take care to indict and prosecute for rebellion and treason such as were liable to prosecution within the intimation of that letter in the Munster circuit, which I was ready to have done, but how that matter stopped is not necessary for my purpose to report.[5]

3   Sidney to the earl of Nottingham: *Cal. S.P. dom., 1693*, p. 198.
4   PRONI, Wilmot papers, T. 3019, pp. 963 and 979.
5   6 May 1693: Surrey Record Office, Guildford Muniment Room, Midleton MS 1248/1, p. 260.

Although Brodrick may have been surprised that more use had not been made of his services, he did not attribute that to any prejudice against him on the part of the lord lieutenant, and it would appear probable that the reason was simply that there was no need for the services of the third serjeant, the senior law officers being more than adequate in number to provide the government with the services which it required. This conclusion is supported by the circumstances in which the post had been created as described in the previous chapter, and by its being left vacant for nineteen years after Brodrick's dismissal in 1692, and for a further ten years following the promotion of John Witherington, the third serjeant, to second serjeant in 1716.

The second serjeant does seem to have been called upon from time to time by the government, although this conclusion must necessarily be somewhat tentative in the absence of substantial evidence. Were the second serjeant seen as unnecessary, then one might have expected the post to be left vacant in the closing years of the seventeenth century, following the precedent set after Brodrick's dismissal. A reference to the activities of the second serjeant (admittedly, an isolated one) which suggests that some significance was attached to the post, occurs in 1701. Payments of five guineas a day were ordered to be made to the attorney general, solicitor general and Serjeant Neave, then second serjeant, for their attendance on the king's behalf before the court of claims to prosecute those whom it was alleged had wrongly claimed the benefit of the treaties of Galway and Limerick.[6] As we shall see, Neave was later a leading member of the government in the commons.

The income of any practitioner is one of the main indicators of the professional standing of the individual concerned. Unfortunately, it is very difficult to form a clear picture of the income which a serjeant could expect to make from his position in this period. Such contemporary evidence as has survived is conflicting. In November and December 1692, the lord lieutenant, Viscount Sidney, had to find a suitable replacement for Osborne, following the latter's dismissal as prime serjeant. He did not find this an easy task, and wrote to London to see whether a suitable candidate could be found there who might be persuaded to come to Ireland, although he doubted whether this could be achieved. His first choice in Dublin had been Sir John Meade who, despite having sat in the Jacobite parliament of

6   *Cal. S.P. dom., 1700–02*, p. 396.

1689 as one of the members for Dublin University, was a staunch Williamite who had been made a king's counsel in December 1690. However, Sidney cryptically remarked, 'there are some exceptions against him which I have already acquainted you with', almost certainly a reference to Meade's wife being a roman catholic, a considerable handicap in the violently anti-catholic atmosphere of the time. Although Meade was eventually offered the post, he declined, ostensibly on the ground that the size of his practice would prevent him from devoting sufficient time to it. Sidney commented to the earl of Nottingham:

I believe you will find it difficult to persuade a man who is good for anything to come hither for that employment, which is only worth £30 a year besides his practice. Therefore I think Mr Donnellan and Mr Pakenham (both king's counsel) will be the fittest who can be picked upon for the king's service.[7]

This disparaging assessment of the financial rewards which a prime serjeant might expect to receive has, not surprisingly, led one modern historian to describe the post of prime serjeant as poorly paid.[8] However, there is considerable evidence that the office of prime serjeant was a lucrative one. Not long after Sidney's assessment, we find an assertion by Sir Richard Stephens that the office of second serjeant was worth £1,000 a year to him when he was dismissed in 1682.[9] At first blush, this claim should be treated with reserve. Stephens was writing seventeen years after his dismissal, and naturally anxious to state his case in the best possible light. His reliability is not enhanced by his statement that he had been removed from the position 'by the prevailing popish interest' when, as we saw in the previous chapter, he had really been dismissed by Ormond because Stephens was unable to satisfy Ormond of his adherence to the established church. Nevertheless, at that time it was certainly possible for successful counsel to earn substantial amounts.[10] When Dennis Daly was nominated a justice of the common pleas in 1686, he asked

---

7 *Cal. S.P. dom., 1695*, pp. 215, 219 and 222. In the eighteenth century Mr Justice Robinson gave the salary at this time as £33 16s. 8d. Dublin Corporation, Gilbert Library, MS 36 (Robinson papers), ff. 354–56.

8 J.I. McGuire in 'The Irish parliament of 1692', in Thomas Bartlett and D.W. Hayton (ed.), *Penal era and golden age* (Belfast, 1979), at p. 13.

9 *Cal S.P. dom., 1697*, pp. 120–21.

10 See T.C. Barnard, 'Lawyers and the law in later seventeenth-century Ireland', in *IHS*, xxviii (1993), 256.

that his appointment be postponed until the following term because he would lose £400 a year. As a puisne judge's salary at the time was £400, together with a circuit allowance of £100, this would imply that Daly's income was in the region of £900 a year.[11] In November 1693, Brodrick wrote that in the twenty working days of the law term starting on 5 November he had made £200 10s. 0d., which he considered 'very fair'.[12] As he was in private practice, Brodrick had no fees for crown work, so his income for this term would suggest that Stephens's claim that he made £1,000 a year was perfectly plausible, given that there were four law terms and two assize circuits each year. By 1717, the financial position of the prime serjeant had improved, because his salary had been increased to £100 a year, whereas the salaries of the attorney general and solicitor general remained at £88 6s. 8d. The second serjeant still received £30 a year, whilst the third serjeant apparently received nothing by way of a salary.[13]

It has to be remembered that Sidney's statement in 1692, that 'the post is only worth £30 a year', whilst strictly correct in that this was the salary of the post, was subject to the caveat that this was 'besides his practice'. A serjeant had the prospect of fees from other sources simply because he was a serjeant. The serjeants were free to represent other clients, provided that this did not conflict with their obligations towards the crown, and they accepted retainers on that basis. Thus we find that Serjeant Osborne and the solicitor general each received a retainer of five guineas from the duke of Ormond, Osborne promising 'never to engage against the Duke of Ormond by any client whatsoever, except his Majesty'.[14]

Some of the serjeants' clients would be impressed by the mark of royal favour conferred by their rank, others would be attracted by the important practical advantage enjoyed by a serjeant in court conferred by his precedence over other counsel, to which reference has already been made. Precedence was valuable because the order in which matters were heard in court was determined by the seniority of the counsel concerned, and not, as is almost invariably the case now, by

11 Clarendon, *State letters*, i, 360–63 and Ball, *Judges*, ii, 281–82.
12 Surrey Record Office, Guildford Muniment Room, Midleton MS 1248/1, p. 206.
13 Gilbert Library, MS 36 (Robinson papers), ff. 354–56. The second serjeant received £30 a year between 1678 and 1722, except in 1717, when he was apparently paid £30 6s. 0d: ibid.
14 'Letters of Lord Longford and others 1689–1702', *Anal Hib*, no. 32 (1989), 96.

their order in a list fixed upon the principle of first come, first served. The prime serjeant took precedence over the attorney general and the solicitor general, who, in turn, took precedence over the second and third serjeants respectively. All the law officers had precedence over all other counsel, although on rare occasions an individual would be granted a patent of precedence by the crown which could alter this precedence, as in the case of Anthony Malone in 1756.

The value in financial terms of the office of prime serjeant naturally tended to be inflated or minimized according to the desire of the incumbent for judicial or other preferment, and his perception as to how this aim could be advanced by his description of his current post. A realistic picture of the value of the office to the incumbent is probably that painted by Prime Serjeant Singleton in 1739, when he unsuccessfully sought the vacant chancellorship, and wrote to the lord lieutenant that, after what he described as thirteen years' faithful service, he hoped he 'might be removed to a place of more ease, though of less profit than my present situation affords'.[15] As the lord lieutenant had been recommended to pay 100 guineas each to Singleton and the solicitor general just a month before, for their work in connection with a marriage settlement,[16] he might be expected to have some idea of the value of the post. However, Singleton had to be content with the chief justiceship of the common pleas, the chancellorship going instead to Robert Jocelyn, attorney general since 1730.

Little definitive evidence has survived as to the earnings of members of the Irish bar in the eighteenth century with which the serjeants' incomes can be compared, and although contemporaries believed that the most successful members of the bar could earn large amounts, it is clear that they were few in number. Chief Baron Willes wrote that whilst he had been told that two or three of the leading counsel earned £2,000 to £3,000 a year, he felt that, in general, earnings at the Irish bar were small for several reasons. Firstly, many more counsel went on circuit than the available business would suggest were necessary; in most venues there were more than twelve, and, in some cases, more than twenty, counsel present. Secondly, a great many interlocutory motions in cases were moved by attorneys themselves, and this represented a substantial loss of

---

15 PRONI, Chatsworth MS, T.3158/100 (268/10).
16 PRONI, Chatsworth MS, T.3158/90 (252/3).

business to the bar. To some degree at least, these factors were offset by the size of the fees charged, which Willes believed to be greater than in England, and by employing many more counsel on each side than was the English practice. In part, this was to ensure that sufficient counsel were available to deal with the case when it came to trial, as some of the counsel retained might well be appearing in other courts at the same time.[17] Ball describes how in 1743 in *Annesley* v. *Anglesey*, the ejectment trial between the lessee of James Annesley and the earl of Anglesey, the plaintiff was represented by thirteen counsel (the second and third serjeants, a king's counsel and ten juniors), and the defendant by fourteen (the prime serjeant, the attorney general, the solicitor general, the recorder of Dublin, two king's counsel and eight juniors). This was exceeded in 1745, in the subsequent perjury proceedings arising out of the case, when the prosecution was represented by twelve counsel and the defendant by fifteen![18] Presumably these were extreme examples of the tendency described by Willes.

One significant source of income, which a serjeant could expect to enjoy on a frequent basis, was the allowance for circuit expenses paid to a judge of assize. Throughout the seventeenth and eighteenth centuries, there were five assize circuits in Ireland until a sixth was created in 1796. Before a fourth judge was added in 1783 to each of the courts of king's bench, common pleas and exchequer, as each circuit required two judges, there was always a need for at least one extra judge. Often more than one would be necessary for other reasons. Sometimes, one or more of the judges was reluctant to go on circuit, or unable to do so because of illness. In the early years of the century dissatisfaction with this led to a resolution being passed in the Irish parliament that the judges go on their circuits and stay for a reasonable time to finish the business.[19]

About this time, doubts appear to have arisen for some reason as to the power of the puisne barons of the exchequer to hear civil and criminal cases on assize, 'their not being sworn serjeants'. As it had never been a requirement in Ireland, unlike England, that any judge had to be a serjeant before his appointment, it is strange that this

---

17 Edward Willes, 'Miscellaneous observations on Ireland, 1750–60', PRONI, T.2855/1, pp. 10 and 20.
18 Ball, *Judges*, ii, 134–35.
19 25 Oct. 1703: *Commons' jn. Ire.*, ii, p. 347.

should have been considered an impediment to the puisne barons of the exchequer acting as assize judges. The opportunity was taken to confirm that the prime serjeant, the attorney general, the solicitor general 'or any other of His Majesty's [counsel] learned in the law' were also entitled to act. Given that, as we have seen, the prime serjeant and other members of the bar had performed this duty for centuries, it is surprising that there was any doubt about their fitness to act.[20]

Parliament itself also contributed to the problem, since it was the practice for two of the judges to be in attendance when parliament was sitting,[21] and, as we shall see, there were occasions when judges could not go on circuit as they were required to remain in Dublin to advise the government. When the commission of assize had to be augmented, Willes described how the place or places were filled by being offered to the prime serjeant first, and thereafter to the attorney general, the solicitor general, the second serjeant and the third serjeant, in that order. Although detailed records have not survived, there is evidence that it was very common for the serjeants and the other law officers to serve as assize judges. Mr Justice Robinson, writing after 1780, listed fifteen occasions between 1750 and 1780 when serjeants acted as assize judges,[22] and the solicitor general, John Scott, went out in 1777. At this period at least, king's counsel were also called upon, Robinson listing seven such occasions. Anthony Marlay went out three times between 1750 and 1759, including both the Leinster Lent assizes and the Connacht summer assizes of 1759. Robinson himself went out in 1752 and 1757, before he became a justice of the king's bench in 1758.[23]

Despite the practice of using temporary judges being very common, it did not meet with Willes's approval:

20 8 Geo I, c.6. I owe this reference to Professor Osborough.
21 'Copies of the claims laid before the commissioners, under act 40 Geo III, c.34, by all persons claiming compensation in consequence of their offices being discontinued, or diminished in value, by the Union: and the evidence laid before the said commissioners, in support of such claim'. H.C. 1805, vii, 1 (hereafter 'Claims to the commissioners of compensation').
22 Gilbert Library, MS 36 (Robinson papers), ff. 245–51, and 343–45. Robinson described some of those who acted as serjeants when they had not yet become serjeants. The figures in the text have been adjusted accordingly.
23 Ibid., and Ball, *Judges*, ii, 210.

[The temporary judge] has not the same *authority* nor can he venture to do justice in the same manner as a judge who, I may say, acts in his own right. He only considers himself as barely executing a commission for a limited time and if he can go through all that without inconvenience or the hazard of doing anything which may prejudice himself in his future preferment is generally as much as he looks to and as in this kingdom the execution of a circuit judge is of the utmost consequence to the peace and good government of the kingdom the man who goes judge should not only have an eye to irreprochable [*sic*] justice but likewise to take care politically of the allowance or disallowance of presentments and other things which though of no great consequence to individuals of the community is material to the good government of the kingdom. And it frequently happens that a powerful man in a county and whom an occasional judge sometimes for his own sake may be willing and desirous to oblige and sometimes for fear of disobliging is tempted and induced to do that which though not properly injustice to any particular man is an injury to the community which it is probable a judge (who has no hopes or fears) would not be induced to do.[24]

Willes had been king's serjeant in England before his appointment as chief baron of the exchequer in Ireland in 1757 (where he served until his retirement in 1766) and, as his experience made him well qualified to comment on both countries, his views must command respect. An intelligent and sensitive man, Willes was a perceptive observer of the Irish legal and political scene.

Burdensome as circuit duty was, the judges and temporary judges could expect to profit from the fees which litigants paid to the judges on each case. Although the judge received 9s.8d. for allowing a writ at assizes,[25] a fee was also payable to the judge on each civil bill, although the fee is unknown, nor is it clear whether the fee was payable when the civil bill was issued, or when it was entered for hearing. In the eighteenth century, the numbers of civil bills were very great. For example, Mr Justice Robinson recorded that on the North East spring circuit of 1760, 12,546 'processes' (civil bills) were 'sold', of which only 2,225 were entered. On the North West summer circuit of the same year, 9,004 processes were 'sold', 1,529 were entered, and

24 Willes, 'Miscellaneous observations on Ireland 1750–60', p. 21. For an account of his career, and some of his letters on Ireland, see *The letters of Lord Chief Baron Edward Willes to the earl of Warwick 1757–62*, ed. James Kelly (Aberystwyth, 1990).
25 Gilbert Library, MS 32 (Robinson papers), f.32.

decrees or other orders were made in 1,124 cases.[26] That the fee was paid when the civil bill was issued is certainly possible, even probable, given the reference to the process being 'sold'. The fact that a record was kept of the total number issued in this way, suggests that each was issued officially. Whether the fee was paid on the civil bill being issued or entered for hearing, the judges certainly profited. In 1780, when Robinson was at the County Down summer assizes on the North East circuit, he was called back to Dublin on being appointed as one of three commissioners of the great seal. He was replaced for the rest of the circuit by Prime Serjeant Browne, Robinson noting, 'whereby I lost fees to the amount of £121 19s. 0d.'[27] What proportion of this represented his circuit fee, or a share of it, is unclear. However, in his account books, he recorded payments of £97 10s. 0d. for two circuits, in 1760 and 1762, and also recorded additional payments of £21 12s. 9½d., and £20 15s. 8½d., respectively, for each of those circuits.[28] These payments were presumably his share of the fees paid by litigants.

The serjeants could also expect to benefit from the generous circuit allowance, which had been increased to £200 by the end of the eighteenth century. In 1762, Lord Chief Justice Aston and Edmund Malone, then second serjeant, were each paid £235 4s. 7½d. for their trouble and expense in going to Munster to try cases against levellers and whiteboys at various venues.[29] On 30 July 1762, the attorney general, solicitor general and Prime Serjeant John Hely-Hutchinson were each paid £155 6s. 8¼d. for preparing the bills of indictment in these cases. In May of the same year, Hely-Hutchinson, Lord Chief Justice Flood and Chief Baron Willes were each paid £103 15s. 9¼d. for 'his attendance on government by order of the lord lieutenant, whereby he was hindered from going circuit and lost his usual allowance for that service'.[30] Whilst these payments are only recorded in the *Commons' journals* for 1761–64,

26 Gilbert Library, MS 36 (Robinson papers), ff. 241–51; *Cal. S.P. dom., 1690*, pp. 203–04, and D.S. Greer, 'The development of civil bill procedure', in John McEldowney and Paul O'Higgins (ed.), *The common law tradition: essays in Irish legal history* (Dublin, 1990), pp. 43 and 54.
27 Gilbert Library, MS 36 (Robinson papers), f. 345.
28 Gilbert Library, MS 29 (Robinson papers), unpaginated.
29 *Commons' jn. Ire.*, vii, p. clxiii. The expenses of circuit were estimated as a quarter of the circuit fee by the time of the Union. See Appendix One.
30 Ibid., p. clxi.

and may be unusual because of the government's preoccupation with agrarian crime at the time, they are examples of payments which could be made to the serjeants for performing various official tasks. Although some of these might be of an irregular and unpredictable nature, the returns of the commissioners appointed following the Act of Union to assess the diminution in value of various offices connected with the Irish parliament – returns which are considered in detail in Appendix One – show, that in the closing years of the eighteenth century, very substantial amounts in fees were paid on a regular basis to the prime serjeant, attorney general, solicitor general and counsel to the revenue, but not to the second or third serjeant, for preparing or scrutinising and approving bills laid before the Irish parliament. In the case of the prime serjeant, the minimum was £826 a year, but it could be almost £1,200 a year, if the prime serjeant was instructed to prepare or settle revenue and other miscellaneous parliamentary bills.

Other payments which the prime serjeant might expect to receive were fees payable in peerage cases. In 1800, these amounted to £234 3s. 6d., but there were no such payments in the three preceding years.[31] Fees were also paid to the prime serjeant (and other law officers) on the granting or renewal of patents. These could also be substantial, because we know that Prime Serjeants Stanley and Browne each received £277 11s.6d. under this heading in the immediate aftermath of the Union.[32] Taking all these figures into account, it would seem that the prime serjeant would certainly expect to receive about £1,200 or £1,300 a year by the end of the eighteenth century.

Detailed figures have not survived for earlier years, although, when the post-Union compensation claims were being considered, some of these amounts were said to have been paid for thirty years, from which one might reasonably assume that comparable fees for work in conjunction with parliamentary bills had been paid to the prime serjeant for many years. However, some material has survived in the case of Prime Serjeant Hely-Hutchinson which is not easily reconciled with the assumption just advanced.

---

31 'Claims to the commissioners for compensation', H.C. 1805, vii, 1–15. All amounts have been converted into pounds, shillings and pence, and a yearly average shown (as appropriate).
32 *Liber mun. pub. Hib.*, iii, 186.

On 27 December 1772, Hely-Hutchinson, who had been prime serjeant since 1761, said, 'I remain in the same inconsiderable post in which I set out, and to which no responsibility is attached'.[33] The fee book has survived in which his professional fees were recorded in meticulous detail between 30 October 1762 and the end of November 1772, and during that period these amounted to £31,456 8s. 9d., or an average of £3,119 a year.[34] Under the heading 'Prime Serjeancy', there are only sixty-seven entries, starting in May 1762 and ending in July 1771. Apart from entries for £211 11s. 6d. in May 1764, and for £117 3s. 3d. in May 1767, most are for small sums. The total for all sixty-seven is £829 15s. 6d., or approximately £100 a year. These amounts are strikingly different from the earnings of the prime serjeant at the end of the century, and from the figure which his contemporaries believed represented the value of the office to Hely-Hutchinson. About this time, an anonymous and highly placed official prepared a memorandum for the lord lieutenant, giving details of the political and personal links of all peers and members of parliament, together with the amounts they received in salaries and pensions. Hely-Hutchinson's income as prime serjeant was given as £1,200, and the attorney general's as £1,500 a year.[35] We know that the attorney general of the day received £2,086 5s. 9d. as compensation following the Union, so why is there such a discrepancy between the earnings of the two posts in the 1770s when thirty years later they were much closer? Was the anonymous official seriously in error in his estimate, or is there another explanation for the modest figures recorded by Hely-Hutchinson?

Whilst the entries are meticulous and detailed, it is noteworthy that payments which we know were made to Hely-Hutchinson have not been recorded, such as the £103 15s. 9¼d. in May 1762 already referred to, nor, for example, did he include payments for acting as an assize judge in July and August 1762, and again in 1763. The entries seem to be for cases where he was briefed in court as prime serjeant, and it seems probable that the fee book only records fees

33 H.M.C., *rep. 12*, app. ix, p. 273.
34 T.C.D., Donoughmore MSS, C/6/2. At some stage, someone has added up the entries on each page, and the total stated in the text has been entered at the end of the book. As it is in a very fragile state, it has only been possible to study the entries up to the end of 1765, and those at the end of the book headed 'Prime Serjeancy'.
35 William Hunt (ed.), *The Irish parliament, 1775* (Dublin and London, 1907), pp. 26 and 50.

paid to him as a barrister, and does not include amounts which were paid to him for other duties which he performed as prime serjeant. If this hypothesis is correct, then the prime serjeant's income from all duties and perquisites associated with his office in Hely-Hutchinson's day was about £1,200 a year, and broadly comparable with that of his successors thirty years later. Hely-Hutchinson was, after all, notorious for his rapacious appetite for posts and sinecures for himself, his family and relations. In 1773, a contemporary remarked '[Hely-Hutchinson] would prostitute his conscience to advance his relations who are very poor'.[36] When Hely-Hutchinson described his post as 'inconsiderable', he was simply trying to obtain further emoluments for himself.

Whilst the second and third serjeants probably benefited financially from their offices, this may have been to a significantly lesser extent, given their lesser status and the limited use made of their services. Apart from the £30 a year salary paid to the second serjeant at the beginning of the century, and no evidence has been discovered to show that this was increased, such income as they could expect would probably come mainly from the circuit allowance and fees as assize judges.

A mark of the status of all three serjeants at the head of the bar was their invariable election as benchers of King's Inns following their appointment as a serjeant, a mark of their professional standing which they shared with the attorney general and solicitor general.[37] However, this position of professional pre-eminence was not always accompanied by an equivalent feeling of respect for either the abilities or character of individual serjeants, whether by the profession or Dublin society in general. One who had the misfortune to be cruelly lampooned was Serjeant Bettesworth. His support in parliament for any measure that would prejudice the clergy of the established church attracted the ire of Swift, who excoriated what he saw as Bettesworth's hypocritical and dissenting practice of addressing every acquaintance as 'brother' in the following lines:

Thus at the bar the booby Bettesworth
Though half-a-crown o'erpays his sweat's worth
Who knows in law, nor text, nor margent,
Calls Singleton his brother serjeant.

36 M. Bodkin (ed.), 'Notes on the Irish parliament in 1773', *RIA Proc*, xlviii–xlix (1942–44), sect. c, p. 183.
37 King's Inns, Green Book (admission of benchers, 1712–41); Admission of benchers, 1741–92.

Swift described how Bettesworth came to his house and angrily demanded to know whether or not he was the author. Failing to obtain a satisfactory answer, he left, threatening that he would be revenged on Swift by his pen. Swift was unimpressed by this threat but Bettesworth, said to have confessed in the house of commons that Swift's satire had cost him £1,200 a year, had his revenge in an unexpected fashion.[38] Emboldened by Bettesworth's reverse at the hands of Swift, Dr Josiah Hort, the Church of Ireland bishop of Kilmore, composed a satire of his own entitled 'A new proposal for the better regulation and improvement of quadrille'. This proposed, among other regulations, that any dispute arising out of this card game should be laid before Bettesworth, but with a right of appeal to a wooden figure in Dublin's Essex street known as the Upright Man. Hort arranged for his satire to be printed by the famous Dublin printer George Faulkner. Incensed by this further attack, in March 1736, Bettesworth had Faulkner arrested and brought before the bar of the house of commons, which found the charge of breach of privilege proved, and committed the unfortunate Faulkner to prison. Such action was quite common at the time, and, after a few days in Newgate, he obtained his release by making his apology to the house for this libel on one of its members, as well as giving a copy of his new edition of Swift's works in lieu of fees payable to the law officers. Swift, perhaps realizing that he was partly responsible for Faulkner's plight, wrote to Hort demanding that he give financial assistance to Faulkner,

who suffered so much upon your lordship's account, confined to a dungeon among common thieves, and others with infectious disease, to the hazard of his life, besides the expense of above twenty-five pounds, and besides the ignominy to be sent to Newgate like a common malefactor.[39]

It is at this point that we turn to consider in detail the role played by the serjeants in Irish political life, and in the house of commons in

---

38 W.M. Mason, *The history and antiquities of the collegiate and cathedral church of St Patrick, near Dublin, from its foundation in 1190, to the year 1819* (Dublin, 1820), pp. 390–91. I owe this reference to Professor Osborough.

39 Sir John Gilbert, *History of the city of Dublin*, 3 vols. (Dublin, 1878), ii, 32; *The correspondence of Jonathan Swift*, ed. Harold Williams, 5 vols. (Oxford, 1963–65), iv, 482; *Prince of printers, the letters of George Faulkner*, ed. R.E. Ward (Lexington, Kentucky, 1972), pp. 12–13; *Commons' jn. Ire.*, iv, pp. 211–16.

particular. Any evaluation of their role in this area has to be viewed in the context of the complex, frequently uneasy and sometimes turbulent relationship between the crown and the Irish parliament, a relationship which changed markedly as the eighteenth century progressed, and was affected by the interplay of many different factors.

After the revolution which placed William and Mary on the thrones of England, Scotland and Ireland, the sovereign still personally directed and controlled the government in all three kingdoms. Although in practice there were many factors which increasingly circumscribed the ability of the sovereign to act in a fashion which did not command support in parliament, nevertheless the views of the sovereign were still extremely important. As the eighteenth century progressed, ministers exercised the sovereign's powers in a more independent fashion, although his or her views were often decisive. The right of the Irish parliament to act independently of the English parliament was severely restricted by the provisions of Poynings's Act which prevented it from initiating and considering legislation which had not been first considered and approved by the English privy council. This controversial power enabled the English government to exercise substantial control over the proceedings of the Irish parliament. However, the development of the practice of the Irish parliament in bringing forward heads of bills meant that this power was far from absolute by the eighteenth century. This procedure involved legislation being initiated in draft by the Irish parliament, and then submitted to the Irish privy council in the form of heads of bills. The Irish privy council then decided whether to transmit the heads to England for approval. Even if the heads were transmitted, the English privy council could still refuse to accept them.[40] The Irish administration was separate from that in England, Ireland having its own civil, military, legal and ecclesiastical establishments, as well as its own revenue and customs. So long as the customary revenues granted to the crown at the beginning of each reign were sufficient to meet the expenses of government, the ability of the Irish commons to exercise a degree of control over the administration was limited.

40　See J.I. McGuire in 'The Irish parliament of 1692', at p. 2, and Declan O'Donovan, 'The money bill dispute of 1758', at p. 58, both in Barlett and Hayton (ed.), *Penal era and golden age*. The evolution of the heads of bill procedure is traced in Mary Hayden, 'The origin and development of heads of bills in the Irish parliament', *RSAI Jn*, lv (1925), 112. I am obliged to Professor Osborough for drawing this article to my attention.

However, when financial constraints compelled the government to seek additional revenue from parliament, opponents of the administration could then seek to extract concessions in return.

At the head of the Irish administration was the lord lieutenant, who was always a prominent politician in England, and, by virtue of his office, a leading member of the government there. Many of the lords lieutenant were great landowners and, because of this and their social and political ties with London, invariably spent the great majority of their terms of office out of Ireland, only coming to Dublin for short periods. These visits generally coincided with the start of each parliamentary session. During the absence of the lord lieutenant, lords justices, who were major office holders and political figures, were appointed to act in his place and controlled the Irish administration on a day-to-day basis. However, when the lord lieutenant was in England, they referred all matters of significance to him. This meant that, in practice, the lords justices exercised great power and influence because the lord lieutenant had to have a good relationship with, and depended upon, them for advice and support, particularly when dealing with the Irish parliament. The freedom of manoeuvre of any lord lieutenant on Irish issues was therefore influenced, and often limited, by his relationship with the lords justices, as well as by his standing with, and instructions from, his cabinet colleagues in London, whom he regularly consulted on Irish affairs whether he was in England or Ireland.

Before 1688, there were only four parliaments (five if the special case of the Jacobite parliament of 1689 is included) in Ireland during the seventeenth century. After 1690, the Irish parliament sat regularly for the first time, and the relationship between the administration and parliament became a matter of continuing importance. To enable the government to get its business through the commons in particular, the lord lieutenant, or the lords justices in his absence, had to ensure that a majority could be assembled in parliament. Because of the composition of the Irish house of commons, this was rarely a straightforward exercise, and one which was fraught with difficulty, particularly at times of tension and controversy.[41]

After 1690, the Irish parliament was exclusively protestant and although the protestant minority as a whole were united by their belief

---

41 D.W. Hayton, 'The beginnings of the undertaker system', in Bartlett and Hayton (ed.), *Penal era and golden age*, pp. 35–37; R.F. Foster, *Modern Ireland 1600–1972* (London, 1989), pp. 226–236.

that it was vital for the preservation of protestantism in Ireland that Ireland was politically united with Great Britain under a common sovereign, there were deep divisions within that minority as to how the government of Ireland was to be carried on, and presbyterians, in particular, were excluded from power for many years. In the house of commons there was nothing resembling the modern system of disciplined parties, although there were recognisable groups of members who broadly shared similar attitudes to certain issues, and who would often act and vote in conjunction with each other. However, such groups were very fluid in their composition, and individuals could be easily influenced and detached from these groups and persuaded to support or oppose the government's measures. With a very limited franchise, the great majority of constituencies were dominated, to varying degrees, by prominent local families. Powerful individuals controlled several seats, in many of which the electorate was so small and tightly controlled that seats were bought and sold. Members of parliament were very responsive to the views of patrons in whose gift the seat was, or who could at least materially influence the electorate, although it by no means followed that popular or local feeling was ignored on important issues.[42]

The interplay of the various factors so far described meant that the administration had to devote a great deal of attention to the management of the house of commons, and to conciliating major political figures and their supporters or allies. Whilst issues of principle were important, personalities and the personal interests of the individuals concerned were at least as important, if not more so.

As the sovereign's representative, the lord lieutenant appointed a very large number of civil, military, ecclesiastical and legal officials, with the exception of a small number of the very highest offices specified in the letters patent issued upon his appointment. In those cases, the appointments were reserved to the sovereign and filled by the cabinet in London. The views of the lord lieutenant as to who should be appointed to important posts were not always decisive, as leading office holders and political figures in Dublin regularly engaged in intense lobbying of the English government to secure their own appointment, or that of a relative or political ally. It was an accepted feature of eighteenth-century life in both England and

---

42 A.P.W. Malcomson, 'The parliamentary traffic of this country', in Bartlett and Hayton (ed.), *Penal era and golden age*; and James Kelly, *Prelude to Union: Anglo-Irish politics in the 1780s* (Cork, 1992), pp. 218–19.

Ireland that the crown's power of patronage should be used to achieve parliamentary support for the government, and this power was the most important weapon in the lord lieutenant's armoury in his continuing efforts to secure a majority in the commons. The weapon was used to reward loyalty, to punish disloyalty, and to recognise ability in a house which was always difficult to control, and where the influence of oratory, as well as clashes of temperament and personality, played a significant part. The house of lords usually presented fewer problems for the government because many peers did not attend, unlike the bishops of the Church of Ireland who did attend regularly and could generally be relied upon to provide the government with a solid block of votes. Nevertheless, the creation of new peerages, or advancement in the peerage for existing peers or members of their families, was a frequent occurrence.

As advancement in the army, the church or the law could only be achieved by appointment to offices which were almost all in the gift of the crown, ambitious individuals had to impress the government to further their fortunes. Although many posts were sinecures which were granted to an individual for life, or a number of lives, thereby restricting the amount of patronage actually available at any one time, many remained which naturally became vacant from time to time, and these included judgeships and other legal posts. From 1690 to the Act of Union, barristers were an important element in the Irish house of commons, both in numbers and influence. Many of the matters which caused the government difficulty in parliament involved legislation or parliamentary procedure, and, naturally, lawyers were particularly prominent in debates and committees involving legislative or procedural issues. It was obviously essential for the government to secure the support of able lawyers in the house of commons, so as to ensure that its arguments were effectively presented and those of its opponents countered. Amongst the offices most frequently used by the government for this purpose were those of the law officers, including the three serjeants at law. We shall see this meant that the serjeants often played an important, and sometimes crucial, part in Irish parliamentary affairs throughout this period. The political activities of the serjeants illustrate the way in which many of those factors described above played a part in the complex and uneasy relationship between the crown and parliament.

Between 1690 and 1800, all but two of the fifty-three individuals who became serjeants were members of parliament at the time of their appointment. That membership of the commons was not merely a desirable, but an essential, qualification for the office in practice is confirmed by the comments of John Bowes. Called to the bar in England in 1718, Bowes was an Englishman who came to Ireland in 1725 under the patronage of his fellow-countryman Richard West, when West was appointed chancellor. Although West died in 1726, Bowes mounted the first rung on the ladder that ultimately led him to the summit of the legal profession when he became third serjeant in 1727. Recognising that a seat in parliament was essential, he wrote in December of that year: 'prudence, not ambition, put me upon asking [for the post of third serjeant] ... my next step is to secure a seat in parliament'.[43] It was not until 1731 that he realised his aim when he became MP for Taghmon. However, as he became solicitor general in 1730, Bowes was almost unique in achieving such substantial professional advancement despite his absence from the house of commons. Interestingly, the only other person to be appointed a serjeant who was not an MP was Henry Purdon, who succeeded Bowes as third serjeant.

That parliamentary service as a serjeant was a frequent stepping-stone to judicial preferment can be seen from an analysis of the pattern of judicial appointments. Eighty-seven appointments were made to the chief or puisne judgeships of the king's bench, common pleas and exchequer in Ireland between William's victory at the Boyne in 1690 and the passing of the Act of Union. Eighteen were made direct from England, leaving 69 to be filled by members of the Irish bar. Of those 69, 20 were serjeants at the time of their appointment to the bench. Two were third serjeants, 6 were second serjeants and no fewer than 12 held the office of prime serjeant. A further 6 judges had been serjeants at some point in their careers. Of the 5 solicitors general appointed judges, 3 had been serjeants, and of 5 attorneys general appointed to the bench, one had been a serjeant. The connection between service as a serjeant and judicial preferment is even more striking when one considers that during the same period, of the 53 individuals who were appointed serjeants, 10 died in office and 2, William Brodrick and Duquerry, resigned, Duquerry due to ill-health. Of the 41 survivors, 24 past or present serjeants were elevated to the

43 To Sir Dudley Ryder, 12 Dec. 1727: *Eighteenth-century Irish official papers in Great Britain private collections*, vol. 2 (Belfast, 1990), pp. 218–19. Ryder became solicitor general in England 1733–36, attorney general 1736–54 and chief justice of the king's bench 1754–56.

bench. In addition, a further 4 serjeants achieved other judicial offices, with Jocelyn becoming lord chancellor, Staunton a master in chancery, Toler chief justice of the common pleas in 1800 after the Union, and Daly a baron of the exchequer in 1801.

These figures show just how important the posts of serjeant, and that of prime serjeant in particular, were as a stepping-stone to the bench, and the extent to which legal preferment was used as a means of rewarding parliamentary support for the crown. One episode that illustrates the operation of several of the factors that could come into play in such situations occurred in 1759, when the government was anxious to gain the support of one of its leading parliamentary opponents by appointing E.S. Pery prime serjeant.[44] To create a vacancy for Pery, the duke of Bedford offered a vacancy in the king's bench to William Scott, prime serjeant and MP for Londonderry City. Unfortunately, this plan miscarried when Pery declined the post out of delicacy towards Lord Belvedere, who was his patron and in a sulk with the Castle at the time. Bedford felt obliged to honour his offer of the vacant judgeship to Scott,[45] who was duly appointed, and the post of prime serjeant went instead to Thomas Tenison. Whilst this manoeuvring was taking place, Richard Malone thought that he would be promoted from second to prime serjeant, but was to be disappointed.[46] Malone died later that year, leaving debts of £10,000, leading Chief Baron Willes to comment that John Gore 'applied for the second serjeancy, reconsidered and recalled his pretensions, he first considered [it] a step to the solicitorship afterwards as an object too small for his ambition'.[47]

Richard Malone was succeeded as second serjeant by his brother Edmund, thereby completing a unique hat-trick by being the third brother to become a serjeant. This achievement was all the more striking because of the suspicions entertained by Archbishop Stone that the protestantism of Anthony Malone, the most distinguished of

---

44 Edmund Sexton Pery, 1719–1806, 1st Viscount Pery. Called to the Irish bar in 1745 and rapidly gained a leading position in the profession. MP for the borough of Wicklow 1751–60 and for Limerick city 1760–85. Speaker of the Irish house of commons 1771–85.

45 *Eighteenth-century Irish official papers*, vol. 2, pp. 218–19.

46 Ibid.

47 Undated letter to an unknown correspondent, Willes papers, PRONI, Mic/236. John Gore, KC 1749, solicitor general 1760–64, MP for Co. Longford 1761–64. Chief justice of the king's bench 1764–84, created Baron Annaly 1766.

the three and prime serjeant at the time, was suspect because their mother had been a roman catholic in her youth.[48]

Although the government looked to office holders in the commons to support and vote for it, it was by no means always the case that 'the king's servants' could be relied upon to support the government. As we shall see, there were several occasions when the serjeants were numbered amongst the leading opponents of the government, and were dismissed because of this, or because they were identified with the previous regime after a change of government.

This phenomenon was to manifest itself in a way that was to become familiar within months of William's victory at the Boyne. In 1689 and 1690, the serjeants were caught up in the struggle between the Jacobites and Williamites, which was ultimately decided upon the battlefield. In February 1689, William and Mary ascended the English throne, James II landed in Ireland in March of that year, and in May summoned a parliament to meet in Dublin. Amongst the members of that parliament was Garrett Dillon, the prime serjeant and one of the members for Mullingar. Dillon later became a colonel in the Jacobite army, and in 1691 was one of the signatories of the civil articles of the Treaty of Limerick. Another signatory of the treaty was Sir Toby Butler, the solicitor general and former third serjeant who was MP for Ennis.[49] Among those proscribed by the Jacobite parliament were Sir Richard Ryves, John Osborne and Sir Richard Stephens, former serjeants who had been dismissed from their posts under James and who threw in their lot with William. In the months immediately following the victory of the Williamite forces in July, they were amongst the first protestants to be appointed as judges or law officers in place of roman catholics who had been appointed to these offices by James II.[50]

One of the earliest appointments was that of Osborne as prime serjeant at the end of September. Further appointments were made

48 C. Litton Falkiner, 'Correspondence of Archbishop Stone and the duke of Newcastle', *EHR*, xx (1905), 512.

49 Thomas Davis, *The patriot parliament of 1689*, 3rd ed. (London and New York, 1893), pp. 159 and 168. Dillon forfeited over 4,700 acres in Co. Mayo (BL, Add. MS 14,405, pp. 5–8). H.M.C., *Stuart MSS*, i, 80.

50 William King, *The state of the protestants of Ireland*, 3rd ed. (London, 1692), appendix, pp. 244–66, lists Ryves, Osborne, Stephens and Henry Echlin among those proscribed as being in open rebellion against James. Osborne and Stephens are recorded by Clarendon as visiting him and waiting on William at court. Clarendon, *State letters*, ii, 189–91.

later in the year, notably that of Alan Brodrick as third serjeant at the end of November. William's initial intention was to appoint Sir Richard Ryves prime serjeant and Richard Pyne as second.[51] Both had retired to London, been appointed as commissioners of oyer and terminer (or assize judges to use the more familiar term) and later as two of the three commissioners of the great seal.[52] Despite these signs of favour, William changed his mind, and both were passed over on this occasion as Sir Richard Stephens was made second serjeant. He only held the post for a short time until he was made a justice of the king's bench on 3 December 1690, Ryves succeeding him early in 1691. Osborne proved a very unsatisfactory appointment because he moved rapidly against those protestants who had acted in any civil office under James, declaring in the chancery court that they were guilty of high treason and filing a motion the next day in the king's bench seeking their prosecution.

Although such a move can hardly be viewed as surprising in the middle of a civil war in the light of the proscription of protestants by the Jacobite parliament, it led William King to declare it 'had startled the whole kingdom', in a long memorandum which he immediately sent to London, arguing that this would be disastrous, and that many protestants had no choice but to remain in office under James.[53] The protests of King and others bore fruit, and the earl of Nottingham wrote to the lords justices conveying the king's displeasure at Osborne's initiative:

I have laid your letter of the 14th. before the king, who has received great complaints from others also, of the proceedings of Serjeant Osborn, of which he highly disapproves, thinking it not prudent to give any occasion of fear to those who have submitted to the government, and it is his pleasure to direct your lordships that the judges should not proceed in declaring this point of law, which, however true, the king does not intend to extend to his protestant subjects. He would have you satisfy those that submit, that they shall enjoy the benefit of his intentions towards them and not be exposed to the penalties which the indiscreet zeal of Serjeant Osborn has given them great reason to fear.[54]

51 Earl of Nottingham to the lords justices: *Cal. S.P. dom., 1690–91*, p. 181.
52 Ball, *Judges*, ii, 4.
53 NLI, MS 2055. I am indebted to Mr J.I. McGuire for drawing this memorandum to my attention.
54 *Cal. S.P. dom., 1690–91*, pp. 168–69.

This direction from the king seems not to have been completely successful in halting or reversing Osborne's actions. In March 1692, one Captain White from Co. Kildare petitioned for relief from his outlawry for treason in 1690 as the result of indictments brought against him in two counties by Osborne.[55] The comment by Brodrick quoted at the beginning of this chapter that he had been instructed to indict individuals for treason on the Munster circuit (although these proceedings were, it seems, dropped) would perhaps indicate that such prosecutions were not initiated by Osborne alone, although it is not possible to establish how common they were. Osborne's action in initiating prosecutions in this manner is of interest because it would be consistent with an independent power to act on behalf of the crown being exercised by the prime serjeant. Certainly, there is no hint in Nottingham's letter that what Osborne had done was beyond his powers, or that the power to initiate prosecutions was vested in the attorney general alone. However, it would be unsafe to draw any definite conclusion as to the power of the prime serjeant to initiate proceedings in the name of the crown at this time from the absence of such a suggestion. It could well have been the case that, with the Jacobite armies still in the field and the final outcome of the war far from certain, neither Nottingham nor the lords justices had time to be concerned whether the prime serjeant had the technical power to institute proceedings of this type, or whether that was a matter for the attorney general.

Osborne's action in bringing these prosecutions was deeply embarrassing to the government, demonstrating as it did that the conciliatory attitude of the king was not shared by all of his servants in the Irish government, some of whom wished to see every possible step taken that would result in the complete subjugation of the roman catholic and Jacobite population, thereby ensuring that the protestant position in Ireland could not be threatened or undermined. It was also the forerunner of a more serious dispute between the king and his protestant subjects in Ireland, a dispute in which Osborne played a crucial part.

In the aftermath of the Treaty of Limerick the government was faced with determined opposition from Irish protestants who regarded the terms of the treaty as too favourable to the roman catholic population. A parliament was summoned in October 1692, but had to be prorogued after four weeks of increasingly acrimonious debate and

55 *Cal. S.P. dom., 1692*, p. 190.

vehement opposition, much of which came from within the government itself. Osborne was one of the most notable and active of the dissidents and the lord lieutenant, Viscount Sidney, identified him as one of the key figures opposing the government. After parliament had been in session for barely a fortnight, Sidney wrote to London:

I am angry with nobody so much as with Serjeant Osborne, who behaves himself every day most treacherously and ungratefully; he must certainly be turned out of his place, and Sir John Meade ought to be in it, for he has done extremely well, and is a man of most excellent parts; all the exception that can be made against him is that his wife is a papist.[56]

Sidney's anger encompassed the third serjeant, Alan Brodrick, as well, and he decided to assert his authority by dismissing both from office a few days later. Osborne died very shortly afterwards, but Brodrick was destined to be one of the most important legal and political figures in Ireland, in or out of office, during the next thirty years. Reference has already been made to a letter written by Brodrick to his brother in the spring of 1693, and in that letter he gave his account of the events leading up to his dismissal. He explained that he believed that, as the Irish privy council had so much power and because the judges were so subservient to the council, it was necessary to have a parliament. This was an indication that he, as did many others, saw the Irish parliament as a vital safeguard of the interests of Irish protestants,[57] even though the ability of parliament to act effectively to safeguard those interests was restricted by the operation of Poynings's Act.

It was not to be long before the wheel turned full circle and Brodrick was restored to office. The fiasco of the 1692 parliament convinced the government in England that an alternative approach was necessary. In 1695, an accommodation was reached whereby Brodrick became solicitor general, and he and his brother Thomas promised to secure the passage of the necessary money bills through the Irish parliament, in return for a significant share of government patronage and a voice in decisions as to the type of legislation to be brought before parliament. They were the first of what were to become known as 'undertakers', that is, major Irish political figures

56 *Cal. S.P. dom., 1695 (addenda 1689–95)*, p. 215.
57 Surrey Record Office, Guildford Muniment Room, Midleton MS 1248/1, pp. 261–62.

who undertook to the government to get supply bills through in return for these concessions, and who were to be such a feature of the Irish political scene over the next eighty years.[58]

A difficulty faced by all lords lieutenant when they came to make appointments was that personal rivalries had to be taken into account when deciding who should fill any vacant place. An excellent example of the way in which many different factors had to be taken into consideration in such situations is contained in the following account by Lord Capel of his trial of strength with the chancellor, Sir Charles Porter, in December 1695, over Capel's proposal that William Neave be appointed second serjeant:

Last Sunday morning, after we came from church, I acquainted him that I intended to make Mr William Neave, a gentleman of the long robe, his Majesty's second serjeant-at-law. The chancellor after some small pause told me that he could not bear it, that it was to prefer his enemy that had appeared against him this sessions, and that he would write to the King about it. I replied that he might write or do what he pleased, but that I was judge of the persons I thought fit to employ in the King's service, and that I intended to make Mr Ormsby and Mr Wingfield of the king's counsel at law. This morning Mr Neave waited on his lordship with the fiant or bill for his warrant to pass it under the great seal, but he said that he would take time to consider it, and gives for reason that he is not of ability to discharge that employment. His first reason, that Mr Neave was one of those who prosecuted the articles against him will not hold, his lordship having since called to mind the speech he made this session in the House of Commons in his own defence, that he had forgiven those who prosecuted him in former parliaments, and should now bear no resentment against any that might vote against him in this; though Mr Reading, a barrister who had appeared against the chancellor [in] the last parliament, was for that reason hindered from being approved for the recordership of Drogheda. But since my being alone in the government I have made him of the counsel to the commissioners of the revenue, he having been of great use to me in bringing His Majesty's affairs to a good issue. Mr Neave was recommended to me by the Earl of Meath, Lord Lanesborough and others, and I was assured by the Attorney and Solicitor-General of his ability to discharge that office. However, I expected not this reply of the chancellor, having lately, at his instance, made Mr William Porter, his brother, one of the King's counsel, Mr William Molyneaux, at his recommendation, one of the Masters in Chancery, and Sir Thomas Packenham, who always appeared and voted for him, His Majesty's prime serjeant. The influence and

58 Gerard O'Brien, *Anglo-Irish politics in the age of Grattan and Pitt* (Dublin, 1987), p. 21.

power of the lawyers in this kingdom is indeed very great, especially in parliament, and without their concurrence I could not have asserted His Majesty's right as to the beginning of money bills, and therefore I reserved these places at my disposal until the end of the sessions. But the true reason why I have thought fit to prefer these gentlemen was in obedience to His Majesty's commands, signified to me in yours of 23 November, that I should stop all manner of prosecution against the chancellor in the parliament of England. Finding, therefore, after the articles against the chancellor were rejected, that several of the members had meetings in order to accuse him in the parliament of England, and that some of these gentlemen of the law were principally concerned, I prevailed with them to desist; but if the chancellor is so haughty as to stop grants or preferments to those gentlemen that appeared against him, which they tell me they did believing him faulty in his place, I dare not undertake that His Majesty shall be troubled with no further complaints against him in the parliament of England.[59]

Despite Porter's opposition, Neave became second serjeant on 13 January 1696, and was to become an important member of the government, although less active in parliament on legal matters than the attorney general. However, he was a whig, and the arrival of the tory duke of Ormond as lord lieutenant in July 1711 led to the dismissal of Neave, by now prime serjeant, and the second serjeant, William Caulfield, and their replacement by Robert Blennerhassett and Morley Saunders, respectively. In November, John Cliffe's appointment as third serjeant meant that that post was filled for the first time in nineteen years. The events following the death of Queen Anne in August 1714 emphasized that the serjeants were firmly identified with the government of the day, because the accession of George I resulted in the dismissal of the tory administration and a drastic purge of the Irish judiciary and law officers. No fewer than seven new appointments were made in the superior courts, and all three serjeants were replaced in December. William Caulfield returned to office and was promoted to prime serjeant, and in that capacity he acted as one of the government's managers in the commons. He shared this role with Gore, the attorney general, Rogerson, the solicitor general, and Charles Delafye who was the secretary to the lords justices.[60] The law officers, including the prime serjeant, regularly performed this role as the century progressed. Thus, in 1727, we find Rogerson, by now

59 Capel to the duke of Shrewsbury, 17 Dec. 1695: *Cal. S.P. dom., 1695*, p. 128.
60 R.E. Burns, *Irish parliamentary politics in the eighteenth century*, 2 vols. (Washington D.C., 1989–90), i, 58.

attorney general, still acting in this capacity, together with the prime serjeant, Henry Singleton, and the solicitor general, Thomas Marlay.[61]

Although the practice of relying upon the leading law officers to manage the commons was well established by the middle of the century, it was in the period between 1743 and 1784 that the office of prime serjeant came to be regarded as particularly suited to a member of the bar whose parliamentary talents were such that he could act as the main advocate of the government's policies in, and manager of, the commons at a time when it was very difficult for the government to get its business through the house.

A notable example of a prime serjeant appointed because of his potential as a parliamentary manager was Anthony Malone. One of the outstanding advocates at the Irish bar in the eighteenth century, he was regarded as an obvious candidate for the position by the duke of Devonshire, according to the earl of Bessborough, who wrote to his son, 'my lord duke very well knows how useful this man must be in parliament, how necessary it may be for the king's affairs to have a person of his abilities in his services'.[62] Malone was made prime serjeant in May 1743, and became one of the most powerful figures in the Irish administration. Despite his reservations about the sincerity of Malone's protestantism referred to earlier, in 1747 Primate Stone commended him as 'by his abilities the most considerable man here, and the most useful to the government; at the same time he is of all those in the service of the government the most independent and the least importunate for favours'.[63] However, when Malone came to demonstrate that independence, the very qualities which made him such an asset to the government as prime serjeant and contributed to his high standing in parliament and with the general public, were to make him a formidable dissident in the government of which he was a leading figure. This became evident during the major constitutional crisis of 1753 which became known as the Money Bill dispute. Whilst the ostensible cause of this political convulsion was a dispute as to the way in which a surplus which had accumulated in the Irish treasury should be applied, in reality, the reasons for the dispute were much

---

61 Ibid., p. 22.
62 To his son, Lord Duncannon, Devonshire's chief secretary, 27 Jan. 1743: PRONI, Chatsworth MS, T.3158/235 (299/0).
63 19 Mar. 1747: PRONI, Wilmot papers, T.3019/801.

more complex.[64] The effects of economic difficulties in the linen indus-
try and elsewhere, rising food prices, political issues such as absentee
landlords and the exemption from tax of English pensions charged on
the Irish revenue, combined with a potent and widespread feeling of
resentment against the government. A bitter confrontation took place
between government and opposition, with Malone at the centre of the
storm, a crisis seen by many at the time as calling into question the very
nature of the constitutional relationship between the English government and the Irish parliament. Whilst it is beyond the scope of this
study to trace these events in detail, nevertheless they are significant as
being yet another occasion when the prime serjeant of the day proved
not to be a supporter, but a determined opponent of the government.

One participant in the crisis who was in no doubt that the prime
serjeant's opposition to the government's proposals for the way in
which the surplus was to be applied was merely the outward and visible
manifestation of a hidden agenda directed towards achieving a greater
degree of independence for the Irish parliament, was Archbishop
Stone. On 6 December 1753, he wrote to the duke of Newcastle:

Indeed, my lord, the cause of them [the matters in dispute] is of much longer
growth and lies much deeper. The constitutional dependency upon England is
the object upon which the prime serjeant's eye is constantly fixed.[65]

At the beginning of November, the commons debated whether a tax of
four shillings in the pound on absentee landlords should be dropped,
and the government thought that Malone could be persuaded to
support its position, the chief secretary reporting that when he was
first directed to mention that affair to the king's servants,

I found the Prime Serjeant very averse to it, but by good words and a little
flattery he came into that measure ... the debate lasted about four hours,
and latterly we had the assistance of the Prime Serjeant and others of the
Speaker's friends.[66]

---

64 The definitive account of this dispute is Declan O'Donovan, 'The Money Bill
    dispute of 1753', in Bartlett and Hayden (ed.), *Penal era and golden age*, p. 55.
65 Ibid., p. 63. BL, Add. MSS 32,733, f. 369.
66 Lord George Sackville to Henry Pelham, 11 Nov. 1753: PRONI, Pelham
    MS, T.2863/1/59. Sackville was the chief secretary, and son of the duke of
    Dorset, the lord lieutenant.

Despite this initial show of support, it soon became obvious that Malone could not be relied upon to support the administration. As the weeks went past, public and parliamentary feeling against the government increased and Sackville saw Malone as one of the key figures whose hostility was contributing to this state of affairs. The crisis came to a head on 17 December, with the rejection by the commons of the bill to apply part of the surplus to reducing the national debt. When he wrote to Pelham the next day reporting this defeat, Sackville was in no doubt that Malone's influence had been instrumental in bringing about the rejection of the bill:

It is astonishing to see with what success Mr Prime Serjeant has spread his opinion and alarmed the nation in respect to the alteration that it is thought must be made in the money bill. It is publicly asserted that if the Commons submit in that particular there is an end to all liberty in this country, that they will have nothing to do but to submit implicitly to whatever shall be dictated to them by the English government.[67]

The ministry in London decided that it was essential to take action that would make it clear that the king's servants would be punished when they acted against the government, and on 28 December instructions were sent to Dublin that Malone and several other prominent office holders were to be dismissed, and deprived of pensions which they held. Such was the public support for Malone that when Eaton Stannard was made prime serjeant in his place, Stannard was burnt in effigy.[68] Although an experienced lawyer and parliamentarian,[69] Stannard was not of comparable stature to Malone, and despite the circumstances which led to his dismissal as prime serjeant, Malone's ability and influence were such that in succeeding years the anxiety of the ministry to gain his support was demonstrated by his being granted a patent of precedence at the end of 1756. This was a very rare mark of special favour to a barrister, which had the effect of granting him professional precedence ahead of other counsel, to which he would not otherwise be entitled. In Malone's case, the grant gave him precedence over the prime serjeant, the attorney general, the solicitor general and all of the other king's counsel. A more

67 PRONI, Pelham MS, T. 2863/1/62.
68 PRONI, Bedford MS, T. 2915/11/48.
69 He had been MP for Midleton since 1727, and was recorder of Dublin, 1733–50.

substantial mark of favour was Malone's appointment to the sinecure of chancellor of the exchequer, the salary attached to the post being increased by £700 a year to make it even more attractive.

Malone's dismissal as prime serjeant meant that it was to be some years before the post was again occupied by someone of significant political stature. During the earlier part of John Hely-Hutchinson's tenure of the post, from 1761 until his appointment as provost of Trinity College in 1774, he was one of the government's parliamentary managers. However, he was not the most important manager as that role fell to Philip Tisdall. Third serjeant from 1742 until 1751, solicitor general from 1751 until 1760 and attorney general until his death in 1777, Tisdall was for many years one of the major figures in the Irish administration. With the arrival of Lord Townshend as lord lieutenant in the autumn of 1767, the political landscape soon changed dramatically and, although both Tisdall and Hely-Hutchinson were retained in office, the efforts of Townshend between 1767 and 1772 meant that from then on the lord lieutenant of the day sought to directly control parliament and dispense patronage in order to ensure that the king's business could be got through, rather than relying upon the efforts of the undertakers who had hitherto performed this task in return for a share of patronage and influence upon government.

Although Townshend and his successors exercised power in a more direct and unfettered fashion than had been the case in the past, politicians such as Tisdall and Hely-Hutchinson remained highly influential, and had to be conciliated lest they turn their influence and abilities against the government. The government still had to recruit office holders whose abilities could sway parliament, and, as we shall see, in the decade after 1774 the prime serjeant's post was filled on several occasions by men of great ability chosen to be the government's principal parliamentary champion.

That the choice as to who should be the government's principal lieutenant in the commons at this time generally had to be made between the attorney general and the prime serjeant can be seen from the following extracts from a memoir written by the earl of Buckinghamshire who was lord lieutenant from 1777 to 1780. Throughout his period of office, Buckinghamshire had to contend with the increasingly vociferous demands for legislative independence from the Irish parliament, at a time when the Imperial government was embroiled in the war with the American colonies, a war which gradually expanded until Great Britain was also at war with the French, the Spanish and the Dutch, as well as facing the

Mahratta Confederacy in India. The constant demand for troops for service in North America, the danger of a French invasion of Ireland and the influence of the Volunteer movement in Ireland itself meant Buckinghamshire had enormous difficulty in maintaining the government's position. It would seem that this memoir was written not long after his recall in 1780 to vindicate his actions as lord lieutenant. Buckinghamshire was sworn in as lord lieutenant in January 1777, and among his first and most important tasks was to decide who should lead his administration in the commons. Despite the changes brought about by Townshend, Tisdall and Hely-Hutchinson were the obvious candidates, and the choice fell upon Tisdall, but his death later that year meant that another leader had to be found. In the following passage, Buckinghamshire explained why he came to choose Hussey Burgh to be prime serjeant:

Mr Tisdall in one of his early conversations mentioned Mr Hussey Burgh as the most promising of the rising young men, recommending him to particular notice and, in consequence of Mr Dennis, the prime serjeant, being appointed chief baron, Mr Burgh succeeded, apparently with general approbation, to the office, and every letter from England felicitated the lord lieutenant upon the arrangement.[70]

Burgh became prime serjeant in July 1777, but with Tisdall's death in the autumn a new attorney general had to be found; the choice fell upon John Scott, and Buckinghamshire explained why Burgh became the government's leader in the commons:

At the eve of the opening of the sessions the account of Mr Tisdall's death was received. Mr Scott was immediately appointed attorney general. The lead in parliamentary business naturally devolved either upon him or the prime serjeant, but Mr Scott declining it, the former was necessarily called forth.[71]

Burgh became increasingly sympathetic to the demands for free trade for Ireland, and in June 1780 resigned as prime serjeant.

The loss of his principal lieutenant in the commons was a heavy blow to Buckinghamshire, who commented bitterly in his memoir:

No man ever experienced more political injury than Lord Buckingham [shire] from Mr Burgh; even after his first desertion, had he adhered to his decla-

70 PRONI, Buckinghamshire MS, T.3502/1.
71 Ibid.

rations in parliament, upon the concessions made by England, the remainder of that administration might probably have passed without any material ruffle, and the situation of Ireland would at this time have been very different.[72]

Burgh's successor as prime serjeant was James Browne, MP for Tuam. 'A sensible but heavy man and a tiresome speaker',[73] Browne was not the man to counter the matchless oratory of Burgh, Grattan and others who constantly assailed the government in the commons. That burden fell to the attorney general, John Scott. 'Copper-faced Jack', as Scott was known to his contemporaries, proved equal to the task. His vigour, determination and forensic ability were indispensable as the administration sought to resist the campaign, supported by the Volunteer movement, to repeal Poynings's Act and the Declaratory Act of 1720 (which stated that the British parliament had legislative supremacy over the Irish parliament, and making the British house of lords the final court of appeal in Irish litigation).

Eventually the political tide proved irresistible, and the collapse of Lord North's government in March 1782 and the formation of the Rockingham ministry brought about changes in the Irish administration. In the summer, Browne and Scott were dismissed. Scott is generally believed to have known that he would be removed and to have decided to provoke his dismissal by asserting that Great Britain had no right to bind Ireland by acts of parliament. The duke of Portland (the new lord lieutenant) removed Browne at the same time, Burgh was re-apppointed prime serjeant, but only held the post on this occasion for a few weeks, as he became chief baron of the exchequer in July at the age of thirty-nine.

Scott was replaced as attorney general by Barry Yelverton, an equally distinguished and determined opponent of the government, whose bill (subsequently known as Yelverton's Act) in July 1782 to amend Poynings's Act was a major step towards achieving legislative independence for the Irish parliament. However, Scott's talents were such that it was inevitable that he would return to office in due course, and, when he did, it was to be as prime serjeant. The considerations which led the government to regard Scott as a serious candidate for that post are noteworthy as yet another demonstration

---

72 Ibid.
73 G.O. Sayles (ed.), 'Contemporary sketches of the Irish house of commons in 1782', *RIA Proc*, lvi (1954), sect. c, p. 249.

of the way in which the office of prime serjeant was regarded as one which should be filled by a leading parliamentary figure, if at all possible. In October 1783, Portland, now prime minister, wrote to Thomas Pelham, responding to a suggestion that Scott be made prime serjeant. Whilst acknowledging that Scott had proved untrustworthy in the past, Portland reluctantly recognised that, however unpalatable it might be, something had to be done:

As I believe the removal of Mr Scott to have been one of the best acts of my Administration founded as it was on the extreme profligacy and contempt of principle which he publicly avowed and boasted of, I can not reconcile my mind to so liberal a construction of the principle or more properly speaking of the necessity of the Coalition as to admit the policy of placing a person so circumstanced in a very high office of expectation in the opinion of the public as well as his own. I am persuaded that it is intended by you carefully to guard against his having the conduct or management of the House of Commons, but let me submit to you the difficulty of that measure with such an Attorney General as Fitzgibbon, who as well as Scott has been bred up in habits of thinking respecting the conduct of Government very different from those which are consistent with our professions and principles and which are totally incompatible with that economy which we have bound ourselves to observe in the management of the public finances. Contradictory as it may seem to the caution I have just recommended to you I can not scruple to prefer an expedient suggested by Adair or rather reported by him as a resource which had occurred to some of our friends, which is the placing Scott at the head of the Court of Common Pleas by making such a provision for the Chief Justice as might induce him to retire. This would not be long a burden upon the public, the length of [Chief Justice Patterson's] services would justify it, Scott would not refuse to accept it, and you would get rid of a man who has it in his power to do you much mischief and can never render you any service adequate to the price he has already received and the credit you risk by putting him in an active situation.[74]

Pelham gave a cautious repose to this unenthusiastic yet elaborate proposal, explaining that he had a more modest suggestion in mind which he thought might be adequate:

With regard to Scott it was never my intention to place unbounded confidence in him, I considered his opposition so formidable, I disliked his returning to his former station, and consequently thought that the office of

---

74 27 Oct. 1783 (PRONI, BL, Add. MS. 33,100, T.755/l, pp. 255–57).

prime serjeant gave him legal rank, without the necessity of further confidence that administration might think proper to place in him.[75]

The collapse of Portland's short-lived ministry at the end of the year, and the appointment of William Pitt the younger as prime minister on 19 December, meant that this proposal to make Scott prime serjeant was stillborn. Nevertheless, Pelham's belief that the offer of the prime serjeant's position might prove sufficient to lure a former attorney general into supporting the ministry was to prove well-founded, because Scott was appointed to the post by the new ministry on 31 December 1783. His tenure of office proved to be brief, as he became chief justice of the king's bench the following May, his successor as prime serjeant being James Browne who had been dismissed from the post two years before. Browne's second tenure of office proved no more successful than his first, because he was dismissed in 1787 and replaced by James Fitzgerald, who had been dismissed as third serjeant by Pelham in 1782, then made second serjeant in 1784, and who was later to be dismissed as prime serjeant by Cornwallis in 1799 because of his opposition to the Union.

The events we have considered clearly establish that the prime serjeant was an important political as well as legal office, frequently (though not invariably) held by one of the leading parliamentary figures of the day, chosen to fill the post to act as leader of the government ranks in the commons. It often provided a means whereby the administration could seek to turn a dangerous opponent into a useful, though frequently unreliable, parliamentary champion without having to displace the attorney general. The decade from the first appointment of Burgh as prime serjeant in July 1777 to Browne's dismissal from office for the second time in the summer of 1787 can be said to mark the apogee of the importance of the office of prime serjeant in parliamentary terms.

However, the standing and talents of many of the prime serjeants throughout the period from 1690 to the Act of Union, and during this decade in particular, should not blind us to the reality that, by the end of the eighteenth century, the post of prime serjeant was an anachronism, whose continued survival and precedence over both the attorney general and solicitor general no doubt owed something to inertia and tradition, but was largely because it provided an

---

75 Ibid., Pelham to Portland, undated letter.

additional means whereby the administration could enlist the services of a prominent lawyer in the commons. The rise in importance of the attorney general as both a legal and political office, which we have already noted in both the sixteenth and seventeenth centuries, continued throughout the eighteenth century. Prominent as many of the prime serjeants were during the period covered by this chapter, when one remembers that the post of attorney general was held by men such as Robert Jocelyn from 1730 to 1739, Philip Tisdall from 1760 to 1777 and, most noteworthy of all, by John Fitzgibbon between 1783 and 1789, the latter office was indisputably pre-eminent. Once the Irish parliament ceased to exist, there was no longer a need for such a parliamentary champion, and so the prime serjeant no longer served a purpose which justified the continued existence of the office, and, in particular, the precedence it conferred over the attorney general and solicitor general. Its extinction was probably inevitable and, as we shall see in the next chapter, it did not long survive the parliament which had seen so many of its most outstanding members hold this ancient office.

CHAPTER FIVE

'No longer a prize to be fought for in parliament': the serjeants in post-Union Ireland

THE PASSING OF the Act of Union was marked by passionate debate both inside and outside the Irish house of commons, and just as members of the Irish bar were amongst the most prominent proponents of the arguments for and against, so were the serjeants.[1] One of the most notable casualties of the drive by Cornwallis, the lord lieutenant, to persuade the Irish parliament to pass the Act was the prime serjeant, James Fitzgerald. Dismissed as third serjeant in 1782, he returned to favour in 1784 when he became second serjeant, and had been promoted to prime serjeant in 1787 when James Browne was dismissed from that position for the second time. Fitzgerald had been in parliament since 1776 and was regarded as a sound lawyer and eloquent pleader, yet Cornwallis had no hesitation in dismissing him because of his opposition to the Union.[2] His successor as prime serjeant was St George Daly, MP for Galway since 1798. Although at the bar for seventeen years, Daly had little professional standing and was personally unpopular. Nevertheless, he made strenuous efforts in parliament and elsewhere to rally support for the Union.[3] In August 1799 at a county meeting in Loughrea, Co. Galway which debated the Union, Daly was assisted by the third serjeant, Edmund Stanley.[4] MP for Lanesborough, Stanley had been in the commons since 1790 and, although slightly younger than Daly, was more distinguished professionally, becoming a king's counsel and a bencher of King's Inns after

---

1   It has been estimated that there were 67 barristers (of whom 42 were in active practice) among the 300 members of the commons at the time: G.C. Bolton, *The passing of the Irish Act of Union: a study in parliamentary politics* (Oxford, 1966), pp. 80–81.
2   *Gentleman's Magazine*, March 1835. His great reputation and the reason for his dismissal ensured that Fitzgerald continued to enjoy the respect of the bar, which insisted on giving him the precedence which he had enjoyed as prime serjeant.
3   Ball, *Judges*, ii, 238.
4   Bolton, *The passing of the Irish Act of Union*, p. 102.

only seven years at the bar. Coming as he did from a Co. Roscommon family, Stanley was also active there at this time, seeking to persuade the grand jury to declare for the Union,[5] no doubt influenced by his experiences during the rising of the previous year when he narrowly escaped with his life in Co. Wexford whilst travelling to Cork to sit as a judge of assize.[6] Another prominent lawyer whose talents were deployed on behalf of the government and who was destined to become a serjeant in later years was William Johnston.[7] However the majority of the Irish bar, and its ablest members, were determined opponents of the measure, although several later became serjeants. Amongst the latter was Thomas Goold, whose experiences in Paris during the Revolution led him to write a defence of Burke's *Reflections on the revolution in France*. Goold vigorously opposed the Union in his *An address to the people of Ireland on the subject of the projected Union*, published in 1799, yet, like many others who opposed the Union, he ultimately made his peace with the administration, although it was not until 1823 that he became a serjeant.

As might be expected, those who supported the government at the time were rewarded first, Daly becoming a baron of the exchequer in the summer of 1801, with Stanley being promoted from third serjeant to succeed him as prime serjeant. Unfortunately for Stanley, he was to enjoy this office for less than six months. His affairs were so financially embarrassed that he was unable to appear in Dublin, due no doubt to a fear of being arrested for debt, and he was dismissed in the closing days of 1801. Although Stanley and others were to attribute this purely to the enmity towards him of the lord chancellor, the earl of Clare,[8] the lord lieutenant took the view that, quite apart from the impropriety of his continuing in office when his affairs were in such a state, Stanley's absence from Dublin was impairing his ability to discharge his duties. The earl of Hardwicke appointed Arthur Browne prime serjeant in his place, but softened the blow by giving Stanley Browne's place on the board of accounts, an equally

5 Ibid., p. 148.
6 *New Annual Register for 1805* (London, 1806), p. 86.
7 Bolton, *The passing of the Irish Act of Union*, p. 102.
8 Mr Justice Day to Stanley, 19 July 1802 (PRONI, Pitt/Prettyman papers, T.3319, p. 79).

valuable office,[9] and one which Stanley was subsequently to sell for £5,000.[10]

A distinguished and learned man of wide intellectual attainments, Browne was destined to be the last prime serjeant.[11] MP for Dublin University, he initially opposed the Union but, on reflection, changed his mind, concluding that the Irish parliament had forfeited any claim to a continued existence. In particular, Browne believed that under a Union the government would be able to meet the claims of Irish catholics, whilst preserving the existing order. He had been granted the lucrative post on the board of accounts in return for his support for the Union, and Hardwicke explained his appointment as prime serjeant in part because 'it has the recommendation of satisfying the Engagement [that is, the promise at the time of the Union] to Dr Browne in his own profession'.[12]

Although Browne's change of mind was bitterly criticised, it 'has a certain consistency, he was above all attached to the existing order of church and state and the system of property based upon the English conquest in Ireland'.[13] Browne was not the only prominent opponent of the Union to accept office soon afterwards. Another was Arthur Moore, appointed third serjeant in 1801 and promoted to the new office of first serjeant on Browne's death. A third was Charles Kendal Bushe, who had published an anti-Union pamphlet with the title *Cease your funning, or the rebel detected*, yet succeeded Moore as third serjeant in July 1805, holding office for only three months before becoming solicitor general. As we shall see later in this chapter, many prominent protestant lawyers in the 1820s and 1830s were extremely active politically. A recent study has pointed out that they defended the existing constitution 'as a coherent system which

9 Letter of 26 Dec. 1801 from Hardwicke to Thomas Pelham, 3rd Baron Pelham of Stanmer, secretary of state for the home department 1801–03 (BL, Hardwicke papers, Add. MS 35,732, f. 12).

10 Stanley to Hardwicke, 6 Aug. 1803 (BL, Hardwicke papers, Add. MS 35,741, f. 150). Stanley showed little gratitude for this in later years, and eventually his demands for further recompense for his services were rewarded by a knighthood and appointment at a salary of £3,000 p.a. to the new post of recorder of Prince of Wales Island (now Pinang in Malaysia) in 1807. I hope to publish a separate study of Stanley's unusual career in due course.

11 For an account of Browne's career, see Paul O'Higgins, 'Arthur Browne (1756–1805): an Irish civilian', *NILQ*, xx (1969), 255.

12 26 Dec. 1801 (BL, Hardwicke papers, Add. MS 35,732, f. 12).

13 O'Higgins, 'Arthur Browne', 267.

had stood the test of time, and which had been compatible with economic prosperity and with the extension of "toleration" (in its limited eighteenth-century sense) to catholics and other dissenters from the established church'.[14] Whilst Moore and Bushe no doubt recognised that it was necessary to reach an accommodation with the new order, Browne at least was arguably an early exponent of the conservative philosophy identified above.

Browne's death at the end of June 1805 led to the abolition of the office of prime serjeant and its replacement by the new office of first serjeant which ranked immediately after that of solicitor general. This resulted in little comment at the time,[15] no doubt reflecting a general acceptance of the reality that, despite the prestige and antiquity of the office, it was impossible to defend its continued precedence over the much more important posts of attorney general and solicitor general. The change also provided the opportunity for an examination of the remuneration attached to the serjeants' posts, giving rise to a revealing correspondence between the lord chancellor and the lord lieutenant which throws some light upon the political significance of the serjeants and their offices at that time.

On 20 June 1805, Lord Redesdale[16] wrote to Hardwicke stressing the need to conciliate the bar, and suggesting that salaries be attached to each post:

I have before suggested to Your Excellency how much I consider the good opinion of the bar here as valuable to Government, the strength of Government rests [wholly] in public opinion. There is no body now in Ireland which has so much influence in public opinion as the bar. I believe the appointments of Serjeant Moore and Mr Bushe will be generally approved; and I propose to communicate [this] to those gentlemen tomorrow. The salary both of prime serjeant and second serjeant, charged on the civil list, amount to about £30 a year as I understand from Mr Marsden.[17] I have proposed to him to give a salary of £150 to [the] first, £100 a year to the

---

14 Jacqueline Hill, 'The legal profession and the defence of the *ancien régime* in Ireland, 1790–1840', in Hogan & Osborough (ed.), *Brehons, serjeants and attorneys*, p. 208.

15 On 29 June 1805, the *Belfast Newsletter* referred to the new arrangement believed to be imminent without comment, correctly forecasting that Moore would be promoted from third to first serjeant, with Chatterton remaining as second, and Bushe becoming third, serjeant.

16 John Mitford, 1748–1830. 1st Baron Redesdale, lord chancellor of Ireland, 1802–06.

17 Alexander Marsden, under-secretary to the lord lieutenant, 1801–06.

second, and £50 a year to the third serjeant, who now receives no salary. I remember Lord Thurlow used to say he always wished that those who had rank from the Crown should have salary, however small; and I think his idea is just; and some things which have passed in England show it to be so.[18]

Marsden wrote to Hardwicke on 24 June agreeing to this proposal,[19] and, although there is no definite evidence to confirm that these salaries were actually paid, there is some reason to think that they were, to judge by a letter from Sir James Chatterton, quoted below. Although it would seem that the abolition of the prime serjeant's position did not attract opposition, the proposal to promote Moore from third to first serjeant did. Chatterton had been second serjeant for nine years and third serjeant for two years before that. Despite the established (but by no means invariable) custom that an existing serjeant was promoted within the ranks of the serjeancy when a vacancy arose, he had been passed over for promotion to prime serjeant three times, although he was made a baronet in August 1801, no doubt to compensate him for Stanley's promotion over his head in July of that year. In succeeding years, Chatterton wrote to Hardwicke on several occasions to press his claims for further advancement, going so far as to have a memorial drawn up in July 1804 setting out in detail his professional and political career; and in August, he sent a further memorial showing the grant to him of the freedom of Cork in recognition of his judicial services.[20] Determined to avoid being disappointed again, and having unsuccessfully pressed his claim to be made first serjeant upon Redesdale, Chatterton wrote a long letter to Hardwicke on 29 June in which he sought to justify his claim to further preferment:

I beg leave with great respect, to state to your Excellency, that having received from the Lord Chancellor the honour of a letter, in which he is so good to say, that he is sorry to learn from myself, as well as from your Excellency, that I am disappointed, in consequence of the arrangements proposed to be made, upon the vacancy of the office of prime serjeant, and that his lordship trusted, with my ample fortune, and considering the state of my health, I would not upon reflection be disposed, much to blame these arrangements, and also mentioning the salary intended to be paid to the different serjeants, however that salary could be of no object to me, I have in my answer stated to his

18 BL, Hardwicke papers, Add. MS 35,717, f. 107.
19 BL, Hardwicke papers, Add. MS 35,726, f. 99.
20 3 July 1804 (BL, Hardwicke papers, Add. MS 35,750, f. 288); 15 Aug.1804 (BL, Hardwicke papers, Add. MS 35,751, f. 334).

lordship (as I now beg leave to state to your Excellency) that in returning his lordship my best thanks for the honour of his letter, it would be doing injustice to my own feelings if I did not express my deep sorrow and regret, in finding it to be the intention of Government to pass by, in the arrangement about to take place, the pretensions of an old and faithful servant.[21]

Having somewhat sententiously disclaimed concern about the emoluments of the office, Chatterton concluded by saying that 'it is rank in the profession' that he looked for, and that he had acted as an assize judge in almost every part of Ireland. Chatterton's plea fell on deaf ears, although Redesdale did acknowledge to Hardwicke that Chatterton's disappointment had created a certain amount of sympathy at the bar and elsewhere.[22]

No sooner had these promotions been settled than the death later that year of the chief baron, Lord Avonmore, precipitated further changes amongst the judiciary and law officers. Bushe was promoted solicitor general and succeeded as third serjeant by John Ball in October, although one of those initially considered for the latter post was Edward Mayne. In December 1805, Redesdale wrote to Hardwicke about Mayne's prospects in the light of the vacancy which was thought likely following the conviction of Mr Justice Robert Johnson on a charge of libel in the English king's bench, as the result of which he faced a period of imprisonment. Mayne was appointed a justice of the common pleas in 1806, but in the course of the letter Redesdale explained why Mayne had not been appointed third serjeant when the vacancy arose in October:

It occurred to me, some time ago, that it might be advantageous to appoint Mr Mayne ... third serjeant, but this was objected to by Mr Marsden for reasons which I do not think were considerable *as the office of serjeant is no longer a prize to be fought for in parliament.*[23] (my emphasis)

Redesdale's assessment of the decline in significance of the serjeant's office in parliamentary terms after the Union provides some confirmation of the conclusion in the previous chapter that the prime serjeant had come to be regarded primarily as a parliamentary champion. The demise of the Irish parliament meant that there was no longer a need for such a champion and highlighted the anomaly

21 BL, Hardwicke papers, Add. MS 35,760, ff. 62–63.
22 29 July 1805 (BL, Hardwicke papers, Add. MS 35,718, f. 127).
23 13 Dec. 1805 (BL, Hardwicke papers, Add. MS 35,718, f. 187).

whereby the prime serjeant continued to have precedence over the attorney and solicitor general. The need to provide an office of sufficient prestige to reward Stanley, and then Browne, for their support for the Union ended with Browne's death. That provided the opportunity to rationalize the position by at last formally recognising what had long been the case, namely, that the offices of attorney general and solicitor general were more important than the most senior of the serjeants.

It may also be that the abolition of the post of prime serjeant and its replacement by the lesser office of first serjeant was regarded at the time as bringing the Irish serjeants into line with the English practice. That at least might be what Chatterton had in mind when he wrote to Hardwicke asking to be appointed first serjeant following Browne's death,

should it be the intention of the king's government (as it is said to be) to discontinue the office of prime serjeant, and to appoint first, second and third serjeants as in England, and to give precedence to the attorney and solicitor general.[24]

In England it was common for there to be several king's serjeants at a time, the two most senior of whom had been confirmed as having precedence over the attorney general and solicitor general by a royal warrant of 1623. Although the growth in prestige of the king's counsel meant that the standing of the serjeants at law correspondingly declined over many years, it was not until 1813 that the attorney general and solicitor general were given precedence over the 'two ancientest king's serjeants', who were generally referred to as the king's first (or principal) serjeant and second serjeant.[25] If Chatterton believed that the abolition of the office of prime serjeant was following an English precedent, he was in error.

Whilst it is certainly correct that the serjeants no longer had the importance in parliamentary terms that they enjoyed in the eighteenth century, they continued to enjoy considerable professional prestige and to be closely associated with politics throughout the remainder of their existence. This is clearly seen from an analysis of the careers of the post-Union serjeants.

24 15 June 1805 (BL, Hardwicke papers, Add. MS, 35,760, f. 39).
25 Baker, *Serjeants at law*, pp. 58–61 and 111–113.

As had been the case in the past, appointment as a serjeant and further advancement through the ranks of the law officers to the bench was the norm, although there were periods when the serjeants were more prominent politically and professionally than others. Of the 61 serjeants appointed after the Act of Union came into force, 11 died in office and 4 resigned or were dismissed. As we have seen, Stanley's dismissal was due to his financial problems. The reason for Stock's resignation in 1851 is unknown. Whilst the reasons for the resignation of Jonathan Christian in April 1855 are equally obscure, this did not adversely affect his subsequent career: he became solicitor general in 1856, a justice of the common pleas in 1858 and a lord justice of appeal in 1867. As we shall see, the resignation of Lefroy as first serjeant in 1830 was due to political considerations, but he ultimately became chief justice of the queen's bench. If one therefore adds Stanley and Stock to the 11 serjeants who died in office, of the remaining 48, 8 were appointed to lesser judicial offices such as masters in chancery or county court judges whilst serving as serjeants, and no fewer than 36 became judges of the superior courts.[26] Of these 36, 10 were appointed directly to the bench, and 23 went on to serve first as solicitor general or attorney general.

As in previous centuries, the importance of political affiliations and considerations when judicial appointments came to be made in post-Union Ireland has long been recognized. When one examines the careers of the serjeants appointed during this period, the correlation between political activity and appointment as a serjeant is equally pronounced: no fewer than 30 of the 61 post-Union serjeants were MPs at some stage of their careers. Many of the remainder were politically active; indeed, the non-political serjeant was almost unknown.

Although many of the post-Union serjeants were MPs, nevertheless between 1801 and 1832 (when Perrin was elected MP for Co. Monaghan) no serjeant had a seat in parliament, whereas of the serjeants appointed in the years immediately following the Union, Stanley, Browne, Moore, Bushe, Ball and William Johnson had all been members of the Irish house of commons. As there were initially only 100 Irish seats at Westminster, compared to 300 at College Green,

---

26 That is, of the courts amalgamated into a unified supreme court of judicature, consisting of the court of appeal and the high court, by the Supreme Court of Judicature (Ireland) Act, 1877. In 1897, this process was finally completed when the admiralty and bankruptcy courts were amalgamated with the high court.

there were simply not enough seats to go round. In addition, the great majority of seats were controlled to varying degrees by wealthy patrons, and in those instances where he did not wish to retain the seat for himself, a member of his immediate family or a protégé, the cost of purchasing a seat could amount to thousands of pounds.[27]

Whilst the scarcity of seats and cost of elections were, no doubt, important factors in dramatically reducing the number of practising barristers in parliament in the immediate aftermath of the Union, another factor must surely have been the unwelcome prospect of the disruption of a barrister's practice brought about by absences at Westminster, absences in turn exacerbated by poor communications within Ireland itself and between Ireland and England. It has to be remembered that the first of Bianconi's 'long cars' which revolutionized coach transport in Ireland were not introduced until 1815. Although the advent of the first steamship from Holyhead in 1819 reduced the crossing time from about 15 hours in good weather to about 7 or 8 hours, the mail coach between London and Holyhead still took about 30 hours. These travel difficulties must have presented a formidable disincentive to any barrister contemplating whether a parliamentary career could be combined with practice in Dublin and on assize. However, as communications improved during the nineteenth century, there were dramatic improvements in journey times. By the middle of the century the sea crossing had been reduced to 4 hours, and the rail journey from London to Holyhead took 9 hours. By 1914 the total journey time between Dublin and London had been further reduced to 9 hours. It cannot be entirely coincidental that the numbers of serjeants who were, or aspired to be, elected to parliament greatly increased as communications within Ireland and between Ireland and England started to improve. By the 1830s, we see many of those who were, or were to become, serjeants seeking election. However, improved communications were probably not the sole reason for this development, because it was not until 1848 that the railway and steamer links between Dublin and London were completed.[28]

27 A.P.W. Malcomson, ' "The parliamentary traffic of this country" ', in Bartlett & Hayton (ed.), *Penal era and golden age*, pp. 159–60.
28 D.B. McNeill, *Irish passenger steamship services*, 2 vols. (Newton Abbott, 1971), ii, 13–15 and 23–24; and information from J.J.S. Grey, to whom I am greatly indebted on this topic.

Another possible reason may be the change in the political and electoral landscape associated with O'Connell's campaigns and what has been described as 'the confessional basis of political identification',[29] which accentuated the political and professional profiles of the serjeants. Certainly, there was a sudden increase in the number of serjeants who were members of parliament, or sought election. Between 1801 and 1830 no serjeant was an MP, yet of ten serjeants appointed between 1831 and 1841 several served in parliament. Michael O'Loghlen was a serjeant from 1831 to 1834, stood unsuccessfully as a Liberal candidate for Dublin in 1832, and was elected for Dungarvan in 1835. His successor as third serjeant was Louis Perrin who was elected MP for Dublin in 1831. Perrin was unseated but was elected MP for Co. Monaghan in 1832 and for Cashel in 1835. In 1835 he was succeeded as third serjeant by Joseph Devonsher Jackson. A noted Conservative, Jackson became MP for Bandon the same year.

One of the most prominent Conservative lawyers of this period was Thomas Lefroy. A leading equity practitioner, Lefroy was appointed third serjeant in 1818, and by 1830 had been promoted through the ranks of the serjeancy to first serjeant. In 1820 he refused an appointment to the king's bench, in 1821 to the exchequer and in 1823 to the common pleas. Lefroy stood unsuccessfully for Dublin University in 1827, and in 1829, in a speech to the Brunswick Constitutional Club, made a vigorous attack upon the Emancipation Bill.[30] Whilst they did not deny his professional eminence, Lefroy's political views, and what they regarded as his unctuous and hypocritical protestantism, were anathema to O'Connell and his supporters, to judge by the sustained venom of the attack on him by Richard Lalor Shiel in his *Sketches of the Irish bar.* 'There is something apparently irreconcilable between the ambition and avidity which are almost inseparable from the propensities of a successful lawyer, and any very genuine enthusiasm in religion', commented Shiel, repeating the point later in the sketch:

---

29 R F. Foster, *Modern Ireland, 1600–1972* (London, 1989), pp. 301–07.
30 The other principal speaker on that occasion was William Saurin, attorney general from 1807 until 1822. Brunswick clubs sprang up in 1828 as a means of mobilizing support for the protestant constitution and to defend it against demands for catholic emancipation. Jacqueline Hill, 'The legal profession and the defence of the *ancien régime* in Ireland, 1790–1840', in Hogan & Osborough (ed.), *Brehons, serjeants and attorneys*, p. 181.

1 Colonel Sir Audley Mervyn (*c.*1603–75)

2 Eaton Stannard (*c.*1685–1757)

3 Anthony Malone (1700–76), as chancellor of the Irish exchequer

4 Rt. hon. John Hely-Hutchinson (1724–94)

5 Walter Hussey Burgh (1742–83)

6 Rt. hon. James Fitzgerald (1742–1835)

7 Rt. hon. James Fitzgerald (1742–1835)

8 John Ball (*c*.1754–1813)

9 Arthur Browne, the last prime serjeant (*c.*1756–1805)

10 Thomas Goold (*c*.1766–1846)

11 Mr Justice Perrin (1782–1864)

12 Thomas Lord O'Hagan (1812–85), Irish lord chancellor

13 Thomas Lord O'Hagan (1812–85), Irish lord chancellor

14 Richard Armstrong (1815–80)

15 Sir Colman O'Loghlen, 2nd baronet (1819–77)

16 Charles Hare Hemphill, 1st Baron Hemphill (1822–1908)

17 Denis Caulfield Heron (1824–81)

18 Hewitt Poole Jellett (1825–1911)

Right Hon Mr Justice Do[

C.n.K.
Feb. 1922

19 Mr Justice Dodd (1844–1930)

20 Johnny Moriarty (1854–1915)

21 Serjeant Hanna KC (1871–1946)

22 Serjeant Sullivan KC (1871–1959)

THE KING'S SERJEANTS:
BONES SULLIVAN.   BELLY McSWINEY.   BRAINS MATHESON.

23 The king's serjeants: Bones Sullivan (1871–1959), Belly McSweeny (1865–1923), Brains Matheson (1851–1921)

The person who has accomplished this exemplary reconciliation between characters so opposite in appearance as a devoted follower of the gospel and a wily disputant at the bar, stands in great prominence in the Four Courts, but is still more noted among 'the saints' in Dublin, and I think may be accounted their leader.[31]

On 4 February 1830, O'Connell finally took his seat as MP for Clare, and within weeks this was to have repercussions for Lefroy. Due to illness, Baron McClelland was unable to go on circuit, and, as the law officers rarely acted as assize judges by this time, the invariable practice was to ask the serjeants in order of seniority to go in place of the unavailable judge or judges. Although Lefroy had acted as an assize judge on several occasions since 1818, the Conservative government decided to depart from the usual practice of appointing the first serjeant in place of McClelland. Given Lefroy's experience as an assize judge, his undeniable status as a leader of the bar and a prominent supporter of the government, this startling departure from the accepted practice was seen as a move to placate O'Connell. An approach was made to Lefroy by the attorney general to persuade him to ask for exemption from circuit duty on the basis of his obligations as counsel in the lord chancellor's court, but he declined. On 28 February, the under secretary wrote to Lefroy:

I have received the Lord Lieutenant's command to acquaint you that he considers your nomination to the provisional exercise of the judicial function as inexpedient in the existing circumstances of this country.

Nowhere in the correspondence was it stated what were the 'existing circumstances of this country', which made it 'inexpedient' for Lefroy to act as an assize judge. For his part, Lefroy took his stand upon the need for those exercising judicial functions to be independent, as well as pointing to the obligation to perform such functions as one of the incidents of the serjeant's office:

I confess it does appear to me to be essential to the due administration of public justice, that the officers of the Crown, so far as respects the discharge of their judicial functions, should have the same independence which the law has secured to the judges, so as to place them in like manner beyond the control of popular clamour or the existing circumstances. I also think on the

31 Richard Lalor Shiel, 'Thomas Lefroy', in *Sketches of the Irish bar*, 2 vols. (New York, 1854), i, 216–31.

part of the profession to which I belong, that I ought not to submit in my person to have the office stripped of one of its most honourable incidents by compromise or acquiescence though inconvenient in its exercise to myself.[32]

Dignified though Lefroy's response to this manoeuvre was, he bitterly resented it as a slur upon his integrity and impartiality, and regarded it as being motivated 'merely with a view to court the favour of Mr O'Con[nell]and his adherents of the opposition'.[33]

The *Freeman's Journal* of 2 March commented: 'This passing over of Serjeant Lefroy by the Government evinces at least a desire to listen to the voice and consult the wishes of the people of this country'. The Conservative *Dublin Evening Mail* came to Lefroy's defence in more robust tones:

A correspondence ensued between Mr Lefroy and the Government, in which an effort was made to induce the learned gentleman to alter his determination, or retract his resignation, but in vain. In the absence of this documentary evidence, it will be sufficient to state that attempts were made to induce Mr Serjeant Lefroy to ask as a favour the exemption from circuit duties, on the plea of professional avocations in chancery, because, as it is triumphantly boasted by the popish press, his politics were at variance with those of Mr O'Connell and the radical newspapers. The politics of a judge, and government interference for such an alleged cause! What a question does such an association involve? What a constructive libel does it contain upon the purity of justice?

The public look with an intensity unprecedented to the production of the correspondence which led to the resignation of Mr Serjeant Lefroy.[34]

It is evident that the *Evening Mail* had been fully briefed about the exchange between Lefroy and the government; and the controversy continued with efforts being made by a number of Dublin Corporation aldermen, sheriffs' peers and councillors to petition the lord mayor to convene a meeting of the corporation to discuss Lefroy's resignation. This attempt failed, much to the satisfaction of the *Freeman's Journal*, which, on 9 March, posed the following question:

32 Thomas Lefroy, *Memoir of Chief Justice Lefroy* (Dublin,1871), pp. 112–13.
33 Undated copy letter to an unidentified peer. MS H/18 in the possession of Jeffry Lefroy esq., of Carrigglas, Co. Longford.
34 Quoted, Lefroy, *Memoir of Chief Justice Lefroy*, p. 118.

And we will begin our solution in an Irish way, by asking 'why or wherefore' should the Lord Mayor of Dublin convene a Post Assembly to address Mr THOMAS LEFROY? What have the Corporation to do with the appointment of judges?

The reply to this rhetorical question displayed a bitter partisanship fully equal to that of the *Evening Mail*:

A piece of effrontery so audacious and unparalleled, we never saw, or even heard of. Who is Mr LEFROY that the Lord Mayor of Dublin should convene a meeting to address him? He is by education, by fortune, and by profession, a gentleman, but in politics he has been, and is still a violent opponent to the rights and liberties of seven-eighths of the inhabitants of this country, and as such justice when administered by him would lose half its effect, because it would lose all its character. We do not mean to say that Mr LEFROY would carry his political and his religious prejudices upon the bench – although by the way, we cannot forget his famous charge in the North; but in order that justice may have way – in order that the laws should produce a salutary effect, it is essentially necessary that the mass of the peasantry should respect their dispensers. We now ask the most ardent admirer of the Ex-Serjeant – we ask the most enthusiastic supporter of the political principles which he advocated with such indiscreet vehemence at the Rotunda, on the 5th November, 1828, when he said *the King ought to be dethroned if he signed the emancipation act* – we ask any man imbued with one particle of common sense, if the lower orders of the people of Ireland would respect the judgement seat on which they saw Mr LEFROY seated? The laws may be obeyed through a dread of the consequences of their infringement, but they will not be respected if the Judge be not 'above suspicion'. The Government are aware of this; they know how mischievous an experiment it would be to send Serjeant Lefroy on circuit, and they very properly dispensed with his services.

Paradoxically, Lefroy's resignation had the effect of considerably enhancing his political standing. The *Freeman's Journal* of 8 March carried a report that efforts were being made to persuade him to stand in a pending by-election for Cork, and, although he did not take that opportunity, Lefroy was elected for Dublin University later that year. He was to be re-elected at each subsequent election until he accepted an appointment as a baron of the exchequer in 1841.

To fill the vacancy created by Lefroy's resignation, Thomas Goold was promoted from second to first serjeant, Francis Blackburne from third to second, with the post of third serjeant filled by Edward Pennefather. Blackburne and Pennefather were both prominent

Conservatives. However, when the next vacancy occurred in the serjeants' ranks in 1831, Earl Grey's reform ministry was in power and a momentous change took place in the law officers' ranks. Blackburne, although a Conservative, became attorney general.[35] Grey's experiment in appointing a political opponent to such an important and sensitive office as that of attorney general was not repeated by any subsequent administration, but of greater significance so far as the serjeants were concerned was the appointment of Michael O'Loghlen as third serjeant.

The first roman catholic to be appointed a serjeant (and later a judge) since the reign of James II, O'Loghlen had one of the largest practices at the Irish bar and in an all too short career as master of the rolls proved himself to be 'a giant in judicial spirit'.[36] O'Loghlen's appointment meant that from then on roman catholics were appointed as law officers and judges. Eminent as he was professionally, O'Loghlen was also a close associate of O'Connell, and in 1832, by then second serjeant, stood unsuccessfully as a Liberal for Dublin. Although Lefroy, Blackburne, Pennefather and O'Loghlen were not members of parliament when appointed serjeants, they were politically prominent and thus typical of the nineteenth and twentieth-century serjeants. It fell to Louis Perrin, who succeeded O'Loghlen as third serjeant in 1832, to achieve election to parliament whilst a serjeant. Although returned for Dublin in the reform interest in 1831, Perrin had been unseated. However, he was elected for Co. Monaghan in 1832. His election restored the eighteenth-century link between the serjeancy and parliament, a link that many, though by no means all, of his successors maintained.

Despite the political prominence of so many serjeants, party links were almost never taken into account when a vacancy occurred within the ranks of the serjeancy itself, and in the nineteenth century it became the practice to promote an existing serjeant to fill a vacancy irrespective of his political affiliation. In January 1831, Grey's Whig government promoted Edward Pennefather from second to first serjeant despite his Conservative links, and in 1835 one of the first acts of Peel's Conservative administration was to advance Perrin from third to first serjeant. However, although administrations always promoted existing serjeants when a vacancy

35 He continued in office under Peel and resigned upon the fall of Peel's ministry in 1835.
36 Ball, *Judges*, ii, 280.

occurred, appointments of new serjeants continued to be on the basis of political affiliation. When Perrin was promoted from third to first serjeant in January 1835, the two vacancies were filled by Conservative supporters, Richard Greene being appointed second and John Devonsher Jackson third. Jackson became MP for Bandon later that year, holding the seat until elected for Dublin University in 1842.

Within days of these appointments, the government was again faced with the necessity of supplementing the assize judges from the ranks of the serjeants, and the spectre of the Lefroy controversy surfaced briefly. The *Belfast Newsletter* of 13 February 1835 carried a report that Greene was to be nominated as a judge on the Munster circuit, although junior to Perrin, because of the latter's politics. Despite the furore that accompanied Lefroy's being passed over some years before, in the event Greene's nomination passed without comment.

The practice of sending the serjeants out on circuit was to continue for another half century, although it did give rise to criticism from time to time. By the 1850s, the advancing years and infirmity of several of the judges meant that they were frequently absent from circuit duty, and this gave rise to adverse public comment. In May 1855, the *Law Times* claimed that of the twelve common law judges, no fewer than five were unable to satisfactorily discharge their duties due to ill-health.[37] Chief Baron Pigot had spent six months in Spain, and Lefroy, the chief justice of the queen's bench, was 83 and unable to sit at nisi prius. Baron Pennefather was 84 and suffering from a total loss of sight, whilst Mr Justice Torrens, older than both Lefroy and Pennefather, had for some years constantly absented himself from going on circuit. Observing that the practice of sending barristers on circuit in place of regular judges had become the invariable rule 'and is regarded as the reverse of satisfactory', the paper went on to point out that one such replacement had resigned as an assize judge whilst on circuit to engage in an election contest, a reference to the events of the previous March when Henry Hughes QC resigned as an assize judge to contest – unsuccessfully – an election in Co. Cavan.[38]

The events surrounding this deplorable episode provide a convenient opportunity to consider in detail the role and standing of the

---

37 *Law Times*, xxv (1855), 9 (26 May 1855).
38 *Law Times*, xxiv (1854–55), 242 (10 Mar. 1855).

serjeants in the middle of the nineteenth century. The *Law Times* of 17 March 1855 drew attention to the fact that at the Leitrim assizes all of the offices – from the judges to the criers – were held by roman catholics for the first time since the Reformation.[39] The *Belfast Newsletter* of 21 March took up this topic under the heading 'Irish Legal Appointments', and displayed a much more jaundiced view of the proportion of roman catholics amongst the seven principal law officers of the crown, namely the lord chancellor, the attorney general, the solicitor general, the law adviser and the three serjeants. In the course of a lengthy analysis of the religious and political affiliations of the various office holders, it described the serjeants as follows:

Serjeant Howley is a Roman Catholic, and a legal pluralist, holding a serjeancy along with the valuable chairmanship of the county of Tipperary, and he is constantly put into the commission as a judge of assize. Mr Serjeant O'Brien, a zealous Roman Catholic, is MP for Limerick, and a leading crown prosecutor on the Munster Circuit. Mr Serjeant Christian is a Protestant and a Whig.

The *Belfast Newsletter's* analysis was accurate in most respects, and the careers of the three serjeants can be regarded as broadly representative of the standing of the serjeants in the last century of the existence of the office. It was fair to describe Howley as a noted pluralist. He remained first serjeant until his death in 1866, by which time he had occupied the part-time post of chairman of the Co. Tipperary quarter sessions for thirty years. As it was not until the County Courts (Ireland) Act of 1877 that a full-time county court judiciary, exercising both civil and criminal jurisdictions, was created in Ireland, the posts of chairmen of quarter sessions were held by members of the bar who were able to combine their judicial functions with practice. Some of these were undoubtedly men of the highest ability, such as Thomas O'Hagan, later Lord O'Hagan; others were less distinguished. Political activity was no more an impediment to exercising these lesser judicial offices than it was to that of assize judge, as may be seen from Sir Colman O'Loghlen continuing as chairman of Co. Mayo although elected MP for Clare in 1863. Howley did receive the highly unusual honour of being knighted in 1865, although, as he was by then well into his seventies, this was presumably by way of a consolation prize for the absence of further advancement.

39 Ibid., 256.

The second and third serjeants referred to by the *Belfast Newsletter* were markedly more distinguished. A gold medallist at Trinity College, Dublin, James O'Brien was Liberal MP for Limerick from 1854 to 1858, when he became a justice of the queen's bench, which office he held until his death twenty four years later. A leading equity practitioner, Jonathan Christian had been appointed third serjeant in 1851 by the Whig government of Lord John Russell, although the *Law Times* had remarked the previous year that 'his political opinions were known only to himself'.[40] Whether or not the *Belfast Newsletter* was correct to describe Christian as a Whig in politics, he proceeded to act in a fashion that suggested he was not in sympathy with Palmerston's government by immediately resigning as third serjeant, something which occasioned little comment in the legal or wider press. In 1850, he had resigned from the influential position of law adviser at Dublin Castle because its duties interfered with his equity practice. In his judicial career he was to demonstrate remarkable public contempt from the bench for many of those with whom he disagreed, comments described by a contemporary writer as being uttered in 'the spirit of personal sarcasm, cold, keen and cynical'.[41] It may well be that his resignation was due to pique at being passed over for further advancement, because by this time, as we shall see, apart from the obligation to sit as an assize judge and the right to crown briefs in prosecutions on his circuit, the duties of the serjeants were minimal. Whatever the reason for Christian's resignation from a leading office for the second time, it did not act as an obstacle to his further advancement, because the Liberal government appointed him solicitor general in 1856 and a justice of the common pleas in 1858.

Christian's resignation provided the government with the opportunity to promote one of those who (together with Christian) had been described by the *Belfast Newsletter* as one of the 'Liberal Protestants' of high professional standing whose professional achievements were being overlooked when Walter Berwick QC was made third serjeant.[42] Not only did Berwick's promotion confound the newspaper's belief that only roman catholics would achieve preferment, but he had recently received an unmistakable mark of

---

40 Daire Hogan, ' "Arrows too sharply pointed": the relations of Lord Justice Christian and Lord O'Hagan, 1868–1874', in McEldowney & O'Higgins (ed.), *The common law tradition: essays in Irish legal history*, p. 63.
41 Quoted, ibid., p. 70.
42 Berwick was a grand-nephew of Henry Grattan, *BNL*, 21 Mar. 1855.

professional recognition when appointed an assize judge to fill the vacancy created by the resignation of Henry Hughes to which we have earlier referred.[43]

The appointments of Hughes and Berwick as assize judges, rather than to call upon the serjeants, was due to a significant change that had taken place in the practice of sending out the law officers and serjeants as assize judges. Whilst it remained common until the mid-1880s for additional assize judges to be appointed from the ranks of the bar, by 1855 it was rare for the law officers to serve in this capacity. One who did was Thomas O'Hagan who served as a judge on the spring assizes of the North West circuit in 1860 whilst solicitor general.[44] This was unusual, the last law officer to sit as a judge on this circuit had been the then solicitor general in 1821. It would seem that the solicitor general was not normally involved in directing criminal prosecutions and therefore was felt to be eligible to sit as an assize judge. That at least was the view of the *Belfast Newsletter*. It stated that the attorney general was never named in the commission of assize because of his position as a public prosecutor, whereas the solicitor general was included unless he was in parliament or had directed prosecutions in the absence of, or in conjunction, with the attorney general.[45] Although the *Belfast Newsletter* did not comment adversely on the practice of a member of the government sitting as a judge in criminal trials in O'Hagan's case, the political activities of Serjeant Armstrong were raised in parliament some years later, and led to a statement being made in the house of commons in 1876.

A queen's counsel since 1854 and first serjeant since 1866, Richard Armstrong was one of the foremost advocates of the time. Liberal MP for Sligo borough between 1865 and 1868, he was subsequently held to have spent £1,480 in bribing of electors at the general election of 1865, 65 of whom were identified by name and who received £1,200 between them. When Armstrong's suitability to act as an assize judge was questioned, the chief secretary, Sir Michael Hicks Beach, made a statement on behalf of the Irish lord chancellor which is of interest, both as a definitive statement as to the method of appointment of additional assize judges, and as an example of the robust character of Irish politics at the time:

43 *Law Times*, xxiv (1854–55), 242.
44 List of judges of assize for that circuit from 1820 to 1925, compiled by Alfred Moore Munn, sometime clerk of the crown and peace for the city and county of Londonderry, in the possession of the author.
45 *BNL*, 5 Mar. 1860.

In Ireland there are three Queen's Serjeants, who are always named in the ordinary commissions of assizes with the judges. The Queen's Counsel are not named in this commission, and if one is sent a Special Commission is opened for the purpose. When a judge does not go the proper person to take his place is a serjeant; if there is no serjeant a Queen's counsel is sent. The first serjeant is Serjeant Armstrong. There are two other serjeants, but they are in Parliament and could not go as judges. The objection was on constitutional grounds, and because the payments received might make them vacate their seats. Serjeant Armstrong was, under a Royal commission issued in June, 1869, to inquire into the existence of corrupt practices in the borough of Sligo, found to have been guilty of corrupt practices at the previous election of 1865, when he was returned to Parliament for the borough of Sligo. The Act under which the Commission was held, 15th and 16th Vic. c.57, provides that any person who, like Serjeant Armstrong, is examined before such a commission, and makes a full disclosure, shall be free from all penal actions, forfeitures, punnishments, disabilities, and incapabilities. Mr Serjeant Armstrong was not disturbed in his office of Serjeant either by the Government of the day or by any succeeding Government. He has been named in every succeeding commission as one of the judges. Nearly eleven years have elapsed since the election at which the corrupt practices occurred, and the Lord Chancellor considers that Mr Serjeant Armstrong, as a gentleman of distinguished eminence in his profession, and who ranks next after the law officers of the Crown, would not be disqualified to discharge the duties of his office, and might, therefore, in fulfilment of one of them preside in the absence of a judge at the assizes.[46]

The controversy did not prevent Armstrong acting as an assize judge on the same circuit the following year, nor did political activity prevent a serjeant sitting as a judge once he had left parliament. In 1883, Serjeant Sherlock, a former Liberal MP, was the last member of the bar to act as an assize judge on the North West circuit. Although the practice of appointing the serjeants or queen's counsel as assize judges fell into abeyance after the mid-1880s, the serjeants' obligation to sit as assize judges, if required, was not forgotten. In 1912, Serjeant Moriarty sat at North Tipperary assizes in place of Mr Justice Gibson who was ill.[47] Later still, Serjeant Matheson twice acted as an assize judge,[48] and Serjeant Sullivan was the last serjeant

46 Quoted, *ILT & SJ*, x (1876), 411–12.
47 *ILT & SJ*, xlvi (1912), 69.
48 Matheson to Bonar Law, 10 June 1918 (House of Lords Record Office, Bonar Law papers, folder 83/4/14).

to perform judicial functions, narrowly escaping assassination during Tralee assizes in 1921.[49]

At the time of the statement by Sir Michael Hicks Beach in 1876, a Conservative government was in power, yet all three serjeants were Liberals, and the second and third serjeants were both in parliament: Sir Colman O'Loghlen as MP for Clare and David Sherlock as MP for King's County. Although, as we have seen, unlike the attorney general and solicitor general, the serjeants were not regarded as part of the administration of the day in that they were not expected to resign on a change of government, political considerations continued to be involved in almost every case when the time came to appoint a new serjeant. As before, however, an existing serjeant would almost invariably be promoted within the serjeant's ranks, irrespective of his political affiliation. Thus, within weeks of Lord Salisbury's caretaker government being formed on 23 June 1885, the death of the first serjeant, James Robinson, led to the promotion of the leading Liberal politician Charles Hemphill from second to first serjeant; the Conservative Peter O'Brien was promoted from third to second; and John Gibson, another Conservative, was appointed third serjeant. All three were politically and professionally prominent, and as representative of the political and public standing of the serjeants towards the latter part of the nineteenth century as Lefroy, Blackburne, Perrin and O'Loghlen had been earlier. Hemphill, who had been a Liberal candidate in Cashel in 1857, remained a serjeant until he became solicitor general in 1895. Liberal MP for North Tyrone from 1895 to 1906, he was created Baron Hemphill upon his retirement from active politics in 1906. Peter O'Brien, a redoubtable and courageous crown prosecutor, stood unsuccessfully as a Liberal in Clare in 1879, but later changed allegiance and was made solicitor general, attorney general and finally lord chief justice by the Conservatives. John Gibson, younger brother of Edward Gibson, Lord Ashbourne, the Conservative Irish lord chancellor, was Conservative MP for the Walton division of Liverpool 1885–1888, and was to serve twice as solicitor general and once as attorney general before he was appointed a judge of the queen's bench division.

The only exceptions to these conventions were the promotions of Charles O'Connor and John Moriarty from third to first serjeant in 1907 and 1910 respectively, and the appointment of Charles

---

49 An episode described by him in his autobiographical *The last serjeant* (London, 1952), p. 41.

Matheson as third serjeant in 1911. O'Connor and Moriarty were both promoted over the head of Hewitt Poole Jellett, who had been second serjeant since 1892. However, Jellett was eighty-two when O'Connor was promoted, and, as he had retired from active practice several years before,[50] the government no doubt felt that Jellett's continued possession of the office of serjeant was purely honorific, which justified his being passed over on these occasions. In 1911, the Liberal government again broke with convention in a much more significant way when it came to fill the office of third serjeant. Rather than appointing a Liberal or Nationalist, Augustine Birrell, the chief secretary, made a conciliatory gesture to the Unionist minority by appointing Charles Matheson to the vacant office. For many years chairman of the City of Dublin Unionist Association, Matheson had been MP for Dublin St Stephen's Green between 1904 and 1906.[51] Although subsequently promoted second, and then first, serjeant by the Liberal government, Matheson's appointment was an isolated departure from the practice of filling vacancies with supporters of the government. The last two serjeants to be appointed by the Liberal government were clearly designed to conciliate the Irish Parliamentary Party. A.M. Sullivan was a scion of a distinguished Nationalist family and George McSweeny a former official of that party.[52] Similarly, when the Conservative-dominated government made what proved to be the last appointment of a serjeant in October 1919, its choice fell upon Henry Hanna who stood as a Unionist for the St Stephen's Green seat the year before.

At this stage it is appropriate to consider what duties, apart from the obligation to serve as assize judges, were attached to the office of serjeant, and whether there were any accompanying financial benefits. In later years, the serjeants were rarely, if ever, called upon to advise the government, yet in the immediate aftermath of the Union the emoluments of the offices of prime and second serjeants were considerable. We have already seen how Lord Chancellor Redesdale proposed in 1805 that the first, second and third serjeants should receive annual salaries of £150, £100 and £50 respectively. It is not clear whether these salaries were to be in substitution for, or in

50 On Jellett's retirement from active practice in 1899, the bar presented his portrait to King's Inns. *ILT & SJ*, xxxiii (1899), 458.
51 Lawrence McBride, *The greening of Dublin Castle: the transformation of bureaucratic and judicial personnel in Ireland 1892–1922* (Washington DC, 1991), p. 161; House of Lords Record Office, Bonar Law papers, folder 83/5/4.
52 McBride, *The greening of Dublin Castle*, p. 161.

addition to, the previous emoluments, although it would seem somewhat more likely that the proposed salaries were intended to replace fees previously paid. If that was the position, then not only did the new office of first serjeant lose the considerable income as well as the precedence which the prime serjeant had previously enjoyed, but the second serjeant suffered a corresponding loss of income.

When Stanley was dismissed as prime serjeant in 1801, we have already seen how the earl of Hardwicke softened the blow by giving Stanley Arthur Browne's post on the board of accounts, commenting that the emoluments were 'equal to those of the office of Prime Serjeant, independently of [the chance of] circuit.'[53] As the annual salary attached to a seat on the board of accounts was £800, this meant that, apart from the allowance paid to a judge who went on circuit, the prime serjeant could expect to receive this amount, presumably in fees for crown work of various kinds. Whilst the second serjeant also had the chance of the circuit allowance, it would seem that the income from that office was, as one would expect, somewhat smaller and in the region of £500 a year. That was the figure which Sir James Chatterton, then second serjeant, put upon his office in 1804 when he tried to secure further advancement by holding out to the lord lieutenant the prospect of gaining the disposition of the two offices Chatterton presently held:

Your Excellency will have the disposal of the two places which he has the honour of holding under Government, the Paper Office an honourable sinecure of £500 p.a. on the Establishment, and the place of the King's Second Serjeant at Law, the fourth in rank at the Irish bar, attended with many advantages to a professional man and from the opportunities of going the circuits, reasonably estimated at £500 a year more.[54]

Whether or not the salaries proposed by Redesdale in 1805 were implemented, for many years afterwards the office of serjeant continued to be of value to the holder, though less valuable than in the eighteenth century. Almost certainly the most valuable attribute of the office was that a serjeant was entitled to a brief on behalf of the crown in every criminal prosecution on his circuit. This must have been a very lucrative perquisite indeed, and although some whose practice lay outside the criminal law might not have availed of

53 Hardwicke to Lord Pelham, secretary of state for the home department, 26 Dec. 1801 (BL, Hardwicke papers, Add. MS 35, 732, f. 12).
54 3 July 1804 (BL, Hardwicke papers, Add. MS 35, 750, f. 288).

it, as the Irish bar was predominantly non-specialist, it is probable that many serjeants did. It is recorded that Serjeant Goold regularly prosecuted upon the Munster circuit after becoming third serjeant in 1823,[55] and in its analysis of the law officers of March 1855 which has already been referred to, the *Belfast Newsletter* described Serjeant O'Brien 'as a leading Crown prosecutor on the Munster circuit'. This practice was confirmed as late as 1865, when the crown and treasury solicitor sent a circular to the crown solicitors giving directions as to the number of counsel to be briefed at the assizes, which included the following instruction:

When one of the Serjeants goes the Circuit, it is established that he is entitled to a brief in all the Crown cases, on the ground that his office precludes him from acting in any case against the Crown. In that case the Serjeant will, as he has always done, give his aid in the conduct of the prosecutions, and the necessity of employing Special or Supernumerary Counsel will not then arise.[56]

Although this practice appears to have been discontinued during the 1880s,[57] it was certainly still in operation in 1876 when Serjeant Sir Colman O'Loghlen prosecuted at the Cork summer assizes of that year.[58]

Another source of income for the serjeants occurred when the government required the services of one of its law officers to investigate particular crimes or prosecute cases outside the normal assize sittings. In April 1822, Serjeant Torrens was paid ten guineas a day for prosecuting for fifty-three days at Limerick under the Insurrection Act, a total of £602 17s. 6d.[59] Such occasional duties were not confined to prosecuting, nor indeed to the ranks of the serjeants. Under the Insurrection Act, a serjeant or king's counsel had to preside at quarter sessions and, whilst Serjeants Torrens and Lloyd were initially entrusted with the duty of presiding in certain areas in 1822, the former was recalled from Cork and replaced by Francis Blackburne KC.[60]

55 J.R. O'Flanagan, *The Munster circuit, tales, trials and traditions* (London, 1880), p. 312.
56 21 Feb. 1865 (NAI, CCS 1865/).
57 *ILT & SJ*, xxviii (1894), 123.
58 O'Flanagan, *The Munster circuit*, p. 394.
59 3 Geo. IV, c.1, s.5. NAI, OP/527/16.
60 Edward Blackburne, *Life of the rt. hon. Francis Blackburne* (London, 1874), pp. 36–37.

However, by their very nature, such calls upon the serjeants were infrequent, and whilst the fragmentary nature of the surviving evidence makes it impossible to draw definite conclusions, documents which have survived for the years 1826 to 1831 and for 1865 suggest that governments almost never turned to the serjeants for advice, relying upon the services of the attorney general and solicitor general, and later also upon the new post of law adviser. Of seven cases to advise which have survived for the years 1825–31, in only one did a serjeant (Blackburne) give an opinion jointly with the attorney general.[61] In one of the seven cases the opinion was given jointly by Richard Greene, who was the first to be appointed law adviser,[62] and the attorney general. An analysis of a much larger number of crown briefs in civil matters which have survived for 1865 confirms the lack of use made of the serjeants in an advisory role by the government. Of 29 briefs, 23 were to the attorney general and solicitor general jointly, 3 to the attorney general alone and 1 to the solicitor general alone. One brief was to the law adviser (Barry) and I was to Serjeant Sullivan, second serjeant since 1861. However, as Sullivan combined the post of law adviser (later held by Barry) with that of second serjeant at the time, there can be little doubt that he was briefed in his capacity as law adviser but addressed by the title of serjeant.[63]

Professor Casey agrees with the explanation advanced by Professor McDowell,[64] namely, that the post of law adviser came into being because of the number of legal problems faced by the Irish government, and the fact that either or both law officers were frequently out of the country; but why was it considered necessary to create a new post when the crown had the services of the three serjeants to call upon?

When the post of law adviser was created, the first holder was an opponent of the government. Although a Conservative, Richard Greene KC was appointed by Earl Grey's Whig administration and, as we have seen, Grey also appointed the Conservative Edward Blackburne to be attorney general. That the serjeants were often parliamentary opponents appointed by previous governments no

61 NAI, OP/773.
62 For a description of the origin and role of the law adviser, see J.P. Casey, *The office of the attorney general in Ireland* (Dublin, 1980), pp. 36–37.
63 NAI, CCS/1865. Edward Sullivan was later lord chancellor.
64 R.B. McDowell, *The Irish administration 1800–1914* (London, 1964), pp. 120–21.

doubt influenced successive governments when they sought legal advice. The institution and conduct of prosecutions was a matter which often gave rise to intense controversy, as in 1834 when Serjeant Perrin accused Blackburne in the house of commons of unfairness in the conduct of prosecutions, even though Perrin himself was conducting prosecutions on the North East circuit at the time.[65] The sensitivity of such matters meant that governments naturally wished to take advice from those who were politically sympathetic as well as to reward their supporters, and so, almost invariably, the law adviser came to be a political supporter of the government of the day, certainly if the pattern of appointments in the 1850s and 1860s is representative of the law advisers as a group.

James Lawson QC, Liberal MP for Portarlington 1865–68, became law adviser in 1858, but was replaced by James Robinson QC when Lord Derby's Conservative government took up office. When Lord Palmerston became prime minister again in June 1859, Lawson became law adviser for the second time. He remained in that post until he became solicitor general in 1861, even though he was made second serjeant in 1860. His successor as both law adviser and second serjeant was Edward Sullivan. Liberal MP for Mallow 1865–70 , Sullivan held office as solicitor general, attorney general and lord chancellor in various Liberal governments. Sullivan was both law adviser and second serjeant until he became solicitor general in 1865. However, when Sullivan became solicitor general, the link between the serjeants and the law adviser was broken. His successor as law adviser was another Liberal, Robert Barry. MP for Dungarvan 1865–68, Barry was later solicitor general and attorney general. Sullivan's successor as second serjeant was also a Liberal, Richard Armstrong QC, third serjeant since 1861 and MP for Sligo 1865–68.

Another factor which may have played a part in the decision to create this new post may have been that the nature of the work was not considered appropriate for individuals of the professional eminence of the serjeants, who generally obtained that office when they had been king's or queen's counsel for a considerable number of years, whereas Greene only became a king's counsel the year before his appointment as law adviser. In later years, although the law adviser was often a king's or queen's counsel, this was not always

---

65 Blackburne, *Life of Francis Blackburne*, pp. 161–84, where this is discussed in detail.

the case.[66] If the fees initially paid to Greene in 1831 are a reliable indicator of the income which a law adviser could hope to achieve, the post might not have been attractive to a more established practitioner. For the first six months of 1831 he received £230 15s. 6d., compared with what were described as the 'salaries' of £461 10s. 9d. and £369 4s. 7d. paid to the attorney general and solicitor general respectively, for the same period. However, these figures probably represent only part of the income expected from each of these offices. The attorney general and solicitor general presumably received additional fees for each case in which they were briefed, and all three seem to have been paid fees for other types of legal work. In 1827, the solicitor general was paid a total of £630, £315 for attending Clonmel assizes and £315 for going to Tipperary to investigate a murder, and in September 1831 Greene was paid a further sum of £100 for going to Newtownbarry, Co. Wexford to investigate what was described as 'the conflict between the Yeomanry and the County People'.[67]

Whilst Sir James Chatterton referred in 1804 to 'the many advantages to a professional man' which accompanied the office of second serjeant, it would seem that by the 1830s the only direct advantage in financial terms which a serjeant might enjoy by virtue of his office was the right, which we have already considered, to be briefed as a crown prosecutor on his circuit. It may not be entirely coincidental that in the middle of the century there occurred a modest, though unmistakable, reduction in the professional status of the serjeants.

When a serjeant was appointed in the eighteenth century, he was immediately elected a bencher of King's Inns (if not already one) and took precedence over existing benchers (other than judges) in accordance with precedence at the bar, so that the prime serjeant took precedence over the attorney general, and so on. As late as 1836, although the number of benchers was now fixed and a newly-appointed serjeant had to wait for a vacancy to arise, once elected a bencher, he still took the precedence due to him as a serjeant ahead of more senior barrister benchers. Thus, in Hilary term of 1836, the newly elected Serjeant Woulfe took precedence over Lefroy, who had, it seems, forfeited his precedence as a bencher over the serjeants upon his resignation as first serjeant in 1830. By 1861, although

66 *ILT & SJ*, iii (1869), 114.
67 NAI, OP/972, and Blackburne, *Life of Francis Blackburne*, pp. 109–11.

newly appointed serjeants were elected benchers when the next vacancy arose, thereafter seniority as benchers was solely in accordance with the date of their election.[68]

Whilst we have seen how the serjeants retained their right to prosecution briefs into the 1870s and frequently sat as assize judges into the 1880s, despite the professional eminence of many of the serjeants, there can be no doubt that the office was regarded as one which conferred professional prestige, rather than one which imposed significant duties on the part of, or conferred benefits upon, the holder. Although many serjeants sat in parliament and were promoted to be solicitor or attorney general, only Sir Colman O'Loghlen achieved ministerial office other than as a law officer. He served as judge advocate general (then a political post) between 1868 and 1870 in Gladstone's first administration whilst he was second serjeant. O'Loghlen seems to have had as much difficulty with his finances as Stanley had over sixty years before, as he was pursued by a Dublin moneylender through the English courts for £108 13s. 1d. In a decision that established an important principle of bankruptcy law, the court of appeal in chancery held that O'Loghlen was not resident at his official office in London and the English courts had no jurisdiction over a debtor bona fide resident in Ireland.[69]

By the end of the nineteenth century, the serjeants had been effectively shorn of almost all the incidents of their ancient office. The obligation upon a serjeant not to appear against the crown apparently remained, despite there being a certain amount of doubt about this,[70] probably because the cessation of the privilege of claiming crown briefs, to which reference has been made, removed the quid pro quo for this obligation.

By the twentieth century, it was common for a serjeant to be referred to, not just by the prefix Serjeant, but to have KC added after his name. The addition of what was, in theory, an inferior rank was a sure sign that the ancient title of serjeant alone was felt to confer insufficient prestige upon the holder, although the standing of the serjeants may also have suffered to some extent by association

68 'The Green Book: admission of benchers, 1712–42', 'Admission of benchers, 1741–92', and 'Entries of benchers, 1794–1864', King's Inns MSS.
69 *Ex p. O'Loghlen, In re O'Loghlen* (1870–71) LR 6 Ch App 406.
70 That is said to have been the belief of Serjeant Campion, who died in 1907, and whose anonymous biographer described this as an 'assumption'. *Memoir of William Bennet Campion, serjeant at law* (Dublin, 1911), p. 75.

with the decline in prestige, and eventual extinction, of the English serjeants at law during the nineteenth century. By the twentieth century, the office of serjeant at law in Ireland had become, to all intents and purposes, a mere title.[71] Nevertheless, the title was one which still carried considerable professional and public prestige. Writing many years later of his appointment in 1910, Ignatius O'Brien's assessment of the significance of this milestone in his career was, in his case at least, a fair one, and probably also represented the view of his contemporaries who held this ancient office:

I had been made third serjeant at law prior to the General Election; though it had long ceased to be an office of profit, it was useful in giving one standing at the bar, and no doubt it helped in showing at any rate that my position was more or less prominent.[72]

Despite the many distinguished offices he held, O'Brien was 'a person of no significance either as a lawyer or a politician',[73] and, like a not insignificant number of other serjeants, his professional advancement was due to political considerations. Others who might be regarded as not being at the front rank of the bar are Chatterton, Sir Colman O'Loghlen and Howley. Nevertheless, that the majority of post-Union serjeants were men of considerable intellectual and professional distinction can be illustrated by the career of Denis Caulfield Heron, who was born in 1824 and became third serjeant in 1880.

A roman catholic, Heron first came to public notice in 1843 when he was refused a Trinity foundation scholarship. This occurred because he was not a member of the established church, although otherwise qualified for one of the sixteen scholarships since he was ranked fifth in order of merit. Heron sought to appeal the refusal of the provost and senior fellows to the visitors, who declined to entertain his appeal. Heron applied to the queen's bench, which granted an order of mandamus directing the visitors to hear the appeal.[74] This proved a

---

71 An indication of this decline is that by 1894 Serjeant Dodd was only the junior crown prosecutor at the Dublin commission, the assize court for Dublin. *ILT & SJ*, xxviii (1894), 123.

72 Later lord chancellor and eventually Baron Shandon. 'The reminiscences of Lord Shandon, lord chancellor of Ireland', p. 349. King's Inns MS.

73 R.F.V. Heuston, 'Legal history and the author: some practical problems of authorship', in W.N. Osborough (ed.), *The Irish Legal History Society: inaugural addresses* (Dublin, 1989), p. 28.

74 *R. (Heron) v. Visitors of Trinity College* (1845–46) 9 Ir LR 41.

pyrrhic victory as the visitors (the Church of Ireland archbishops of Armagh and Dublin) rejected his appeal, having been advised by their assessor that whilst the college statutes gave roman catholics the right to obtain degrees, they did not become members of the corporation of the college, the protestant character of which had remained unaltered. These proceedings attracted considerable attention, and were instrumental in leading Trinity to reform its statutes and to provide non-foundation scholarships for those who could not subscribe to the religious tests.[75]

Of the four queen's bench judges at that time, three had been serjeants, as had Keatinge, the judge of the prerogative court who acted as assessor to the visitors. Chief Justice Pennefather had been, in turn, third, second and first serjeant, then solicitor general. Burton J became a judge of the king's bench in 1820, having been third and second serjeant. Perrin J was successively third and first serjeant, then attorney general. Keatinge had been appointed to the prerogative court in 1843 when third serjeant.

Of those who were counsel in the case, leading counsel for Trinity was Richard Moore, who had been briefly third serjeant and then solicitor general, and was to be appointed attorney general in 1847. Amongst Heron's counsel was Thomas O'Hagan, a fellow Ulsterman whose official career really started when he was made second serjeant in 1859. O'Hagan was later solicitor general, attorney general, a judge of the common pleas and lord chancellor of Ireland in Gladstone's first and second administrations.

Heron was to become a QC in 1860, a bencher of King's Inns in 1872, Liberal MP for Tipperary 1870–74, before he became third serjeant in 1880. Tragically, his career was cut short the following year when he died, aged 56, whilst fishing in April 1881. He also served as law adviser, and early in his career was professor of jurisprudence and political economy at the Queen's College, Galway from 1849 to 1859. Heron was also the author of two works on jurisprudence. *An introduction to the history of jurisprudence* was published in 1860, and *The principles of jurisprudence* in 1873. The former was sufficiently well thought-of to remain required reading at Trinity College, Dublin for many years.[76] Like several other leading

75 V.T.H. Delany, *Christopher Palles, lord chief baron of … the exchequer in Ireland 1874–1916* (Dublin, 1960), pp. 21–23.
76 I owe the information about Heron's academic career and writings to Professor Osborough.

lawyers of the time, Heron's intellectual interests were not confined to the law. He was a member of the Statistical and Social Inquiry Society of Ireland, and served as vice-president of the society 1871–81.

Other prominent members of the society who served as serjeants were Thomas O'Hagan and James Lawson. Lawson was Whateley professor of political economy in Trinity College, Dublin from 1841 to 1846 and acted as secretary of the society.[77] Other serjeants who distinguished themselves academically at Trinity included James O'Brien and Dodgson Hamilton Madden, both gold medallists, and John Gibson, double gold medallist and vice-chancellor's prizeman. In later life, Madden was the author of a number of professional books, as well as several works on Shakespearean subjects, notably *The diary of Master William Silence*. Although now largely forgotten, this was widely regarded as a masterpiece of Shakespearean learning.

With the turmoil in Ireland in the aftermath of the First World War, the serjeants were destined to fade from the Irish scene, in which they had long been an historic and attractive anomaly. Of the last three serjeants, Serjeant McSweeny KC left little impression. Serjeant Sullivan KC and Serjeant Hanna KC, however, were both leading members of the Irish bar. Hanna was a representative of that tradition of political activity which, as we have seen, was so strongly associated with the serjeants throughout the later part of their history in particular. Sullivan was a notable public figure, and both were worthy holders of this ancient office. There is considerable irony in the contrast between their subsequent careers.

Destined to be the last person appointed a serjeant at law when made third serjeant by the Conservative-dominated government in October 1919, Hanna was a Belfast presbyterian who contested St Stephen's Green as a Unionist in the general election of 1918. As the tide of political and sectarian violence engulfed the whole of Ireland in the summer of 1922, he was a spokesman on behalf of the beleaguered protestant community in Southern Ireland, and played a prominent role in a convention of protestants held in the Mansion House in May of that year. In the course of the convention he said:

77 J.F. McEldowney and Paul O'Higgins, 'Irish legal history and the nineteenth century', in McEldowney and O'Higgins (ed.), *The common law tradition*, p. 206.

We are a defenceless minority in Southern Ireland, and all we ask, or have ever asked, is for liberty to live our harmless lives in whatever occupation we follow in the paths of peace. We could be easily driven out of Ireland but we claim it as our country as well as other peoples.[78]

As Ireland, North and South, slowly subsided into an uneasy and bitter state of exhaustion that only partially resembled peace, Hanna, like many others, practised before the courts of both Northern and Southern Ireland. Indeed, such were his abilities that he was one of the counsel for the government of the Irish Free State before the Irish Boundary Commission in 1924. He was appointed a judge of the high court of the Irish Free State in 1925.

Although Hanna came to terms with the new régime in Ireland, Sullivan did not. Despite his Nationalist background and his defence of Casement, justly described as 'unquestionably his greatest legal battle, which he fought with very great courage and tenacity, evoking warm attributes from the Bench',[79] Sullivan's forcibly expressed detestation of violence and illegality meant that he had little sympathy for the new order and, mindful no doubt of his narrow escape from death at the Tralee assizes, he went to England and practised there with distinction until he retired in 1948. With his death on 9 January 1959, the ancient office of king's serjeant at law in Ireland was finally extinguished, having existed for almost seven centuries.

78 *Irish Times*, 12 May 1922.
79 George W. Keeton, *Trial for treason* (London, 1959), p. 211.

Epilogue

FOR ALMOST SEVEN hundred years the king's serjeants at law in Ireland occupied a central position in the Irish legal system. Initially the sovereign's retained pleader in the courts, he soon evolved into the senior law officer of the crown, a position which remained essentially unchallenged until the middle of the Elizabethan period. Thereafter, its position, whilst nominally superior in rank to that of the attorney general, in fact became less important than the latter office. Nevertheless, the serjeants at law achieved a new lease of life due to their status in parliamentary affairs in the century or so before the Act of Union. With the abolition of the Irish parliament, the office slowly declined in importance as its remaining functions were progressively removed, so that, in the last four decades of its existence, the office was reduced to little more than a title, albeit a badge of professional distinction, borne by many of the ablest members of the Irish bar.

We have seen how, in the early days of the 'first adventure of the common law',[1] the king's serjeants emerged from the ranks of the embryonic legal profession when they were selected by the king's representative to act on his behalf, closely following comparable developments in England. However, the parallels with the serjeants in England were soon to diverge with the contraction of effective control of the English government during the fourteenth century.

It is tempting to speculate that had the English government at this early stage established control over the entire island, a separate order of serjeants at law might have evolved in Ireland as it did in England, with an exclusive right of audience in the common pleas and the panoply of creation ceremonies, giving of rings and distinctive robes. There is no evidence of the development of an order of serjeants at law in Ireland, and a prerequisite of such a development would surely have been a much larger and more prosperous community

---

1   W.J. Johnston, 'The first adventure of the common law', *LQR*, xxxvi (1920), 9–30.

than was served by the courts of the Pale, even though its legal system replicated that of England, with courts of chancery, king's bench, common pleas and exchequer.

The king's serjeant at law in Ireland evolved into a distinct office with the features of the law officer which we see in both England and Ireland in later periods. He represented the sovereign in the courts, although he continued to represent private clients. A significant aspect of his duties was to perform judicial and quasi-judicial functions when required. The scarcity of contemporary records makes it impossible to evaluate the intellectual abilities and professional skill of the early Irish serjeants in a meaningful way. As it soon became common for them to be appointed as judges, we may assume that they were generally amongst the ablest practitioners before the Irish courts at the time, although the frequency with which the same names appear as serjeants strongly suggests that family ties often counted for as much as, if not more than, professional ability. During the first three centuries of the history of the king's serjeant he was an integral, and important, part of the administrative and legal system of the Irish lordship. It is in the interstices of government as much as, if not more than, in the law courts that we see him discharging the many and varied functions which he was called upon to perform.

With the attorney general gradually supplanting the king's serjeant in importance as the chief law officer of the crown by the reign of Charles I, one might have expected the office of king's serjeant in Ireland to atrophy, if not wither away. That did not prove to be the case. It is debatable whether there was a need for a second serjeant in 1627, and it is significant that the government managed to dispense with the services of both serjeants during the Cromwellian era. Despite this, a third serjeant was appointed in 1682 as a means of pacifying a disappointed aspirant to judicial office. Despite the office of third serjeant remaining vacant between 1692 and 1711, and again from 1716 to 1726, it was revived and survived for almost two hundred years.

The survival, and continued importance, of the king's serjeants in Ireland was, no doubt, due in part to the force of tradition, but it was also because they were generally, though by no means invariably, drawn from the leading members of the Irish bar. As we have seen, all but two of the eighteenth-century serjeants were MPs when they were appointed, and the prestige of the bar in Ireland in the eighteenth and nineteenth centuries meant that the administration was always alert to the need to conciliate the bar. In 1695, Lord

Capel complained that 'The influence and power of the lawyers in this kingdom is indeed very great, especially in parliament'.[2] This belief was echoed by Lord Chancellor Redesdale in 1805, when he wrote to the earl of Hardwicke:

I have before suggested to Your Excellency how much I consider the good opinion of the bar here as valuable to Government. The strength of Government rests [wholly] in public opinion. There is no body *now* in Ireland which has so much influence as the bar.[3]

The three serjeants provided a means whereby the administration could secure the parliamentary support of members of the bar by appointing them to offices of prestige. In the cases of the prime serjeant and second serjeant, these were also offices which were lucrative, and, for all three serjeants, were usually stepping-stones to further advancement. An important element in the standing of the serjeants was the precedence which they had at the bar. Another was that the ranks of the assize judges were usually supplemented from their ranks. These factors combined to ensure that the serjeants were amongst the leaders of the bar and politically active in the Irish parliament, with the office of prime serjeant probably reaching the height of its prestige in the 1740s to the 1780s.

During the first half of the nineteenth century, the English serjeants at law waged a long, and ultimately forlorn, campaign to maintain their status and privileges in the common pleas. Although they succeeded in obtaining a judgment confirming their exclusive right of audience in that court from the common pleas in 1840, this proved a short-lived victory and was effectively reversed by act of parliament in 1846.[4] Such was the decline in their status by the 1860s that Professor Baker concludes that the majority of English serjeants were 'never eminent', and 'the coif was now recognised as a consolation prize for the less successful'.[5]

Although the position of the Irish serjeants declined after the Union, at this time they occupied a much greater degree of professional eminence than their English namesakes. If they wished, they were still briefed in every crown prosecution on their circuit,

2   17 Dec. 1695, *Cal. S.P. dom., 1695*, p. 129.
3   26 June 1805 (BL, Hardwicke papers, Add. MS 35,717, f. 107).
4   9 & 10 Vict., *c*.54; Baker, *Serjeants at law*, p. 122.
5   Baker, *Serjeants at law*, p. 123.

were elected benchers of King's Inns, and, from time to time, acted as assize judges. Although the lucrative privilege of receiving crown briefs was abolished by the mid–1880s, the office still enjoyed considerable prestige to the end. This was largely on sentimental grounds, providing as it did a line of succession back to the earliest days of the common law in Ireland. However, sentiment would probably not have ensured the survival of the serjeants into the twentieth century, by which time their English counterparts had become extinct, had this ancient office not provided the government with a useful and inexpensive means of conferring professional status on those whom it wished to reward or conciliate for political reasons. Nevertheless, the majority of those appointed in the 119 years after the Union were in the front rank of the Irish bar.

Partition and the division of Ireland into two political and legal entities meant that no further serjeants were appointed, although the existing serjeants continued to be referred to by this title.[6]

The words of Bartholemew Duhigg about a number of eighteenth-century prime serjeants may be thought to provide a fitting epitaph for all those who held the office of king's serjeant at law in Ireland:

If a few weak or worthless men have been Prime Serjeants, be it remembered that the legal talents of a Bernard, and Singleton, the eloquent powers of a Hutchinson, and a Burgh, were displayed in that official situation.[7]

6   See the report of the proceedings in 1923 in the High Court and the Court of Appeal in Northern Ireland in *Macura* v. *The Northern Assurance Co. Ltd.* [1925] NI 141. Serjeant Sullivan and Serjeant Hanna were leading counsel for the plaintiff and defendant respectively, and were referred to by the judges as serjeants, although the law reporters described them as Serjeant Sullivan KC and Serjeant Hanna KC.
7   B.T. Duhigg, *History of the King's Inns* (Dublin, 1806), pp. 210–11.

PART TWO

Succession list of the king's serjeants at law in Ireland

NO COMPLETE LIST of the king's serjeants at law in Ireland has been compiled before, although a list of those known to have been appointed prior to 1627, and thereafter as prime (and later as first) serjeants is to be found in volume IX of *A new history of Ireland*.[1] Further research has enabled a number of additions and corrections to be made to that list. Details of second and third serjeants were included in Smyth's *Chronicle of the law officers of Ireland*, published in 1839, and in Hayden's *Book of dignities*, the third edition of which was published in 1894. A list of those appointed between 1861 and 1919 is also to be found in V.T.H. Delany's *Christopher Palles*.[2] Although Delany gave the year of their appointments, he did not differentiate between first, second and third serjeants.

The list which follows is therefore the first complete list of all of those known to have been appointed king's or queen's serjeants at law in Ireland, with details of their tenure of office. The details for the period *c*.1261–1377 are based upon those given in the list in *A new history of Ireland* prepared by Dr Paul Brand, who revised the details contained in Richardson & Sayles's *The administration of Ireland, 1172–1377*. Smyth's *Chronicle of the law officers of Ireland* has provided most of the details given for the period 1377–1836, although some additional names are to be found in Ellis, 'The administration of the lordship of Ireland under the early Tudors'.[3] For the period 1836–1922, a number of sources have been used, principally the *Dublin Gazette*, the *Book of dignities* and the *Irish Law Times and Solicitors' Journal*.

The destruction of original records over the centuries has meant that, save in a few modern instances, all details have been drawn from secondary sources. Richardson & Sayles identified the serjeants appointed between 1261 and 1377 by a detailed study of the surviving

1   *A new history of Ireland: vol. ix* (Oxford, 1984), pp. 521–25.
2   V.T.H. Delany, *Christopher Palles, lord chief baron of her majesty's court of exchequer in Ireland 1874–1914, his life and times* (Dublin, 1960).
3   Ph.D. thesis, Queen's University, Belfast, 1979.

financial records of the period. Smyth appears to have drawn upon
Lascelles's *Liber munerum publicorum Hiberniae*[4] for his lists, and where
Smyth's lists can be checked against other primary or secondary
sources, they have generally been found to be reliable. Wherever
possible, the dates given have been checked against all the surviving
sources. Considerations of space make it impossible to list all the
sources referred to against each entry, but where all the sources agree,
the dates are given without sources being cited. Where the principal
sources listed above do not agree, or there is uncertainty about dates,
the footnotes refer to the relevant material relied upon.

It may be helpful at this point to describe the procedure by which
a serjeant at law was appointed, at least from the late eighteenth
century onwards. As he held office by letters patent, several steps
had to be gone through before the patent was sealed and he thereby
formally assumed office.[5] If the appointment was initiated or
approved in England, a king's letter was despatched to Dublin.
Before the age of steam this might take some time, and in one or two
instances where a considerable gap elapsed between the issue of the
king's letter and the eventual sealing of the patent, the earlier date
has been given. In the great majority of cases, either a more informal
message was sent to Dublin or the decision was made by the chief
governor there. The chief governor would then sign a warrant
directed to one of the law officers (or in his absence to one of the
king's counsel) directing him to prepare a fiant for letters patent. The
fiant was then drawn up in the exact form of words to be used in the
letters patent themselves. The fiant was then signed by the chief
governor and by the lord chancellor. The clerk of the crown then
engrossed the patent, presented it to the lord chancellor and the
patent was sealed. Although the patent had to be enrolled in the rolls
office within six months, the sealing of the patent was effectively the
final stage of the process. From the early years of the nineteenth
century, it became the custom for a formal announcement to be
made in the *Dublin Gazette* to the effect that the letters patent had
'passed the great seal' on the date upon which the seal was affixed.
However, this was not invariably the case, and even when such an
announcement was made, it did not always give the date on which

4   Rowley Lascelles, *Liber munerum publicorum Hiberniae*, 2 vols. (London, 1824–30).
5   Paper received in Mar. 1794 by Sylvester Douglas, chief secretary for Ireland, 1793–94, later 1st Lord Glenbervie. PRONI T. 3294, ii, pp. 12–14.

the patent passed the great seal. It is sometimes the case, therefore, that even in the nineteenth century an appointment may have become generally known for some time before an official, or any, announcement was made. In the absence of an announcement, the date of the appointment can only be approximately established. By the early years of the nineteenth century, it was the custom that each new law officer, including the serjeants, was formally called within the bar by the lord chancellor upon assuming their new office. This occurred even where a serjeant was being promoted second or first serjeant. Such ceremonies were often reported in the press or law reports, and in several instances such reports provide the only method of establishing the date of an appointment with some precision.[6] Save where otherwise stated, the date given is the date of the letters patent. All dates have been converted to New Style.

(I) KING'S SERJEANTS, 1261–1627

a) 1261–1393/1400

1261–70	Roger Owen *c.*1261/1266	
1270–80	Roger Owen until 1280	Robert of St Edmund 1270
1281–85	John Fitzwilliam Mich. 1281	Robert of St Edmund until *c.*1285
1285–92		
1292–97	John de Neville *c.*25 Dec. 1293 until Trin. 1297	John de Ponz *c.*25 July 1292 until *c.*1297

6   The *Law Reporter*, iii (1829–30), 226 reported: 'April 26 – First day of term, this day, before the sitting of the court of chancery, Thomas Goold, esq., was sworn first serjeant, Francis Blackburne, esq., second serjeant and Edward Pennefather, esq., third serjeant.' *BNL,* 20 Feb. 1835, reported that on 14 Feb. 1835 the lord chancellor called Perrin as first, Greene as second, and Jackson as third serjeant. *ILT & SJ,* xliv (1910), 20 reported Moriarty's call as first serjeant on 14 Jan. 1910.

1297–1307	William of Bardfield c.Trin. 1297 until c.Mich.1307[1]	Richard le Blond c.Mich. 1297	
1307–10		Richard le Blond	
1310–14	Matthew of Hanwood c. Feb. 1311[2] until Mich. 1315	Richard le Blond	
1314–19		Richard le Blond	
1319–22	John of Staines 21 Aug. 1319	Richard le Blond until 21 Mar. 1322	
1322–27	John of Staines until 20 Aug. 1327	Simon Fitzrichard 21 Mar. 1322	
1327–31	John of Cardiff c. 29 Sept. 1327 until 22 Nov. 1330	Simon Fitzrichard until c.Jun. 1331	John Gernoun c.29 Sept. 1327 until 24 June 1330[3]
1331–34	Thomas of Dent c.Jun. 1331 until c.3 Mar. 1334	Hugh Brown c.3 Jun 1331	
1334–38		Hugh Brown[4]	John Gernoun from 2 Nov. 1334 until 6 June 1338
1338–46		Hugh Brown until 3 Jun. 1346	William Petit 17 July 1338
1346–47			William Petit
1347–48	Edmund of Barford c.19 Nov. 1347		William Petit
1348–50	Edmund of Barford	Robert of Preston c.11 Dec. 1348	William Petit until 21 Mar. 1350[5]

1   He was only paid to Mich. 1307, but may have acted as a serjeant until appointed a justice of common pleas in June 1308.

2   Although Hanwood was paid from Mich. 1310, as he did not take his oath of office until Feb. 1311, he probably did not act as king's serjeant until then. He is referred to as king's serjeant in March 1315. NAI RC 8/5, p. 426 and RC 8/10, p. 546. I owe these references to Dr Brand.

3   No payments are recorded between 22 Nov. 1330 and 2 Nov. 1334.

4   No payments are recorded between 24 June and 2 Nov. 1334.

5   He acted as a temporary justice in the justiciar's court between 26 Nov. 1347 and 27 Apr. 1348. No payments are recorded between 21 Sept. 1348 and 21 Sept. 1349.

1350–58	Edmund of Barford	Robert of Preston until 17 July 1358	
1358–60	Edmund of Barford until *c*.19 Feb. 1360	Richard Plunkett *c*.Easter 1358[6] Richard White[6]	John Keppok 19 Aug. 1358
1360–65		Richard Plunkett[7]	John Keppok until 8 Feb. 1365
1365–66		Richard Plunkett	
1366–72	John Tyrell *c*.8 Feb. 1366	Richard Plunkett	
1372–76	John Tyrell	Richard Plunkett until *c*.7 Aug. 1376	Walter Coterell *c*.1372[8]
1376–77	John Tyrell		Walter Coterell
1377–82	John Tyrell	Roger Lenfant *c*.12 Jun. 1377 until *c*.13 Jan. 1382[9] Walter Coterell	Peter Rowe *c*.2 May 1381
1382–84	John Tyrell until between 1382 and 1384[10]	Walter Coterell	Peter Rowe
1384–86		Walter Coterell	Peter Rowe

6 Whilst there are a number of gaps in the payments to him, it would seem probable that he acted as a serjeant until appointed as a justice in the justiciar's court on 8 Aug. 1376. He was absent on the king's service in 1359, when Richard White was appointed to act as his deputy between 19 June and 19 July 1359. Richardson & Sayles, *Admin. Ire.*, p. 179.

7 No payments are recorded between 18 Oct. 1363 and 18 Oct. 1364. Richardson & Sayles, *Admin. Ire.*, p. 180.

8 Smyth, *Law officers*, p. 183, states that Coterell had been appointed by patent for the counties of Wexford and Waterford in the time of Maurice, earl of Kildare, and Robert de Asheton. Coterell was in office until at least 12 July 1388, *Rot. pat. Hib.*, p. 141 b, no. 200. I owe the latter reference to Dr Brand.

9 Lenfant is to be found acting in Cork on 12 June 1377 and is recorded as still in office on 13 Jan. 1382. *Rot. pat. Hib*, p. 103, no. 90 and p.116 b, no. 27. I owe these references to Dr Brand.

10 Although Tyrell was still in office on 10 July 1382 (Richardson & Sayles, *Parliaments and councils*, p. 122, no. 68), he is recorded as being paid as a justice of the justiciar's court by 18 Aug. 1384. *Rot. pat. Hib.*, p. 136 b, no. 205. I owe the latter reference to Dr Brand.

1386–88	Richard Glynon *c.*11 Feb. 1386	Walter Coterell until 12 July 1388	Peter Rowe until *c.*27 Jan. 1387
1388–92	John Bermingham 24 Sept. 1388 until *c.*4 Oct. 1392[11]		
1392–93	John Haire *c.*Nov. 1392		Nicholas White 25 Jan. 1393[12]
1393–1400			

b) *1400–1627*

1400–03	John Bermingham	16 Jan. 1400 until *c.*Mar. 1403[13]
1403–06		
1406	James Uriell	
1406–22		
1422–34	Christopher Barnewall	20 Oct. 1422 until *c.*6 Apr. 1434[14]
1434	Thomas Plunkett	8 Nov. 1434[15]
1435	Robert Dowedall	20 Jun. 1435[16]
1435–38		
1438–47	Edward Somerton	4 Feb. 1438 until 18 Jan. 1447[17]
1447–55	Thomas Snetterby	24 Jun. 1447 until 1455[18]
1455–60		
1460	Peter Trevers	*c.*Feb. 1460[19]
1460–62		
1462–69	Thomas Dowedall	Philip Bermingham

11 Licensed to go to England to study law.
12 White was in office on this date: *Proceedings of the king's council, Ireland*, pp. 108 and 110. I owe this reference to Dr Brand.
13 Bermingham is still styled king's serjeant on 19 Mar. 1403: H.J. Lawlor, 'A calendar of the Liber Niger and Liber Albus of Christ Church Dublin', *RIA Proc*, xxvii (1907–09), 21. I owe this reference to Dr Brand.
14 Good behaviour when appointment renewed in Sept. 1430.
15 During pleasure.
16 Appointed for life. Dowedall was still in office on 28 Nov. 1435. *Rot. pat. Hib.*, p. 259, no. 12. I owe this reference to Dr Brand.
17 Appointed for life.
18 Good behaviour. It would seem that he was still in office in 1455, as there is a reference in that year to his having difficulty in obtaining the fees due to him. *Stat. Ire., Hen. VI*, p. 349.
19 Licensed to go to England. *Stat. Ire., Hen. VI*, p. 793.

	*c.*4 Mar. 1462 until	*c.*Nov. 1463 until
	*c.*Dec. 1469[20]	Feb. 1464
1469–71		
1471–76	Henry Duffe	3 Dec. 1471 until *c.*Dec. 1476[21]
1477–87	John Estrete	July 1477 until *c.*Mar. 1487[22]
1487–96		
1496	Thomas Kent	8 Nov. 1496[23]
1496–1501		
1501–02	John Egyr	
1504–06	John Barnewall[24]	
1506	Clement Fitzleones[25]	
1506–09		
1510	Patrick Finglas[26]	
1511–15	Thomas Rochford	11 Apr. 1511 until *c.*1515[27]
1516	Thomas Fitzsimon	12 May 1516[28]
1520–27	Robert Barnewall	*c.*Mich. 1520 until *c.*Trin 1527[29]
1527–32		
1532–34	Thomas Luttrell	9 Sept. 1532

20 Dowedall was confirmed in office during the parliamentary session which started in Dec. 1469: *Stat. Ire.,1–12 Edw. IV*, p. 549. By 10 Sept. 1471, he had reverted to being a countor, ibid., pp. 735–37, no. 13. I owe these references to Dr Brand.

21 Appointed for life.

22 H.J. Lawlor, 'A calendar of the Liber Niger and the Liber Albus of Christ Church Dublin', *RIA Proc*, xxvii (1907–09), 30. I owe this reference to Dr Brand. Estrete was no longer in office by 26 Mar. 1487, when he was described as the 'king's servant and councillor' and granted the office of master of the coinage in Ireland. *Cal. pat. rolls, 1485–94*, pp. 148 and 169.

23 S.G. Ellis, 'The administration of the lordship of Ireland under the early Tudors', pp. 531–32, citing memoranda roll, 14 Hen. VII, m. 25–5d. NAI, RC 8/43, p. 47

24 Still acting 10 May 1506. NAI, Ferguson MS, iv, 9–10.

25 Ball, *Judges*, i, 188, says 1505 but gives no source. Since Barnewall was still in office on 10 May 1506, Fitzleones must have assumed office after that date.

26 Ellis, 'The administration of the lordship of Ireland under the early Tudors', pp. 531–32, gives 20 Jan. 1508, and cites Ball, *Judges*, i, 188. However, no source is given in Ball at p. 193 for the statement that Finglas appears as serjeant in 1509. He does appear early in 1510 in Hilary term of 1 Hen. VIII: NAI, Ferguson MS, iv, 8.

27 W.M. Mason, *Historical annals of the collegiate and cathedral church of St Patrick*, pp. 142–44.

28 Found acting on 12 May 1516. Memoranda roll, 8–9 Hen. VIII m.8: NAI, Ferguson MS, iv, 39.

29 Ellis, 'The administration of Ireland under the early Tudors', pp. 531–32. PRO, E.101/248/21. Barnewall was still in office in Trinity term of 1527. Memoranda roll, 18 Hen. VIII m.26: NAI, Ferguson MS, iv, 130–31.

1534–50	Patrick Barnewall	17 Oct. 1534
1550–54	John Bathe	16 Oct.1550[30]
1554–74	Richard Finglas	11 Sept.1554
1574–94	Edward Fitzsimon	21 Feb.1574[31]
1594–97	Arthur Corye	9 May 1594
1597–1601	Edward Loftus	1 Nov. 1597
1601–09	Nicholas Kerdiff	8 Jun. 1601
1609–17	John Beere	9 Feb. 1609
1617–27	John Brereton	13 May 1617

(II) KING'S SERJEANTS, 1627–1682

	Principal, Prime from 1661	Second
1627–29	John Brereton	Nathaniel Catelyn 23 May 1627[32]
1629–34	James Barry 6 Oct. 1629	Nathaniel Catelyn
1634–37	Maurice Eustace Aug. 1634	Nathaniel Catelyn
1637–40	Maurice Eustace	William Sambach 16 Apr. 1637 until 23 Jun. 1640
1640–49	Maurice Eustace	
1649–60		
1660–66	Sir Audley Mervyn 20 Sept. 1660[33]	Robert Griffith 4 Mar. 1661[34] until Nov. 1666
	Sir Audley Mervyn	Vacant to 1670
1670–73	Sir Audley Mervyn	Henry Henn 6 Apr. 1670

30 For life.
31 Smyth, *Law officers*, p. 186.
32 *Cal. pat. rolls Ire., Chas. I*, p. 211.
33 Mervyn was appointed under the privy seal on 20 Sept. 1660; the letters patent were not enrolled until 21 May 1661. Good behaviour.
34 Appointed under the privy seal.

1673–74	Sir Audley Mervyn	Richard Reynell 10 May 1673
1674–75	Sir Audley Mervyn	John Osborne 26 May 1674
1675–81	Sir William Davys 26 Oct. 1675	John Osborne Prime serjeant in reversion to Davys 29 Aug. 1676[35]
1681–82	John Osborne 2 May 1680	Sir Richard Stephens 3 May 1680

(III) KING'S SERJEANTS, 1682–1805

	Prime	Second	Third
1682–83	John Osborne	William Beckett 24 Oct. 1682[37]	John Lyndon 24 July 1682[36]
1683–87	John Osborne	William Beckett	Richard Ryves 19 Feb. 1683
	John Osborne	Richard Ryves c.13 July 1683[38]	Henry Echlin 3 Aug. 1683
1687–88	Garrett Dillon 15 Feb. 1687	Vacant from May 1687 until 1690	John Barnewall 6 May 1687
1688–90	Garrett Dillon		Theobald Butler Mar. 1688
1690	John Osborne 29 Sept. 1690[39]	Richard Stephens 14 Nov. 1690	Alan Brodrick 27 Nov. 1690[40]

35 Smyth, *Law officers*, pp. 187–88.
36 Ibid., p. 194. Privy seal 24 July, letters patent 5 Sept. 1682.
37 Ibid., p. 195. Privy seal 24 Oct., letters patent 11 Nov. 1682.
38 Following Beckett's death on 11 July 1683, Ryves was immediately promoted to second in his place. H.M.C., *Ormond MSS (n.s.)*, vii, 69–72, 83 and 91.
39 Smyth, *Law officers,* at p. 188, gives the date of his patent as 29 Sept. 1690. However, a letter was sent from London on 3 Nov. containing details of warrants to be issued under the great seal, one of which was for John Osborne 'the king's first serjeant at law of the court of common pleas of Ireland' *(Cal. S. P. dom., 1690–91*, pp. 156–57). This reference to the common pleas of Ireland is an obvious mistake by the writer, who did not appreciate that the Irish serjeants were not solely connected with the common pleas, unlike their namesakes in England. There was much chopping and changing, with appointments being made and then revoked. It seems probable that the letter was merely confirmatory, and the earlier date is the correct one.
40 A warrant under the great seal of Ireland which appointed Brodrick third

1691–92	John Osborne	Richard Ryves 5 Jan. 1691	Alan Brodrick
1692–95	Nehemiah Donnellan c.29 Nov. 1692[41]	Thomas Packenham c.29 Nov. 1692[41]	Vacant from 1692 until 1711
1695	Thomas Packenham 5 Nov. 1695		
1696– 1703	Thomas Packenham	William Neave 13 Jan. 1696	
1703–08	Robert Saunders 28 Feb. 1703	William Neave	
1708–11	William Neave 1 Dec. 1708	William Caulfield 1 Dec. 1708	
1711–12	Robert Blennerhassett 11 Aug. 1711	Morley Saunders 14 Aug. 1711	John Cliffe 29 Nov. 1711
1712–14	Morley Saunders 9 Feb. 1712	John Cliffe 12 Feb. 1712	John Staunton 25 Feb. 1712
1714–15	William Caulfield 8 Dec. 1714	Robert Fitzgerald 18 Dec. 1714	John Witherington 14 Dec. 1714
1715–16	Godfrey Boate 13 Jun. 1715	Robert Fitzgerald	John Witherington
1716–18	Robert Fitzgerald 23 Jun. 1716	John Witherington 23 Aug. 1716	Vacant from 1716 until 1726
1718–24	Robert Fitzgerald	William Brodrick 23 Dec. 1718	
1724–26	Francis Bernard 26 Jan. 1724	William Brodrick	Robert Jocelyn 28 Mar. 1726
1726–27	Henry Singleton 22 Jun. 1726	William Brodrick	Robert Jocelyn

serjeant was issued on 27 Nov. 1690. *Cal. S. P. dom., 1690–91*, p. 172. The letters patent were dated 19 Feb.1691. Smyth, *Law officers*, p. 195.

41 The earl of Nottingham wrote to the lord lieutenant on 29 Nov. 1692, saying that the king had appointed Donnellan and Packenham. *Cal. S. P. dom., 1691–92*, p. 537. Their letters patent were dated 8 Feb. 1693. Smyth, *Law officers*, pp. 188 and 196.

1727–28	Henry Singleton	William Brodrick	John Bowes 4 May 1727
1728–30	Henry Singleton	Robert Dixon 5 Jan. 1728[42]	John Bowes
1730–32	Henry Singleton	Robert Dixon	Henry Purdon[43] 23 Oct. 1730
1732–38	Henry Singleton	Richard Bettesworth 29 Apr. 1732	Henry Purdon
1738–40	Henry Singleton	Richard Bettesworth	Robert Marshall 18 Apr. 1738
1740–41	Vacant from 1740 until 1741	Richard Bettesworth	Robert Marshall
1741–42	Arthur Blennerhassett 14 Jan. 1741	Robert Marshall 21 Jan. 1741	Philip Tisdall 21 Jan. 1741
1743–51	Anthony Malone 9 May 1743	Robert Marshall	Philip Tisdall
1751–54	Anthony Malone	Robert Marshall	Richard Malone 28 Oct. 1751
1754–57	Eaton Stannard 24 Jan. 1754	Robert Marshall	Richard Malone
1757–59	William Scott 6 Oct. 1757	Richard Malone 25 Nov. 1757	Marcus Patterson 24 Nov. 1757
1759–61	Thomas Tenison 27 July 1759	Edmund Malone 10 Sept. 1759	Marcus Patterson

42 Ball, *Judges*, ii, at 202 and 206 states that Bowes became third serjeant in 1727, and Dixon second serjeant in 1728. This is supported by Hayden, *Book of dignities*, p. 592. Smyth, *Law officers*, at pp. 197 and 244, states Dixon became third serjeant on 5 Jan. 1728 on the resignation of Brodrick as second, and, at p. 197, that Bowes was continued as second, implying that Bowes had been promoted when Brodrick resigned. However, *Lib. mun. pub. Hib.*, states that Dixon became second on Brodrick's resignation. The preponderance of the evidence is, therefore, that Dixon became second and Bowes remained third.

43 Smyth, *Law officers*, p. 245 gives the date of his appointment as 23 Oct., although at p. 197 merely states that his patent was Oct. 1730, but was not inrolled.

1761–64	John Hely-Hutchinson 11 Dec. 1761	Edmund Malone	Marcus Patterson
1764–67	John Hely-Hutchinson	Edmund Malone	James Dennis 10 Oct. 1764
1767–70	John Hely-Hutchinson	James Dennis 14 Jan. 1767	Godfrey Lill 15 Jan. 1767
1770–74	John Hely-Hutchinson	James Dennis	Maurice Coppinger 12 July 1770
1774–76	James Dennis 18 July 1774	Maurice Coppinger 19 July 1774	George Hamilton 20 July 1774
1776–77	James Dennis	Maurice Coppinger	Hugh Carleton 15 May 1776
1777–79	Walter Hussey Burgh 24 July 1777	Hugh Carleton 5 Nov. 1777	Attiwell Wood 6 Nov. 1777
1779–80	Walter Hussey Burgh	Attiwell Wood 8 May 1779	James Fitzgerald 8 May 1779
1780–82	James Browne 14 June 1780	Attiwell Wood	James Fitzgerald
1782–83	Walter Hussey Burgh 1 June 1782	Attiwell Wood	James Fitzgerald
1782–83	Thomas Kelly 13 July 1782	Attiwell Wood	Peter Metge 25 July 1782
1783–84	John Scott 31 Dec. 1783	Attiwell Wood	Peter Metge
1784–87	James Browne 21 May 1784	James Fitzgerald 8 Apr. 1784	John Toler 15 Jan. 1784
1787–89	James Fitzgerald 21 June 1787	John Toler 27 June 1787	Joseph Hewitt 27 June 1787
1789–91	James Fitzgerald	Joseph Hewitt 17 Aug. 1789	Henry Duquerry 17 Aug. 1789

1791–93	James Fitzgerald	Henry Duquerry 30 July 1791	James Chatterton 30 July 1791
1793–99	James Fitzgerald	James Chatterton 10 Dec. 1793	Edmund Stanley 10 Dec. 1793
1799– 1801	St George Daly 28 Jan. 1799	James Chatterton	Edmund Stanley
1801	Edmund Stanley 1 July 1801	James Chatterton	Arthur Moore 10 Nov. 1801
1801–05	Arthur Browne 29 Dec. 1801[44]	James Chatterton	Arthur Moore

(IV) KINGS SERJEANTS, 1805–1919

	First	Second	Third
1805–06	Arthur Moore 25 July 1805	Sir James Chatterton	Charles Kendal Bushe 25 July 1805 John Ball 25 Oct. 1805
1806–13	Arthur Moore	John Ball 23 Apr. 1806	William MacMahon 23 Apr. 1806
1813–14	Arthur Moore	William MacMahon 3 Dec. 1813	William Johnson 4 Dec. 1813
1814–16	Arthur Moore	William Johnson 4 Mar. 1814	Henry Joy 19 Mar. 1814
1816–17	William Johnson 25 July 1816	Henry Joy 26 July 1816	Richard Jebb 27 July 1816
1817–18	Henry Joy 28 Oct. 1817	Richard Jebb 29 Oct. 1817	Charles Burton 30 Oct. 1817
1818–20	Henry Joy	Charles Burton 1 Dec. 1818	Thomas Lefroy 1 Dec. 1818

44 Smyth, *Law officers*, pp. 191 and 260 gives Browne's appointment as 29 Dec. 1802. This is incorrect as Browne was in fact appointed on 29 Dec. 1801. *BNL* of 5 Jan. 1802 had an official announcement dated 1 Jan. 1802 of the changes, the decision to replace Stanley with Browne having been taken a few days earlier (BL, Add. MSS. 35,732, ff. 12–13).

1820–21	Henry Joy	Thomas Lefroy 3 Dec. 1820	
1821–22	Henry Joy	Thomas Lefroy	Thomas Burton Vandeleur 13 Feb. 1821[45]
1822–23	Thomas Lefroy 13 May 1822	John Lloyd 13 May 1822	Robert Torrens 13 May 1822
1823–26	Thomas Lefroy	John Lloyd	Thomas Goold 13 July 1823
1826–30	Thomas Lefroy	Thomas Goold *c.*22 July 1826[46]	Francis Blackburne *c.*22 July 1826[46]
1830–31	Thomas Goold 26 Apr. 1830[47]	Francis Blackburne 26 Apr. 1830[47]	Edward Pennefather 26 Apr. 1830[47]
1831–32	Thomas Goold	Edward Pennefather 18 Jan. 1831	Michael O'Loghlen 18 Jan. 1831
1832–35	Edward Pennefather Feb. 1832	Michael O'Loghlen Feb. 1832	Louis Perrin Feb. 1832
1835–36	Louis Perrin 27 Jan. 1835[48]	Richard Wilson Greene 27 Jan. 1835[48]	Joseph Devonsher Jackson 27 Jan. 1835[48]

45 Hayden, *Book of dignities*, p. 593.
46 Blackburne, *Life of Francis Blackburne*, pp. 53–54. The post of third serjeant was offered to Blackburne on 22 July, and so Goold must have been promoted second about the same time. Their undated appointments appear in *DG* of 12 Aug. 1826.
47 Called before the lord chancellor on 26 Apr. 1830: *Law Reporter*, iii (1829–30), 226. *DG* of 1 May 1830, no date of appointment.
48 Smyth, *Law officers*, does not record Perrin as first serjeant, and p. 269 gives Jackson as becoming second serjeant on 27 Jan. 1835. However, Perrin is recorded as first serjeant and Greene as second serjeant in 'King's Inns Entry of Benchers 1794–1864', so when Pennefather became solicitor general on 27 Jan. 1835, *Reporter* Perrin was promoted to first, Greene became second and Jackson became third serjeant then or shortly afterwards. *BNL* of 10 Feb. 1835 carried a report of a trial in which Greene was described as Serjeant Greene. On 13 Feb., it said he was going as a judge on the Munster circuit in preference to Perrin because of the latter's politics, and on 20 Feb. reported that on 14 Feb. the lord chancellor called Perrin as first, Greene as second and Jackson as third serjeant.

	Richard Wilson Greene 23 May 1835	Joseph Devonshire Jackson 23 May 1835	Stephen Woulfe 23 May 1835
1836–38	Richard Wilson Greene	Joseph Devonsher Jackson	Nicholas Ball 10 Nov. 1836
1838–40	Richard Wilson Greene	Joseph Devonsher Jackson	William Corry 20 July 1838
1840–41	Richard Wilson Greene	Joseph Devonsher Jackson	Richard Moore May 1840
	Richard Wilson Greene	Joseph Devonsher Jackson	Joseph Stock 21 Aug. 1840
1841–42	Richard Wilson Greene	Joseph Stock 18 Nov. 1841	Richard Benson Warren 18 Nov. 1841
1842–43	Joseph Stock 4 Nov. 1842	Richard Benson Warren 4 Nov. 1842	Richard Keatinge 4 Nov. 1842
1843–48	Joseph Stock	Richard Benson Warren	John Howley Sept. 1843[49]
1848–51	Joseph Stock	John Howley July 1848[50]	James O'Brien July 1848[50]
1851–55	John Howley June 1851[51]	James O'Brien June 1851[51]	Jonathan Christian June 1851[51]
1855–58	John Howley	James O'Brien	Walter Berwick Mar. 1855[52]
1858–59	John Howley	Walter Berwick 2 Feb. 1858[53]	Rickard Deasy 5 Feb. 1858[53]

49 Not in *DG*. Hayden, *Book of dignities*, p. 593 gives Sept. 1843; the *Gentleman's Magazine* gives Oct. 1843.

50 10 Ir LR noted that Warren died in July and O'Brien was appointed third serjeant that month. The *Law Times* of 15 July reported O'Brien's appointment and presumably Howley was promoted second at the same time.

51 *DG* of 10 June 1851, no date of appointment.

52 Not in *DG*. Christian's resignation, and the appointment of Berwick in his place, were reported in the *Law Times* of 24 Mar. 1855, and his call was reported in the issue of 28 Apr. 1855.

53 Not in *DG*. Hayden, *Book of dignities*, p. 593 gives 5 Feb. as the date of appointment of both. However, *BNL* of 2 Feb. reported Berwick as second, and, on 6 Feb., that Deasy had been appointed a serjeant.

1859–60	John Howley	Thomas O'Hagan 13 July 1859	Gerald Fitzgibbon July 1859[54]
1860–61	John Howley	James Anthony Lawson Feb. 1860[55] *1/u/60*	Gerald Fitzgibbon
	John Howley	James Anthony Lawson	Edward Sullivan 24 Oct. 1860[56] *1/u/10*
1861–65	John Howley	Edward Sullivan 21 Feb. 1861[57]	Richard Armstrong 21 Feb. 1861[57]
1865–66	Sir John Howley	Richard Armstrong 18 Feb. 1865[58]	Sir Colman O'Loghlen 18 Feb. 1865[58]
1866–69	Richard Armstrong 24 Feb. 1866[59]	Sir Colman O'Loghlen 24 Feb. 1866[59]	Charles Robert Barry 24 Feb. 1866[59]
1869–70	Richard Armstrong	Sir Colman O'Loghlen	Richard Dowse 12 Jan. 1869
1870–77	Richard Armstrong	Sir Colman O'Loghlen	David Sherlock 18 Mar. 1870[60]
1877–80	Richard Armstrong	David Sherlock 29 Nov. 1877[61]	James Robinson 29 Nov. 1877[61]

54 Not in *DG*. O'Hagan was appointed second serjeant on 13 July, so presumably Fitzgibbon was appointed on, or shortly after, that date.

55 Not in *DG*. The *Law Times* of 25 Feb. 1860 reported Lawson had succeeded O'Hagan as second serjeant, and Hayden, *Book of dignities*, p. 593, gives 25 Feb. as the date of his appointment.

56 Hayden, *Book of dignities*, p. 593, gives 24 Oct., *BNL* referred to him as serjeant on 31 Oct., *DG* of 2 Nov. announced his appointment, but with no date.

57 Not in *DG*. Hayden, *Book of dignities*, p. 593, gives 21 Feb. *BNL* of 23 Feb. 1861 referred to Armstrong as 'Serjeant Armstrong' in its report of the trial of *Longworth* v. *Yelverton*.

58 Not in *DG*. Reported in *BNL* of 18 Feb. 1865. Hayden, *Book of dignities*, p. 593, gives that as the date of their appointments.

59 Not in *DG*. Howley died 13 Feb. Hayden, *Book of dignities*, p. 593 gives 27 Feb. for Armstrong's promotion to first, but gives 24 Feb. for the promotion of O'Loghlen to second, and the appointment of Barry as third. If the latter dates are correct, Armstrong must have been promoted on or before 24 Feb.

60 Undated notice of appointment in *DG* of 22 Mar. 1870, *ILT & SJ*, iv (1870), 214, says he was called 18 Mar. 1870.

61 Hayden, *Book of dignities*, p. 593, gives 29 Nov. 1877, but *ILT & SJ*, xi (1877), 629, says they were called on 11 Dec. 1877.

1880–81	David Sherlock 25 Oct. 1880	James Robinson 25 Oct. 1880	Denis Caulfield Heron 25 Oct. 1880
1881–84	David Sherlock	James Robinson	John O'Hagan 30 May 1881
	David Sherlock	James Robinson	Charles Hare Hemphill 10 Sept. 1881[62]
1884–85	James Robinson 20 May 1884	Charles Hare Hemphill 20 May 1884	Peter O'Brien *c.*20 May 1884[63]
1885–87	Charles Hare Hemphill 18 July 1885[64]	Peter O'Brien 18 July 1885[64]	John George Gibson 18 July 1885[64]
1885–87	Charles Hare Hemphill	Peter O'Brien	William Bennett Campion 5 Dec. 1885
1887–88	Charles Hare Hemphill	William Bennett Campion 14 July 1887	Dodgson Hamilton Madden 14 July 1887
1888–92	Charles Hare Hemphill	William Bennett Campion	Hewitt Poole Jellett 14 Feb. 1888
1892– 1907	William Bennett Campion 17 Nov. 1892	Hewitt Poole Jellett 17 Nov. 1892[65]	William Houston Dodd 17 Nov. 1892
1907–08	William Bennett Campion	Hewitt Poole Jellett	Charles Andrew O'Connor 23 Mar. 1907

62 Hayden, *Book of dignities*, p. 593, gives 13 Sept. 1881, but *ILT & SJ*, xv (1881), 486, reported his appointment on 10 Sept. 1881.
63 O'Brien's appointment is not in *DG*, but was probably on, or shortly after, 20 May, when Hemphill was promoted second.
64 Hayden, *Book of dignities*, p. 593, says Gibson was appointed third on 18 July, with Hemphill and O'Brien being promoted to first and second, respectively, on 19 July, but they must have been promoted on 18 July, and this is confirmed by *DG* of 31 July 1885.
65 Although Dodd's appointment appeared in *DG* of 2 Dec. and that of Campion in *DG* of 16 Dec., no announcement appeared of the promotion of Jellett, but this must have occurred on 17 Nov.

	Charles Andrew O'Connor 5 Dec. 1907	Hewitt Poole Jellett	Matthew J Bourke 5 Dec. 1907
1908–10	Charles Andrew O'Connor	Hewitt Poole Jellett	John Francis Moriarty 5 June 1908
1910–11	John Francis Moriarty 14 Jan. 1910[66]	Hewitt Poole Jellett	Ignatius John O'Brien 14 Jan. 1910[66]
1911–12	John Francis Moriarty	Ignatius John O'Brien 18 May 1911[67]	Thomas Francis Molony 18 May 1911[67]
		Thomas Francis Molony 9 Dec. 1911[68]	Charles Louis Matheson 9 Dec. 1911[68]
1912–13	John Francis Moriarty	Charles Louis Matheson 20 July 1912[69]	Alexander Martin Sullivan 20 July 1912[69]
1913–19	Charles Louis Matheson 5 July 1913[70]	Alexander Martin Sullivan 5 July 1913[70]	George McSweeny 5 July 1913[70]
1919	Alexander Martin Sullivan 29 Oct. 1919	George McSweeny 29 Oct. 1919	Henry Hanna 29 Oct. 1919

66 The letters patent were dated 15 Mar. 1910. *ILT & SJ*, xliv (1910), 20, reported their being called on 14 Jan. 1910.
67 *ILT & SJ*, xlv (1911), 137, said both were called on 18 May 1911.
68 *ILT & SJ*, xlv (1911), 304, said both were called on 9 Dec. 1911.
69 Not in *DG*. In *ILT & SJ*, xlvi (1912), 182, the issue of 20 July carried an undated announcement.
70 Not in *DG*. In *ILT & SJ*, xlvii (1913), 187, the issue of 5 July carried an undated announcement.

PART THREE

Biographical details of the
serjeants at law

THESE HAVE BEEN compiled from various sources. If a serjeant went on to hold high judicial office, a reference is given to Ball's *The judges in Ireland, 1221–1921*, where much more information is to be found of the career of the individual concerned. In other cases references are given to the *Dictionary of national biography* and to obituaries in the *Irish Law Times & Solicitors' Journal* as appropriate. Whenever possible, these details have been verified against, or supplemented from, other sources, principally *Alumni Dublinenses*,[1] *King's Inns admission papers, 1607– 1867*,[2] *Return of members of parliament*,[3] *Parliamentary election results in Ireland 1801–1924*,[4] and Thom's *Irish almanac and official directory*, although many other works listed in the bibliography have been consulted.

To avoid unnecessary repetition, certain abbreviations have generally been employed. 'Called' means 'called to the Irish bar', and where the individual concerned died in office, 'when he died' follows the last date on which he held that office. For example, Nicholas Ball was called to the Irish bar in 1814, and died in 1865, whilst a justice of the court of common pleas, having held that office since 1839.

Armstrong, Richard. Born 10 May 1815, Inner Temple 1837. Called 1839. QC 1854. Third serjeant 1861–65, second serjeant 1865–66, first serjeant 1866–80. Bencher of King's Inns 1861. MP (L) for Sligo borough 1865–68, when he was unseated for election mal-practices. Although a Liberal in politics, was always retained for the crown in cases of exceptional difficulty even when a Conservative

---

1 *Alumni Dublinenses: a register of students, graduates, professors and provosts of Trinity College in the University of Dublin*, ed. G.D. Burtchaell and T.U. Sadlier 2nd ed. (Dublin, 1935).
2 Ed. E. Keane, P.B. Phair and T.U. Sadlier (Dublin, 1982).
3 2 vols. (London, 1878).
4 B.M. Walker, *Parliamentary election results in Ireland 1801–1924* (Dublin, 1978).

administration was in office. One of the leaders of the common law bar in Ireland. As a serjeant, he served as an assize judge on several occasions. In 1876, questions were raised as to the propriety of this, leading to a statement in parliament as to the circumstances in which serjeants were named in commissions of assize. Died 1880, obituary *ILT & SJ*, xiv (1880) 452.

Ball, John. Born *c*. 1754, entered TCD 1771, Lincoln's Inn 1776. Called 1778. MP for Drogheda 1796–97 and 1798–1800. Third serjeant 1805–06, second serjeant 1806–13, when he died. *d* 24/8/1813

Ball, Nicholas. Born 1791. Entered Lincoln's Inn 1812. Called 1814. KC 1830. MP (L) for Clonmel 1836–39. Third serjeant 1836–38, attorney general 1838, a justice of the common pleas 1839–65, when he died. Ball, *Judges*, ii, 351–52. *DNB*.

Bardfield, William of. King's serjeant 1297–1307. A justice of the common bench 1308–12 and 1316–1319. Described as 'primes en office de seriance'. Ball, *Judges*, i, 61.

Barford (or Berford), Edmund of. Appointed as king's serjeant 1347 and appears to have served until 1360.

Barnewall, Christopher. King's serjeant 1422–34. A justice of the king's bench 1434–35 and chief justice of the king's bench 1435–37 and 1437–46. Also granted patents appointing him vice-treasurer in 1430, 1432 and 1435. Ball, *Judges*, i, 176.

Barnewall, Sir John. Inner Temple 1673. Recorder of Dublin and knighted in 1687, third serjeant 1687–89. Second baron of the exchequer in 1689. Dismissed after William III's victory at the Boyne in 1690. Ball, *Judges*, i, 364–65.

Barnewall, John. The great-grandson of Christopher Barnewall (above). Attorney general, then king's serjeant and solicitor general 1504–06. Second justice of the king's bench 1514, deputy treasurer 1522 and treasurer 1534, chancellor 1534–38. Succeeded his father as Lord Trimleston 1514. Ball, *Judges*, i, 193. *DNB*.

Barnewall, Patrick. Nephew of Lord Trimleston (above). Entered Gray's Inn 1527. King's serjeant and solicitor general 1534–50, master of the rolls 1550–52. Ball, *Judges*, i, 204–05.

Barnewall, Robert. Appears as king's serjeant between 1520 and 1527.

Barry, Charles Robert. Born 3 Jan. 1823. Entered Lincoln's Inn 1843. Called 1845, QC 1859, a bencher of King's Inns 1863. Law adviser 1865–66. MP (L) for Dungarvan 1865–68. Third serjeant 1866–68, solicitor general 1868–70, attorney general 1870–72. A justice of the king's bench 1872–83 and a lord justice of appeal 1883–87, when he died. Ball, *Judges*, ii, 369.

Barry, James. Educated at TCD, entered Lincoln's Inn 1621 and was called to the bar by Lincoln's Inn 1628. King's serjeant 1629–34. Admitted to King's Inns 1630. MP for Lismore 1634. Second baron of the exchequer 1634, knighted 1640, was superseded during the interregnum, but allowed to practise in 1653 and acted as a justice of assize in 1655. After the restoration of Charles II, was chief justice of the king's bench 1660–73, when he died. Created Baron Santry in 1661. Ball, *Judges*, i, 335–36. *DNB*.

Bathe, John. Lincoln's Inn 1539. Chief or principal solicitor 1547–50. Noted as recorder of Drogheda 1548. King's serjeant 1551–54. Appointed for life and, by a separate patent dated the same day, was also appointed solicitor general during pleasure. Chief justice of the common bench 1554–59, when he was either superseded or died. Ball, *Judges*, i, 206.

Blond, Richard le. King's serjeant 1297–1322. A justice of the bench 1323. Ball, *Judges*, i, 66.

Beckett, William. Middle Temple. Called 1659. KC, second serjeant 1682–83, when he died.

Beere, John. King's serjeant 1609–17. MP for Carlow borough 1613, knighted 1615 and served as a commissioner of the court of wards in 1610, 1613 and 1615. He served as an assize judge on at least nine occasions. Appears to have died or been superseded in 1617.

Bermingham, John. King's serjeant 1388–92, and 1400–03. Second justice of the king's bench 1403–15, when he died. Ball, *Judges*, i, 172.

Bermingham, Philip. Acted as king's serjeant 1463–64; although appointed chief justice of the common bench in 1464, he does not appear to have taken office. Chief justice of the king's bench 1474–90, when he died. Ball, *Judges*, i, 184.

Bernard, Francis. Born 1662. Educated TCD, entered the Middle Temple 1683. MP for Clonakilty 1692–93, and for Bandon 1695–99, 1703–13 and 1715–25. Chief justice of the palatinate of Tipperary 1704, solicitor general 1711–14. Prime serjeant 1724–26. A justice of the common pleas 1726–31, when he died. Ball, *Judges*, ii, 199.

Berwick, Walter. Born 26 April 1800. Entered TCD 1815, Gray's Inn 1823, called 1826. QC 1840. Third serjeant 1855–58, assistant barrister for the east riding of Co. Cork and a bencher of King's Inns 1856. Second serjeant 1858–59. Bankruptcy judge 1859–68. Burnt alive in the Irish Mail train disaster in North Wales in Aug. 1868.

Bettesworth, Richard. Entered Middle Temple 1710, called 1716. KC 1728, second serjeant 1732–41. MP for Thomastown and for Midleton 1727–41. Lampooned by Swift. Died of fever whilst an assize judge in 1741.

Blackburne, Francis. Born 11 November 1782, entered TCD 1798. Called 1805, KC 1822, commissioner under the Insurrection Act 1823–24. Third serjeant 1826–30. Bencher of King's Inns 1826. Second serjeant 1830–31. Attorney general 1831–35 and 1841–42. Master of the rolls 1842–46, chief justice of the queen's bench 1846–52, chancellor 1852. A lord justice of appeal 1856–66, chancellor 1866–67, and died later that year. Edward Blackburne, *Life of the rt hon Francis Blackburne, late lord chancellor of Ireland* (London, 1874). Ball, *Judges*, ii, 355–56. *DNB*.

Blennerhassett, Arthur. Eldest son of Robert Blennerhasset (below). Born 1687, Middle Temple 1708, called 1714. MP for Tralee 1727–43, KC 1726, prime serjeant 1741–43. A justice of the king's bench 1743–58, when he died. Ball, *Judges*, ii, 207–08.

Blennerhassett, Robert. Born *c.*1652. Entered TCD 1667 and admitted King's Inns 1678. MP for Clonmel 1695–99 and for Limerick city 1703–12. Prime serjeant 1711–12, when he died.

Boate, Godfrey. Born 1673, entered TCD and Gray's Inn 1692. A master in chancery 1711–12, when he resigned. Prime serjeant 1715–16. Third justice of the king's bench 1716–21, when he died. Ball, *Judges*, ii, 194.

Bourke, Matthew J. Born 17 July 1849. Educated Queen's University. Entered Inner Temple 1872. Called 1874, KC 1892, a bencher of King's Inns 1897. Third serjeant 1907–08, recorder of Cork 1908–24. Died 1936.

Bowes, John. Born 1691, entered the Inner Temple 1712 and called to the bar in England 1718. Came to Ireland and started to practise in 1725. Third serjeant 1727–30, solicitor general 1730–39. MP for Taghmon 1731–42, attorney general 1739–42, chief baron of the exchequer 1742–57, chancellor 1757–1767, when he died. Created Baron Bowes of Clonlyon 1758. Ball, *Judges*, ii, 206. *DNB*.

Brereton (or Bereton), John. King's serjeant 1617–29. Received a new patent after the accession of Charles I on 16 Apr. 1625. Was knighted during his period of office. Died 1629.

Brodrick, Alan. Born 1656, entered the Middle Temple 1670 and Magdalen College, Oxford 1672. Called to the bar in England 1678. Recorder of Cork 1690. Third serjeant Nov. 1690–92, when dismissed. MP for Cork 1692, 1695, 1703–09. Speaker 1703. Solicitor general 1695–1704, attorney general 1707–09, chief justice of the queen's bench 1709–11, when he was removed from office. MP for Co. Cork 1713–14. Speaker 1713. Chancellor 1714–25. Created Baron Brodrick 1715 and Viscount Midleton 1717. MP for Midhurst in the British commons 1717–28. Died 1728. Ball, *Judges*, ii, 69–70. *DNB*.

Brodrick, William. Brother of Alan Brodrick (above). Attorney general of Jamaica 1692, returned to Ireland 1715. MP for Mallow 1717–27, second serjeant 1718, resigned at the end of 1727 or the beginning of 1728.

Brown, Hugh. Appointed a king's serjeant 1331 and appears to have served until at least 1346. There is a record that on 22 Oct. 1344 he was to receive arrears of £13 15s. for the period he was 'king's narrator' from 3 Dec. 1341 to 3 Sept. 1344.

Browne, Arthur. Born *c*.1756, admitted TCD 1772, Lincoln's Inn 1777. Regius professor of laws 1785–1805 and regius professor of Greek 1797–99 and 1801–05 at TCD. MP for Dublin University 1783–1800. KC 1795 and prime serjeant 1801–05, when he died. A bencher of King's Inns 1803. The last prime serjeant. A full account of his career and extensive published writings, on both legal and non-legal subjects, is to be found in O'Higgins, *NILQ*, xx (1969), 255.

Browne, the hon. James. Entered the Middle Temple 1755 and called 1760. MP for Jamestown 1769–76, Tuam 1776–83 and Castlebar 1783–90. Prime serjeant 1780 until his dismissal in 1782. Reappointed as prime serjeant 1784, but dismissed again in 1787. Died 1790.

Burgh, Walter Hussey. Born Walter Hussey 23 Aug. 1742, married Anne Burgh 1767 and added Burgh to his name from 1776. Entered TCD 1758 and the Middle Temple 1761. Called 1769. MP for Athy 1769–76 and Dublin University 1776–82. Prime serjeant 1777–80, served as an assize judge in 1779. Resigned 1780 and was reappointed prime serjeant 1 June 1782, became chief baron of the exchequer in July 1782. Died 1783. Ball, *Judges*, ii, 219. *DNB*.

Burton, Charles. Born 1760, entered Lincoln's Inn 1781. Called 1792. KC 1806, third serjeant 1817–18, second serjeant 1818–20. A justice of the king's bench 1820–47, when he died. Ball, *Judges*, ii, 341.

Bushe, Charles Kendal. Born 13 Jan. 1767, entered TCD 1782 and Lincoln's Inn 1786. Called 1790, MP for Callan 1796–99 and for Donegal borough 1799–1800. Third serjeant 1805. Solicitor general

1805–22 and chief justice of the king's bench 1822–41. Died 1843. Ball, *Judges*, ii, 342. *DNB*.

Butler, Theobald. Third serjeant, then solicitor general and knighted 1689. MP for Ennis in the Jacobite parliament of 1689. Superseded after William III's victory at the Boyne in 1690. One of the Jacobite signatories of the Treaty of Limerick in 1691, continued in practice afterwards. Died *c*.1721.

Campion, William Bennet. Born 1817, educated TCD. Entered Gray's Inn 1836. Called 1840, QC 1868, a bencher of King's Inns 1884. Third serjeant 1885–87, second serjeant 1887–92 and first serjeant 1892–1907, when he died. Obituary *ILT & SJ*, xli (1907), 247.

Carleton, Hugh. Born 11 Sept. 1739, entered TCD 1755 and the Middle Temple 1758. Called 1764, KC 1768. Recorder of Cork 1769, MP for Tuam 1772–76, Philipstown 1776–83, Naas 1783–87. Third serjeant 1776–77, second serjeant 1777–79 and solicitor general 1779–87. Chief justice of the common pleas 1787–1800. Created Baron Carleton 1789 and Viscount Carleton 1797. Died 1826. Ball, *Judges*, ii, 222–23. *DNB*.

Catelyn, Nathaniel. Possibly the Nicholas Catlin of Suffolk who entered Lincoln's Inn in 1605 and King's Inns in 1622. Was recorder of Dublin when became the first to be appointed as second serjeant 1627. Second serjeant 1627–37. MP for Dublin and speaker of the commons 1634. Was knighted by Lord Deputy Wentworth. Died 1637 whilst on assize.

Caulfield, William. MP for Tulsk 1692, 1695–99 and 1703–13, when he failed to win a seat. Entered the Middle Temple 1700. Called 1705. Second serjeant 1708–11, when he was dismissed. Prime serjeant 1714–15. Second justice of the king's bench 1715–34. Died 1737. Ball, *Judges*, ii, 193–94.

Chatterton, James. May be the James Chatterton who entered the Middle Temple in 1770. Called 1774. MP for Baltimore 1783 and for Doneraile 1783–97. Third serjeant 1791–93 and second serjeant 1793–1806, when he died. Created a baronet 1801.

Christian, Jonathan. Born 17 Feb. 1808, entered TCD 1824 and Gray's Inn 1831. Called 1834, QC 1846. Law adviser 1850. Third serjeant 1851–55, when he resigned. A bencher of King's Inns 1852. Solicitor general 1856–58, a justice of the common pleas 1858–67, a lord justice of appeal 1867–78. Died 1887. Ball, *Judges*, ii, 359–60. Hogan, ' "Arrows too sharply pointed": the relations of Lord Justice Christian and Lord O'Hagan, 1868–74', in J.F. McEldowney and P. O'Higgins (ed.), *The common law tradition*.

Cliffe, John. MP for Bannow 1695, 1695–99, 1703–13, 1713–14, 1715–27. Third serjeant 1711–12, second serjeant 1712–14, when he was dismissed.

Coppinger, Maurice. Born *c*.1727, entered TCD 1743, Middle Temple 1747, called 1753. MP for Ardfert 1758–83, Roscommon 1783–90 and for Belturbet 1790–97. Third serjeant 1770–74, second serjeant 1774–77, when he was dismissed. Acted as an assize judge 1776.

Corry (or Curry), William. Born *c*.1785, entered TCD 1798, called 1806. MP for Armagh borough 1837–40. Third serjeant 1838–40, appointed a master in chancery 1840.

Corye, Arthur. King's serjeant 1594–97, when he died.

Coterell, Walter. Served as a supernumerary king's serjeant 1372–88.

Daly, St George. Born *c*.1757. Entered TCD 1773 and Lincoln's Inn 1781. Called 1782. MP for Galway borough 1798–1800. Prime serjeant 1799–1801. A privy councillor. A baron of the exchequer 1801–03, a justice of the king's bench 1803–22. Died 1829. Ball, *Judges*, ii, 332–33.

Davys, Sir William. Called to the English bar by Lincoln's Inn 1657, and to the Irish bar 1661. Recorder of Dublin and MP for the city 1661, knighted 1662. Acted as an assize judge 1663 and 1667. Appointed a justice of the palatinate of Tipperary 1669. Dismissed as recorder, but reinstated 1672. Prime serjeant 1675–80. Chief justice of the king's bench 1680–87, when he died. Ball, *Judges*, i, 357–58.

Deasy, Rickard (or Richard). Born 23 Dec. 1812, entered TCD 1828 and Gray's Inn 1833. Called 1835, QC 1849. MP(L) Co. Cork 1855–61. Third serjeant 1858–59. A bencher of King's Inns 1858. Solicitor general 1859–60, attorney general 1860–61. A baron of the exchequer 1861–78 and a lord justice of appeal 1878–1883, when he died. Ball, *Judges*, ii, 363–64.

Dennis, James. Born 1721, entered TCD 1735 and the Middle Temple 1739. Called 1746, KC 1757. MP for Rathcormack 1761–68, Youghal 1768–77. Third serjeant 1764–67, second serjeant 1767–74 and prime serjeant 1774–77. Acted as an assize judge 1771 and 1774. Chief baron of the exchequer 1777–82, when he died. Created Baron Tracton 1781. Ball, *Judges*, ii, 218.

Dent, Thomas of. A king's serjeant 1331–34. Second justice of the bench 1334, second justice of the justiciar's court 1337–41, chief justice of that court 1341–44 and chief justice of the bench 1344–58. Ball, *Judges*, i, 74.

Dillon, Gerard (or Garrett). Probably admitted to Gray's Inn in 1669. Called 1674. Recorder of Dublin and KC 1685, prime serjeant 1687–90. MP for Mullingar in the Jacobite parliament of 1689, held the rank of colonel in the Irish army and was one of the Jacobite signatories of the Treaty of Limerick. Attainted and followed James II to France where he retained his military rank and was appointed ensign in James's regiment of Irish guards in 1693.

Dixon, Robert. Born 1685. Entered TCD 1701 and the Middle Temple 1704. Appears at the Irish bar 1711. KC 1716, MP for Kildare 1727–31. Second serjeant 1728–31. A justice of the common pleas 1731–32, when he died. Ball, *Judges*, ii, 201–02.

Dodd, William Houston. Born 28 Mar. 1844, educated at the Queen's College of Belfast, entered the Middle Temple 1871, called 1873. QC 1884, a bencher of King's Inns 1893. Unsuccessful Liberal candidate for Antrim North in 1892 and Londonderry South in 1895. MP(L) for Tyrone North 1906–07. Third serjeant 1892–1907. A justice of the king's bench division 1907–24. Died 1930. Ball, *Judges*, ii, 382.

Donnellan, Nehemiah. Born 1649, entered TCD 1666 and the Middle Temple 1669. Practised in Ireland and became a commissioner of appeals in revenue cases 1677. Went to England in 1688 and called to the bar by the Middle Temple 1689. Returned to Ireland in 1690 when he became KC. Recorder of Galway 1691–94 and of Dublin 1693–95. Prime serjeant 1692–95. Third baron of the exchequer 1695–1703. Chief baron of the exchequer 1703–05, when he died. Ball, *Judges*, ii, 62–63.

Dowedall, Robert. Appointed king's serjeant 1435. Chief justice of the common bench 1438–82, when he died. Ball, *Judges*, i, 177–78.

Dowedall, Thomas. Son of Robert Dowedall (above). Appears in Lincoln's Inn 1459. Appointed king's serjeant 1462 and appears to have served until at least 1469. Keeper of the rolls in chancery 1471–92. Ball, *Judges*, i, 182–83.

Dowse, Richard. Born 8 June 1824. Entered TCD 1845, scholar 1848. Entered Lincoln's Inn 1849. Called 1852, QC 1863. Third serjeant 1869–70. MP (L) for Londonderry city 1868–72. A bencher of King's Inns 1869. Solicitor general 1870–72, attorney general 1872 and a baron of the exchequer 1872–90, when he died. Ball, *Judges*, ii, 369.

Duffe, Henry. King's serjeant 1471 and served until at least 1476. Chief baron of the exchequer 1478. Second justice of the common bench 1479. Ball, *Judges*, i, 185.

Duquerry, Henry. Entered the Middle Temple 1769, called 1774. KC and a bencher of King's Inns 1779. MP for Armagh borough 1789–90 and Rathcormack 1790–97. Third serjeant 1789–91, second serjeant 1791–93, when he resigned, having 'lost his intellect due to sunstroke' on a tour of the Holy Land. Presumably he recovered because he was suggested as a possible counsel for the defence at the trial of William Drennan in 1794, and a speech he made to the commons on negotiations with France was published in 1795. Died 1803.

Echlin, Henry. Born 1652, entered TCD 1667, Lincoln's Inn 1672, called 1677. Third serjeant 1683–87, when he was dismissed. Second baron of the exchequer 1690–92, third justice of the king's bench 1692–93. Second baron 1693–1715. Superseded 1715. Knighted 1692 and created a baronet 1721. Died 1735. Ball, *Judges*, ii, 56–57.

Egyr, John. Appears as king's serjeant 1501–02.

Estrete, John. Appears as king's serjeant in 1477, was confirmed in office 1485 and appears to have served until 1487, by which time he had been appointed a privy councillor in England. In 1487, he was appointed master of the coinage in Ireland and then deputy chief baron of the exchequer. Ball, *Judges*, i, 187.

Eustace, Sir Maurice. Educated at TCD, where he was a scholar and later a fellow. Entered Lincoln's Inn 1619, called to the English bar 1625, and to the Irish bar 1627. Received a king's letter in 1629 appointing him king's serjeant, but the post had already been filled. MP for Athy and king's serjeant 1634. Acted as an assize judge 1637–41. MP for Kildare 1639 and speaker of the commons 1640–47. Knighted 1640. Confidant of Ormond. Imprisoned at Chester 1648–55. Resumed practice in Dublin in 1656 and received favour from Henry Cromwell. Appointed chancellor in 1660 upon the restoration of Charles II, refused a peerage. Died 1665. Ball, *Judges*, i, 344–46.

Finglas, Patrick. Entered Lincoln's Inn 1503. Appears as king's serjeant in 1510. Second justice of the common bench 1519–20, chief baron of the exchequer 1520–34, chief justice of the king's bench in 1534, was superseded almost immediately. Chief baron of the exchequer 1535–37, when he died. Ball, *Judges*, i, 193–94. *DNB*.

Finglas, Richard. Principal solicitor 1550–54, queen's serjeant and solicitor general 1554–74.

Fitzgerald, James. Born 1742, entered TCD 1759. MP for Fore 1776–83, Tulsk 1783–97 and Kildare 1797–1800 in the Irish commons. MP for Ennis 1802–08 and 1812–13. Third serjeant 1779–82.

Dismissed as third serjeant 1782. Second serjeant 1784–87 and prime serjeant 1787–99. Dismissed as prime serjeant in 1799 because of his opposition to the Union. Acted as an assize judge on the Connacht circuit 1793. Died 1835. *DNB*.

Fitzgerald, Robert. Born *c.*1671, entered TCD 1686. Called 1700, MP for Charleville 1703–13. Second serjeant 1714–16, prime serjeant 1716 until he died at the end of 1723 or early in 1724. *d* ϑ 1/1/172ϟ

Fitzgibbon, Gerald. Born 31 Dec. 1793. Entered TCD 1818, Gray's Inn 1827. Called 1830. QC 1841, a bencher of King's Inns 1858. Third serjeant 1859–60. A master in chancery 1860–78. Died 1882. *DNB*.

Fitzleones, Clement. Deputy chief baron of the exchequer 1493, king's attorney 1502, king's serjeant 1506. Ball, *Judges*, i, 188.

Fitzrichard, Simon. One of the king's serjeants, served between 1322 and 1331. Second justice of the bench 1331–34 when he became chief justice of the bench. Superseded as chief justice in 1337 when he became a justice of the bench. Reappointed chief justice of the bench 1338 and served until 1341. Ball, *Judges*, i, 71.

Fitzsimon (Fitzsymon), Edward. Entered the Inner Temple 1555. Commissioner for Munster 1561–68, justiciar in the liberties of Wexford 1563. Attorney general 1570–74. King's serjeant 1574–93, when he died. Acted as master of the rolls 1578. Ball, *Judges*, i, 219.

Fitzsimon, Thomas. Appears as king's serjeant in 1516.

Fitzwilliam, John. Appears as king's serjeant Michaelmas 1281.

Gernoun, John. King's serjeant 1327–30 and 1334–38. A justice of the bench 1338. Chief justice of the bench 1341–44, second justice of the bench 1348. Ball, *Judges*, i, 77.

Gibson, John George. Born 14 Feb. 1846. Entered TCD where he was a scholar, double gold medallist and vice-chancellor's prizeman. Called 1870, QC 1880. Third serjeant 1885 until appointed solicitor general later that year. MP (C) for Liverpool Walton 1885–88. Resigned as solicitor general on the fall of the Conservative government in January 1886. Reappointed solicitor general in July upon the return of the Conservative government. Attorney general 1887–88. A justice of the queen's (later king's) bench division 1888–1921. Died 1923. Ball, *Judges*, ii, 377–78.

Glynon, Richard. King's serjeant 1386.

Goold, Thomas. Born *c.*1766, entered TCD 1781 and Lincoln's Inn 1786. Called 1791. MP for Kilbeggan 1800. KC 1806. Third serjeant 1823–26, second serjeant 1826–30 and first serjeant 1830–32. A master in chancery 1832–46, when he died. *DNB*.

Greene, Richard Wilson. Born *c.*1791, entered TCD 1806, where he was a scholar and gold medallist. Entered Gray's Inn 1811. Called 1814. KC 1830 and law adviser 1831. First serjeant 1835–42. Solicitor general 1842–46, attorney general 1846 and resigned upon the fall of the Conservative government in June. A baron of the exchequer 1852–61. Died 1861. Ball, *Judges*, ii, 358–59.

Griffith, Robert. Appointed second serjeant under the privy seal 1661. Died 1666.

Haire, John. Appears as 'Serjeant at law of our lord the King in his common pleas of Ireland' in the response to a petition presented to parliament in 1392.

Hamilton, George. Born *c.*1732, entered TCD 1747, where he was a scholar. Entered the Middle Temple 1750. Called 1756. KC 1767 and MP for Belfast 1768–76. Third serjeant 1774–76. A baron of the exchequer 1776–93, when he died. Ball, *Judges*, ii, 218.

Hanna, Henry. Born 4 Jan. 1871, educated at Queen's College, Belfast and London University. Called 1896, KC 1911, called to the English bar 1913. A bencher of King's Inns 1915. Stood as a Unionist for Dublin St Stephens Green 1918. Third serjeant 1919–25. The last serjeant to be appointed. A judge of the high court of the Irish Free State 1925–42. Author of *The law of workmen's compensation*; *The pals at Suvla Bay* (1916), an account of the 7th battalion of the Royal Dublin Fusiliers at the Dardanelles in 1915; and *The statute law of the Irish Free State* (1929). Died 1946.

Hanwood, Matthew of. King's serjeant 1311–15.

Hely-Hutchinson, John. Born 1724, son of John Hely, later added the surname of Hutchinson. Entered the Middle Temple 1740 and TCD 1744. Called 1748, KC 1758. MP for Lanesborough 1759–60, for Cork city 1761–90 and for Taghmon 1790–94. Prime serjeant 1761–74. Obtained the reversion to the sinecure of secretary of state in 1766, succeeding to that position in 1777. Acted as an assize judge on at least five occasions between 1762 and 1773. Provost of TCD 1774–94, when he died. *DNB*.

Hemphill, Charles Hare. Born 22 Aug. 1822, entered TCD 1839, where he was a scholar and gold medallist. Entered the Middle Temple, called 1845. Stood unsuccessfully as a Liberal for Cashel in 1857. QC 1860. Between 1863 and 1877 he was successively chairman of quarter sessions of Counties Louth, Leitrim and Kerry when these were part-time posts. Resigned upon the creation of full-time county court judgeships in 1877. Third serjeant 1881–84, second serjeant 1884–85, first serjeant 1885–92. A bencher of King's Inns

1882. Solicitor general 1892–95. MP (L) for Tyrone North 1895–1906. Created Baron Hemphill 1906. Died 1908. *DNB.*

Henn (or Hene), Henry. Entered the Inner Temple 1645, called to the English bar 1653 and became a bencher of the Inn 1668. Went to Ireland and became a member of King's Inns 1669. Second serjeant 1670–73. Commissioner of revenue appeals 1671–72 and 1673. Third baron of the exchequer 1673–80, chief baron of the exchequer 1680–87, when he was superseded. Died 1708. Ball, *Judges*, i, 354.

Heron, Denis Caulfield. Born 16 Feb. 1824 and entered TCD, where he was refused a scholarship because he was a roman catholic. Entered Lincoln's Inn 1845. Professor of jurisprudence and political economy, Queen's College, Galway, 1849–59. Author of *Constitutional history of the University of Dublin* (1847), *An introduction to the history of jurisprudence* (1860) and *The principles of jurisprudence* (1873). Called 1848, QC 1860 and a bencher of King's Inns 1872. MP (L) for Tipperary 1870–74. Law adviser. Third serjeant 1880–81, when he died. Obituary *ILT & SJ*, xv (1881), 219.

Hewitt, Joseph. Born 1754, entered the Middle Temple 1768. Called 1776. MP for Belfast 1784–91. Third serjeant 1787–89, second serjeant 1789–91. A justice of the king's bench 1791–94, when he died. Ball, *Judges*, ii, 227.

Howley, John Bourke. Born 1789. Called 1815, KC 1835, a bencher of King's Inns 1843. Third serjeant 1843–48, second serjeant 1848–51 and first serjeant 1851–66, when he died. Knighted 1865.

Jackson, Joseph Devonsher. Born 1783, entered TCD 1800, and the Middle Temple 1804. Called 1806, KC 1827. Third serjeant 1835, second serjeant 1835–41. MP for Bandon 1835–41, and for Dublin University 1842. Solicitor general 1841–42, a justice of the common pleas 1842–57, when he died. Ball, *Judges*, ii, 355.

Jebb, Richard. Born 1766, entered TCD 1781, where he was a scholar. Entered Lincoln's Inn 1786, called 1789. KC 1806, third serjeant 1816–17, second serjeant 1817–18. A justice of the king's bench 1818–34, when he died. Ball, *Judges*, ii, 340. *DNB.*

Jellett, Hewitt Poole. Born 5 Jan. 1825, entered TCD 1843 and the Middle Temple 1845. Called 1847, QC 1864. Chairman of quarter sessions for King's County 1865–77, when he retired and resumed practice. A bencher of King's Inns 1875. Third serjeant 1888–92, second serjeant 1892 until his death in 1911, although he appears to have retired from active practice in 1899 when the Irish bar presented his portrait to the benchers of King's Inns. Obituary *ILT & SJ*, xlv (1911), 79.

Jocelyn, Robert. Born 1688, entered Gray's Inn 1709, called to the Irish bar 1718. MP for Granard 1725 and for Newtown 1727–39. Third serjeant 1726–27, solicitor general 1727–30, attorney general 1730–39. Chancellor 1739–57, when he died. Created Baron Newport 1743 and Viscount Jocelyn 1755. Ball, *Judges*, ii, 203–04. *DNB*.

Johnson, William. Born 1760, entered TCD 1774, Lincoln's Inn 1782. Called 1785. MP for Roscommon 1799–1800. KC 1808. Third serjeant 1813–14, second serjeant 1814–16 and first serjeant 1816–17. A justice of the common pleas 1817–41. Died 1845. Ball, *Judges*, ii, 340.

Joy, Henry. Born 1763, entered TCD 1780 and the Middle Temple 1783, called 1788. KC 1808, third serjeant 1814–16, second serjeant 1816–17 and first serjeant 1817–22. Solicitor general 1822–27 and attorney general 1827–31. Chief baron of the exchequer 1831–38, when he died. Ball, *Judges*, ii, 347.

Keatinge, Richard. Born 1793, entered TCD 1805, called 1813 and KC 1835. Third serjeant 1842–43. Bencher of King's Inns 1843. Judge of the prerogative court 1843–57 and of the probate court 1857–68. Died 1876. *ILT & SJ*, x (1876), 113.

Kelly, Thomas. Entered the Middle Temple 1747. Called 1753. KC 1767 and acted as a judge of assize 1772. Prime serjeant 1782–83. MP for Portarlington 1783. A justice of the common pleas 1783–1801. Died 1809. Ball, *Judges*, ii, 220.

Kent, Thomas. Escheator of the exchequer 1495. King's serjeant 1496, chief baron of the exchequer 1504–11. Appears as a knight in 1509. Ball, *Judges*, i, 191. Kenny, *King's Inns and the kingdom of Ireland*, pp. 21–22.

Keppok, John. A king's serjeant 1358–65, although the payment recorded probably includes arrears because he was appointed chief baron of the exchequer in 1364. Chief justice of the justiciar's court 1367–70, when he was superseded and reduced to a justice of that court. Reappointed as chief justice of the justiciar's court 1372 and served until he was again superseded and reduced to a justice of the court in 1382. Deputy to the chancellor 1375. Died 1404. Ball, *Judges*, i, 84.

Kerdiff, Nicholas. Probably the Nicholas Kerdiff who was admitted to the Middle Temple in 1594 and called to the English bar in 1600. Appointed king's serjeant 1601 and served until 1609, during which time he served as an assize judge on at least seven occasions.

Lawson, James Anthony. Born 10 Feb. 1817, entered TCD 1833, where he was a scholar, and professor of political economy 1841–46.

Entered Gray's Inn 1838. Called 1840. QC 1857. Law adviser 1858
and 1860–61, combining that post with that of second serjeant
1860–61. A bencher of King's Inns 1861. Solicitor general 1861–65,
attorney general 1865–68. MP(L) for Portarlington 1865–68. A
justice of the common pleas 1868–82 and of the queen's bench
1882–87, when he died. Ball, *Judges*, ii, 367–68. *DNB*.

Lefroy, Thomas Langlois. Born 8 Jan. 1776, entered TCD 1790 and
Lincoln's Inn 1793. Called 1797. KC 1816, third serjeant 1818–20.
A bencher of King's Inns 1819. Second serjeant 1820–22 and first
serjeant 1822–30. As a serjeant, frequently acted as a judge of
assize. Declined appointment to the king's bench 1820, to the
exchequer 1821 and to the common pleas 1823. Resigned as first
serjeant in 1830 because the government refused to appoint him as
an assize judge for political reasons. MP (C) for Dublin University
1830–41. A baron of the exchequer 1841–52, chief justice of the
queen's bench 1852–66. Died 1869. T. Lefroy, *A memoir of Chief
Justice Lefroy* (Dublin, 1871). Ball, *Judges*, ii, 354–55. *DNB*.

Lenfant, Roger. A supernumerary king's serjeant 1377–82.

Lill, Godfrey. Born 1719, entered TCD 1734 and the Middle Temple
1738. Called 1743. A master in chancery 1749–60. KC 1760. MP
for Fore 1761–68 and Baltinglass 1768–74. Counsel to the board of
revenue 1766. Third serjeant 1767–70, acted as an assize judge
1768. Solicitor general 1770–74, a justice of the common pleas
1774–83, when he died. Ball, *Judges*, ii, 217.

Lloyd, John. Second serjeant 1822–26. Appointed judge of the
insolvency court 1826.

Loftus, Edward. Second son of Archbishop Adam Loftus. Queen's
serjeant 1597–1601. Recorder of Dublin. Knighted by the earl of
Essex in 1599 and died at the siege of Kinsale in May 1601.

Luttrell, Thomas. King's serjeant and solicitor general 1532–34. Chief
justice of the common bench 1534–54. Knighted 1540. Died 1554.
Ball, *Judges*, i, 199–200.

Lyndon, John. Entered TCD *c.*1655 and Lincoln's Inn 1557, in which
year he became recorder of Carrickfergus. Joined King's Inns 1663.
MP for Killybegs 1665. The first to be appointed as third serjeant
when appointed under the privy seal in 1682. A judge of the king's
bench 1682–99. Ball, *Judges*, i, 359–60.

MacMahon, William John. Born 12 July 1776, entered TCD 1791,
where he was a scholar, and Gray's Inn 1796. Called 1799. Third
serjeant 1806–13, KC 1807, second serjeant 1813–14. Master of

the rolls 1814–37, when he died. Created a baronet 1815. Ball, *Judges*, ii, 339. *DNB*.

McSweeny, George. Born 4 Feb. 1865. Called 1896, KC 1911. Third serjeant 1913–19, second serjeant 1919–23, died Nov. 1923. Obituary *ILT & SJ*, lvii (1923), 284.

Madden, Dodgson Hamilton. Born 28 Mar. 1840, educated TCD, where he was a scholar and gold medallist. Entered the Middle Temple 1862. Called 1864. QC 1880, MP (U) for Dublin University 1887–92. Third serjeant 1887–88, a bencher of King's Inns 1887, solicitor general 1888–89, attorney general 1889–92, a justice of the queen's bench (later king's bench) division 1892–1919. Vice-chancellor of Dublin University 1895–1919. Author of: *Treatise on registration of deeds* (1868); *Practice of the land judge's court* (1870); *The diary of Master William Silence, a study of Shakespeare and of Elizabethan sport* (1897); *Some passages in the early history of classical learning in Ireland* (1907); *Shakespeare and his fellows: an attempt to decipher the man and his nature* (1916); and *A chapter of medieval history: the fathers of literature, of sport, and horses* (1923). Died 1928. Ball, *Judges*, ii, 378–79.

Malone, Anthony. Born 5 Dec. 1700, educated at Christ Church, Oxford and called 1726. MP for Westmeath 1727–60, Castlemartyr 1761–68, and Westmeath 1769–76. Prime serjeant from 1743 until his dismissal in 1753, because of his opposition to the government in the money bill dispute of that year. Granted a patent of precedence in 1755, giving him precedence at the Irish bar over the prime serjeant, attorney general and solicitor general. Between 1757 and 1761 he held the largely sinecure post of chancellor of the exchequer and exercised the previously nominal right of that office to sit in, and preside over, the court of exchequer, despite the failure of a bank with which he was involved in 1759. Died 1776. *DNB*.

Malone, Edmund. Brother of Anthony Malone (above). Born 1704, entered the Middle Temple 1722 and was called to the English bar 1730. Practised in England until called to the Irish bar in 1740. KC 1745, MP for Askeaton 1753–60 and Granard 1761–67. Second serjeant 1759–67, acted as an assize judge in 1763. A justice of the common pleas 1767–74, when he died. Ball, *Judges*, ii, 214.

Malone, Richard. Brother of Anthony and Edmund Malone (above). Born 13 Nov. 1706. Called 1730. MP for Fore 1741–59. Third serjeant 1751–57, second serjeant 1757–59, when he died.

Marshall, Robert. Entered the Middle Temple 1718, called 1723. Recorder of Clonmel. MP for Clonmel 1727–53. Third serjeant

1738–42 and second serjeant 1742–57, acted as an assize judge in 1750 and 1754. A justice of the common pleas 1757–66. Died 1774. Ball, *Judges*, ii, 209.

[handwritten marginal note: 1753 – ?]

Matheson, Charles Louis. Born 3 Feb. 1851, called 1874. QC 1892. A bencher of King's Inns 1895. MP(U) for Dublin St Stephen's Green 1904–06. Third serjeant 1911–12, second serjeant 1912–13 and first serjeant 1913–19. Acted as a judge of assize whilst serjeant. Recorder of Belfast and county court judge of Antrim 1919–21, when he died. Obituary *ILT & SJ*, lv (1921), 135.

Mervyn, Audley. Born *c.*1603 and educated at Christ Church, Oxford. MP for Tyrone 1640. A leading opponent of the government in the Irish parliament in 1641. After the uprising of Oct. 1641 fought on the royalist side for most of the 1640s before siding with Cromwell. Called to the bar by King's Inns 1658 and played a leading role in the restoration of Charles II in Ireland. In 1660 he was knighted and appointed prime serjeant under the privy seal. Elected speaker of the commons in 1661 and held this post until parliament was dissolved in 1666. Although he fell from favour in 1663, Mervyn remained prime serjeant until his death in 1675. See 'Audley Mervyn: lawyer or politician?' in Osborough (ed.), *Explorations in law and history: Irish Legal History Society discourses 1988–1994* (1995).

Metge, Peter. Entered TCD 1758 and the Middle Temple 1762. Called 1769. MP for Ardee 1776–83 and for Ratoath 1783–84. Judge of the admiralty court and then third serjeant 1782–83. A baron of the exchequer 1783–1801. Died 1809. Ball, *Judges*, ii, 221–22.

Molony, Thomas Francis. Born 31 Jan. 1865, called 1887. QC 1899. Fought Toxteth West as a Liberal 1910. Third serjeant and a bencher of King's Inns 1911, second serjeant 1911–12. Solicitor general 1912–13, and attorney general 1913. A judge of the king's bench division 1913–15, a lord justice of appeal 1915–18 and chief justice of Ireland 1918–20. Chief justice of Southern Ireland and then of the Irish Free State 1921–24. Created a baronet 1922, died 1949. W.N. Osborough, 'The title of the last lord chief justice of Ireland', *Ir Jur*, ix (1974), 87. Ball, *Judges*, ii, 383–84. *DNB*.

Moore, Arthur. Born *c.*1764, entered TCD 1781 and the Middle Temple 1786. Called 1788. KC 1798, MP for Tralee 1798–1800. Third serjeant 1801–05. The first appointment as first serjeant 1805, with the new post having precedence over the second and third serjeants and other members of the bar only. First serjeant 1805–16. Chairman of Kilmainham sessions 1816. A justice of the common pleas 1816–39. Died 1846. Ball, *Judges*, ii, 340–41.

Moore, Richard. Born 1783, entered TCD 1798 and the Middle Temple
1804. Called 1806. KC 1827. Third serjeant, a bencher of King's
Inns, then solicitor general 1840. Solicitor general 1840–41,
attorney general 1846–47, a justice of the queen's bench 1847–57,
when he died. Ball, *Judges*, ii, 357–58.

Moriarty, John Francis. Born 17 Dec. 1854. Educated at TCD, entered
the Middle Temple 1875. Called 1877. QC 1900. Third serjeant
1908–10 and first serjeant 1910–13. In 1913 he became solicitor
general, then attorney general, and finally a lord justice of appeal,
which office he held until he died in 1915. Ball, *Judges*, ii, 384.

Neave, William. MP for Tulsk 1692, 1695–99 and 1703–13. Second
serjeant 1696–1708. Prime serjeant 1708–11, dismissed 1711.

Neville, John de. King's serjeant 1293–97.

O'Brien, Ignatius J. Born 31 July 1857, entered the Middle Temple 1879.
Called 1881. QC 1899, a bencher of King's Inns 1907. Third serjeant
1910–11. Second serjeant 1911. Solicitor general 1911–12, attorney
general 1912–13 and chancellor 1913–18. Created a baronet in 1916
and Baron Shandon 1918. Died 1930. Ball, *Judges*, ii, 383. *DNB.*

O'Brien, James. Born 27 Feb. 1806, entered TCD 1822, where he was a
gold medallist. Entered Gray's Inn 1829. Called 1831. QC 1841,
third serjeant 1848–51, a bencher of King's Inns 1849, second
serjeant 1851–58. MP(L) for Limerick 1854–58, a justice of the
queen's bench 1858–82, when he died. Ball, *Judges*, ii, 360.

O'Brien, Peter. Born 29 June 1842, educated TCD and entered the
Middle Temple 1862. Called 1865. Unsuccessful Liberal candidate
for Clare 1879, later a Conservative supporter. QC 1880. Third
serjeant 1884–85, a bencher of King's Inns 1884, second serjeant
1885–87. Solicitor general 1887–88, attorney general 1888–89. Chief
justice of Ireland 1889–1913. Created a baronet 1891 and Baron
O'Brien of Kilfenora 1900. Died 1914. G. O'Brien, *Reminiscences of
the rt hon Lord O'Brien* (1916). Ball, *Judges*, ii, 378. *DNB.*

O'Connor, Charles Andrew. Born 31 Dec. 1854, educated at TCD,
entered the Middle Temple 1876. Called 1878, QC 1894, a bencher
of King's Inns 1896. Third serjeant then first serjeant 1907, first
serjeant 1907–09, solicitor general 1909–11, attorney general
1911–12. Master of the rolls 1912–24 and a justice of the supreme
court of the Irish Free State 1924–25. Died 1928. Ball, *Judges*, ii, 383.

O'Hagan, John. Son-in-law of Lord O'Hagan (below). Born 19 Mar.
1822, entered Lincoln's Inn 1843. Called 1845. QC 1865. A
bencher of King's Inns 1878. Third serjeant 1881, a judicial

commissioner of the court of the Irish Land Commission (with the rank of a justice of the high court) 1881–90, when he died.

O'Hagan, Thomas. Born 1812, entered Gray's Inn 1834. Called 1836. Assistant barrister for Co. Longford 1847–57 and Co. Dublin 1857. QC 1849, second serjeant 1859–60, solicitor general 1860–61, attorney general 1861–65. MP (L) for Tralee 1863–65. A justice of the common pleas 1865–68. Chancellor 1868–74 and 1880–81. Created Baron O'Hagan 1870. Made a knight of St Patrick 1881. Died 1885. J.F. McEldowney, 'Lord O'Hagan (1812–1885): a study of his life and period as lord chancellor of Ireland (1868–1874)', *Ir Jur*, xiv (1979), 360. Daire Hogan, ' "Arrows too sharply pointed": the relations of Lord Justice Christian and Lord O'Hagan, 1868–1874', in McEldowney and O'Higgins (ed.), *The common law tradition*, p. 61. Ball, *Judges*, ii, 364. *DNB*.

O'Loghlen, Sir Colman. Eldest son of Sir Michael O'Loghlen (below). Born 20 Sept. 1819, educated London University. Called 1840. QC 1852. Chairman of Co. Carlow quarter sessions 1856–59 and of Co. Mayo 1859–64. MP (L) for Clare 1863–77. Third serjeant 1865–66 and a bencher of King's Inns 1865. Second serjeant 1866–77. A member of Gladstone's government as judge advocate general 1868–70, a privy councillor 1868. Died 1877.

O'Loghlen, Michael. Born Oct. 1789, entered TCD 1805, and the Middle Temple 1809. Called 1811. KC 1830. Third serjeant 1831–32 (the first roman catholic to be appointed a serjeant since the reign of James II), second serjeant 1832–34 and a bencher of King's Inns 1832. Solicitor general 1834. MP (L) for Dungarvan 1835–36, reappointed solicitor general 1835, attorney general 1835–36. A baron of the exchequer 1836–37, master of the rolls 1837–42, when he died. Created a baronet 1838. Ball, *Judges*, ii, 349–50. *DNB*.

Osborne, John. Second serjeant 1674–80. In 1676, whilst second serjeant, was granted a patent as prime serjeant in reversion to Sir William Davys, and upon Davys's appointment as chief justice of the king's bench in 1680, Osborne became prime serjeant. Dismissed in 1687 under James II but was reappointed in 1690 by William III. MP for Co. Meath 1692 and again dismissed in Nov. 1692. Died later that year.

Owen, Roger. The first king's serjeant. Known to have been appointed between 1261 and 1266 and to have served until his death in 1280.

Packenham, Sir Thomas. Educated TCD, entered Lincoln's Inn 1674. KC 1685, second serjeant 1692–95, prime serjeant 1695–1703, when he died. MP for Augher 1695.

Patterson, Marcus. Born 1712, entered TCD 1732, where he was a scholar. Entered the Middle Temple 1737. Called 1742. KC 1756. MP for Ballinakill 1756–60 and 1761–68, and for Lisburn 1768–70. Third serjeant 1757–64, acted as an assize judge twice in 1750 and again in 1759. Solicitor general 1764–70 and chief justice of the common pleas 1770–87, when he died. Ball, *Judges*, ii, 216–17.

Pennefather, Edward. Born 22 Oct. 1773, entered TCD 1789 and the Middle Temple 1792. Called 1795. KC 1816. Third serjeant 1830–31, second serjeant 1831–32 and first serjeant 1832–35. Solicitor general in 1835 and 1841. Chief justice of the queen's bench 1841–46, and died 1847. Ball, *Judges*, ii, 353–54. *DNB*.

Perrin, Louis. Born 15 Feb. 1782, entered TCD 1796 and the Middle Temple 1804. Called 1806. KC 1827, MP for Dublin 1831 but was unseated. MP for Monaghan 1832–34 and for Cashel 1835–36. Third serjeant 1832–35 and first serjeant 1835. Attorney general 1835–36, a justice of the king's bench 1836–60, and died 1864. Ball, *Judges*, ii, 349. *DNB*.

Petit, William. Served as a king's serjeant 1338–50. Acted as a justice of the justiciar's bench in 1347. He was later pardoned at the request of the earl of Ormond for the death of Robert de Lynham in 1351, was nominated by the countess of Ormond as her attorney in 1355, and appears as chief justice of the justiciar's court in 1359. Ball, *Judges*, i, 83.

Plunkett, Richard. A serjeant at law in England when he crossed to Ireland and served as the king's serjeant 1358–78, also a justice of the bench 1376 and chief justice of the justiciar's court 1388. Chancellor 1388, and died later that year. Ball, *Judges*, i, 88–89.

Plunkett, Thomas Fitz Christopher. King's serjeant 1434–35. Later found acting as a judge of assize in 1450, knighted 1460. Chief justice of the king's bench 1461 and between 1463 and 1468. Ball, *Judges*, i, 180–81.

Ponz, John de. King's serjeant 1292–97. A justice of the bench 1304. Ball, *Judges*, i, 58. Brand, 'The judges of the lordship of Ireland', p. 28, says he served as a serjeant until 1300.

Preston, Robert of. Served as a king's serjeant 1348–58. Chief justice of the bench 1358–78, when he was superseded. Knighted 1361. Acted as keeper of the great seal 1388, and as deputy justiciar 1389. Chancellor of the exchequer 1391, died 1396. Ball, *Judges*, i, 83.

Purdon, Henry. Entered the Middle Temple 1707. KC 1716. Third serjeant 1730–37, when he died.

Reynell, Richard. Entered the Middle Temple 1642 and called to the English bar 1653. Came to Ireland and called to the Irish bar 1658. MP for Athboy 1661. Acted as a judge of assize 1670 and 1672. Second serjeant 1673–74. Knighted 1673 and created a baronet in 1678. A justice of the king's bench 1674–86, when he was superseded. He returned to England and was MP for Ashburton 1690. Returned to Ireland and was chief justice of the king's bench 1691–95 when he was again superseded. Died 1699. Ball, *Judges*, i, 354–55.

Robinson, James. Born 1814, educated at TCD, entered Gray's Inn 1834, called 1836. QC 1852, law adviser 1859. Chairman of quarter sessions for Co. Roscommon 1859–63, Co. Tyrone 1869 and Co. Cavan 1878. A bencher of King's Inns 1870. Third serjeant 1877–80, second serjeant 1880–84 and first serjeant 1884–85. Acted as an assize judge on several occasions as a serjeant. Died 1885.

Rochford, Thomas. Dean of St Patrick's cathedral 1506–22. King's serjeant and solicitor general 1511–15. Appears as a clerk in chancery 1515 and as keeper of the rolls 1520. Died 1522. Ball, *Judges*, i, 192. W.M. Mason, *Historical annals of the collegiate church of St Patrick*, pp. 142–44.

Rowe, Peter. Acted as a king's serjeant 1381–1387. Chief justice of the justiciar's court 1388, when he had custody of the great seal. Served as chief justice until 1395. Reappointed 1397 but was again superseded. Ball, *Judges*, i, 167.

Ryves, Sir Richard. Born 1643, entered TCD 1657 and the Middle Temple 1663. Called to the English bar 1669. Returned to practise in Ireland. Recorder of Kilkenny 1671 and of Dublin 1680. Knighted 1681. Acted as an assize judge between 1682 and 1686. Third serjeant 1683. Second serjeant 1683–1687. Dismissed 1687, restored as second serjeant 1691 and served until 1692. A baron of the exchequer 1692–93, when he died. Ball, *Judges*, ii, 60.

Sambach, William. Recorder of Carrickfergus. Second serjeant 1637–40. MP for Carrickfergus and solicitor general 1640. Supported Charles I in the civil war.

Saunders, Morley. MP for Enniscorthy 1703–14. Second serjeant 1711–12, prime serjeant 1712–14. Acted as a judge of assize 1713. Dismissed at the end of 1714 during a sweeping reconstruction of the Irish judiciary and law officers.

Saunders, Robert. MP for Cavan borough 1692, 1695–99 and 1703–08. Prime serjeant 1703–08, when he died. Acted as an assize judge 1703.

Scott, John. Born 8 June 1739, entered TCD 1756, where he was a scholar. Entered the Middle Temple 1758. Called 1765, KC 1770. MP for Mullingar 1768–83 and for Portarlington 1783–84. Counsel to the board of revenue 1772, solicitor general 1774–77. Acted as an assize judge in 1777 whilst solicitor general. Attorney general 1777–82, when he was dismissed. Prime serjeant 1783–84. Chief justice of the king's bench 1784–98, when he died. Created Baron Earlsfort 1784, Viscount Clonmell 1789 and earl of Clonmell 1793. Ball, *Judges*, ii, 222. *DNB*.

Scott, William. Born *c*.1704. Entered TCD 1723 and the Middle Temple 1729. Called 1732. Recorder of Londonderry 1734–64. MP for Londonderry city 1739–59. Prime serjeant 1757–59. Acted as an assize judge twice in 1750 and again in 1759 whilst prime serjeant. A justice of the king's bench 1759–68 and a baron of the exchequer 1768–76, when he died. Ball, *Judges*, ii, 210.

Sherlock, David. Born 6 Sept. 1814, educated TCD, entered the Middle Temple 1834. Called 1837. A bencher of King's Inns 1866. MP (L) for King's County 1868–80. Third serjeant 1870–77, second serjeant 1877–80 and first serjeant 1880–84, when he died. Acted as an assize judge in 1877 and 1883. Senior crown prosecutor on the Leinster circuit at the time of his death in 1884. Obituary *ILT & SJ*, xviii (1884), 215.

Singleton, Henry. Born 1682, entered TCD 1698 and the Middle Temple 1702. Called 1707. Recorder of Drogheda 1708. MP for Drogheda 1713–14 and 1715–40. Prime serjeant 1726–40. Chief justice of the common pleas 1740–53. Surrendered the chief justiceship in 1753 and was master of the rolls (at that time a non-judicial sinecure) 1754–59, when he died. Ball, *Judges*, ii, 205.

Snetterby, Thomas. King's serjeant 1447–1455.

Somerton, Edward. King's serjeant 1438–47. Acted as counsel for the city of Waterford. Second justice of the king's bench 1447–61. Ball, *Judges*, i, 179.

Staines, John of. King's serjeant 1319–27.

Stanley, Edmund. Born 1760. Entered TCD 1773, where he was a scholar, and the Inner Temple 1780. Called 1782. KC and a bencher of King's Inns 1789. MP for Augher 1790–97 and for Lanesborough 1798–1800. Third serjeant 1791–1801, prime serjeant 1801. Forced to resign 1801 when overwhelmed by debt. Knighted and appointed recorder of Prince of Wales Island (the present-day Pinang in Malaysia) in 1807, where he served until appointed a judge of the supreme court of Madras 1816. Chief justice of Madras 1820–25, when he retired. Died 1843.

Stannard, Eaton. Born *c*.1685, entered TCD 1702 and the Middle Temple 1710. Called 1714, KC and a bencher of King's Inns 1726. Recorder of Dublin 1733–1750. MP for Midleton 1727–57. Acted as an assize judge in 1741. Prime serjeant 1754–57, when he died.

Staunton (or Stanton), John. MP for Galway city 1703–13, 1713–14 and 1715–25. Third serjeant 1712–14, when he was dismissed as a serjeant (together with Morley Saunders and Cliffe). A master in chancery 1725–31, when he died.

Stephens, Sir Richard. Entered Lincoln's Inn 1658. Called 1663. MP for Ardee 1665. Sometime recorder of Waterford and of Clonmel. Knighted 1679. Second serjeant 1680–82, when he was dismissed by Ormond because of his non-conformity. Reappointed as second serjeant 1690. A justice of the king's bench 1690–92, when he died. Ball, *Judges*, ii, 58.

Stock, Joseph. Born *c*.1784, entered TCD 1803. Called 1812. QC 1835, a bencher of King's Inns 1838. MP for Cashel 1838–47, third serjeant 1840–41, second serjeant 1841–42, and first serjeant 1842–51, when he retired. Judge of the court of admiralty (a part-time appointment) whilst a serjeant. Died 1856 or 1857. *1855/20/10*

Sullivan, Alexander Martin. Born 14 Jan. 1871, a journalist in early life. Called 1892, KC 1908. Third serjeant 1912–13, second serjeant 1913–19 and first serjeant 1919. Called to the English bar by the Middle Temple 1899 and became a KC in England 1919. Acted as an assize judge in 1921 when he survived an assassination attempt during Tralee assizes. From the early 1920s he practised in England where he was referred to as serjeant. A bencher of King's Inns and of the Middle Temple. He retired from active practice after the second world war and lived in Dublin until a short time before his death in 1959. The last serjeant at law. Author of *Old Ireland-reminiscences of an Irish KC* (1927), and *The last serjeant* (1952). Obituary *ILT & SJ*, xciii (1959), 31–32.

Sullivan, Edward. Born 10 July 1822, entered TCD 1839 where he was a scholar. Entered Lincoln's Inn 1846. Called 1848. QC 1858, third serjeant 1860–61. A bencher of King's Inns 1861. Second serjeant 1861–65. Law adviser 1862–65. Solicitor general 1865–66. MP (L) for Mallow 1865–70. Attorney general 1868–70. Master of the rolls 1870–83, chancellor 1883–85, when he died. Created a baronet 1881. Ball, *Judges*, ii, 368–69. *DNB*.

Tenison, Thomas. Born 1707, entered TCD 1725 and the Middle Temple 1726. MP for Dunleer 1728–61. Called 1732, a commissioner for revenue appeals 1732–38 and 1741–59. Prime serjeant 1759–61. A justice of the common pleas 1761–79, when he died. Ball, *Judges*, ii, 212.

Tisdall, Phillip. Born 1703, called 1733. MP for Dublin University 1740–60 and for Armagh borough 1761–77. Third serjeant 1741–51. Solicitor general 1751–60, attorney general 1760–77, when he died. Judge of the prerogative court 1745 until his death. As attorney general was a leading figure in the Irish administration. *DNB*.

Toler, John. His date of birth is unclear. *King's Inns admission papers* says he matriculated at TCD on 2 Dec. 1756, which would mean that he was born in either 1739 (Ball, *Judges*, ii, 331–32) or 1740, but *DNB* says he was born on 3 Dec. 1745. Entered TCD 1756, Lincoln's Inn 1761, called 1770. MP for Tralee 1776–83, Philipstown 1783–90 and for Gorey 1790–1800. KC 1781. Third serjeant 1784–87, second serjeant 1787–89. Solicitor general 1789–98, attorney general 1798–1800. Chief justice of the common pleas 1800–27. Created Baron Norbury 1800 and earl of Norbury on his retirement in 1827. Died 1831. Ball, *Judges*, ii, 331–32. *DNB*.

Torrens, Robert. Born 4 Oct. 1774, entered TCD, where he was a scholar, in 1791, and the Middle Temple 1796. Called 1798. KC and chairman of quarter sessions for Co. Dublin 1817. Third serjeant 1822–23 and acted as a chairman of sessions under the Insurrection Act of 1822. A justice of the common pleas 1823–56, when he died. Ball, *Judges*, ii, 343.

Trevers, Peter. Appears as king's serjeant in February 1460, became keeper of the rolls 1461, died *c*.1468. Ball, *Judges*, i, 181–82.

Tyrell, John. A king's serjeant from 1366 until sometime between 1382 and 1385, although he was appointed a justice of the justiciar's court in 1376, and so may not have served as a serjeant for part of this period. Chief justice of the bench 1386–95, when he died. Ball, *Judges*, i, 88.

Uriell, James. King's serjeant 1406. Chief baron of the exchequer 1419–20, died *c*.1423. Ball, *Judges*, i, 174.

Vandeleur, Thomas Burton. Born *c*.1767. Entered TCD 1783 and Lincoln's Inn 1785. Called 1790. KC 1816. Acted as a judge of assize 1820. Third serjeant 1821–22, a justice of the king's bench 1822–35, when he died. Ball, *Judges*, ii, 343.

Warren, Richard Benson. Born *c*.1783, entered TCD 1800. Called 1806. KC 1824. A bencher of King's Inns 1839. Third serjeant 1841–42, second serjeant 1842–48, when he died.

White, Nicholas. Appears as a king's serjeant in 1393.

White, Richard. Appears as a king's serjeant in Leinster and Munster for 31 days in 1359 whilst Richard Plunkett was absent.

Witherington, John. Called 1706. Third serjeant 1714–16, second serjeant 1716–18, when he died.

Wood, Attiwell. Born *c*.1728, entered TCD 1744, the Middle Temple 1747, called 1753. MP for Castlemartyr 1769–76 and Clonakilty 1776–84. Third serjeant 1777–79, second serjeant 1779–84, when he died.

Woulfe, Stephen. Born 1789, entered TCD 1808 and the Middle Temple 1812. Called 1814, KC 1833. MP (L) for Cashel 1835–38. Third serjeant 1835–36. Bencher of King's Inns 1836. Solicitor general 1836–37, attorney general 1837–38. Chief baron of the exchequer 1838–40, when he died. Ball, *Judges*, ii, 351. *DNB*.

Payments to the serjeants and law officers at the Union

BY THE ACT 40 Geo. III, c. 34, of the Irish parliament, provision was made for the appointment of commissioners to assess claims lodged by various office holders whose offices were to be discontinued by the Union (accomplished in Ireland by the act 40 Geo. III, c.38 and in Great Britain by the act 39 & 40 Geo. III, c.67), or were to be diminished in value with the disappearance of certain functions connected with the Irish parliament. The commissioners received sworn evidence from various officials in support of these claims, and ultimately assessed compensation in those claims which they accepted. Details of the amounts claimed are to be found in the British Parliamentary Papers for 1805 (H.C. 1805, vii). Compensation was payable to all those who held office when the Union came into effect on 1 January 1801, and appears to have been assessed upon the basis of payments made in each of the four years before that, namely 1797, 1798, 1799 and 1800. The amounts paid are also to be found in *Liber munerum publicorum Hiberniae*, part vii, pp. 178–81, and certain fees payable to the law officers in respect of offices granted by letters patent are detailed at p. 186. These fees were paid in respect of dates after 1801, and therefore seem to have continued for a time at least, as they were being paid to the attorney general and solicitor general in 1803.

From these sources it is possible to establish that substantial amounts were paid to the prime serjeant, attorney general, solicitor general and the counsel to the revenue. No payments seem to have been made to the second or third serjeants. Some of the fees were very large, and were paid annually. For example, the prime serjeant, attorney general and solicitor general were paid £700 each year by the solicitor to the commissioners of customs for settling money bills to be laid before parliament. Other payments were irregular, or were paid to certain office holders only. Because the attorney general received a fee when a new peerage was created, or when an existing peer received a step in the peerage, the large number of new peerages, or promotions in the peerage, that were granted in the period leading up to the Union, meant that significant amounts were received by the attorney general under this head.

Some evidence of the frequency with which the serjeants served as assize judges also appears in these claims. As two judges were required to attend parliament when it was in session to advise both houses, replacement judges had to be found from amongst the law officers. The exception was the attorney general, who did not go out, presumably because this was felt to be improper since he was responsible for crown prosecutions. John Stewart, the attorney general, testified to the commissioners that the prime serjeant had lost fees amounting to £400 a year for two circuits, less 100 guineas expenses. He said that the prime serjeant always went on the spring circuit, implying that one of the two circuits was as a replacement for a judge on parliamentary duty. When the prime serjeant was unavailable, the solicitor general and the other two serjeants were called upon, as they were also included in the general commission.

In the following tables the fees have been converted to £ *s. d.* as necessary.

1 By the solicitor to the commissioners of customs for preparing and settling money bills each year.

	£	*s.*	*d.*
Prime serjeant	700	0	0
Attorney general	700	0	0
Solicitor general	700	0	0
First counsel to the revenue	700	0	0

2 By the solicitor to the revenue board for perusing and settling revenue bills.

	1797			1798			1799			1800		
	£	*s.*	*d.*	£	*s.*	*d.*	£	*s.d.*		£	*s.*	*d.*
Prime serjeant[1]	398	2	6	227	10	0	227	10	0	626	2	6
Attorney general	391	2	6	227	10	0	227	10	0	626	2	6
Solicitor general	398	2	6	227	10	0	227	10	0	626	2	6
First counsel to the revenue	1,080	12	6	227	10	0	227	10	0	1,194	17	6

1 At p. 2 the prime serjeant is credited with two separate fees for preparing revenue bills in 1800, but no fee appears for doing so in 1799. The other three counsel have fees for 1799 and only one fee for 1800. It seems probable that the first fee for the prime serjeant was for 1799 and not 1800, and that there was a misprint. The more likely figure is given in the text.

3 By the law agent to the general post office for perusing the annual duty bill.

	£	s.	d.
Prime serjeant	52	10	0
Attorney general	52	10	0
Solicitor general	52	10	0

4 By the solicitor to the stamp office for preparing stamp bills annually since 1796.

	£	s.	d.
Prime serjeant	73	10	0
Attorney general	73	10	0
Solicitor general	73	10	0

5 By the crown solicitor for preparing various bills for parliament.

	1797			1798			1799			1800		
	£	s.	d.	£	s.	d.	£	s.	d.	£	s.	d.
Prime serjeant										234	2	6
Attorney general	11	7	6	56	17	6	85	6	3	262	11	3
Solicitor general										251	3	9

6 In dormant peerage cases the claimant (and cross-claimant, if there was one) paid the attorney general a fee on the reference itself, and on further appearances, except the second. The attorney general was also retained, and paid, by both the crown and the claimant (and cross-claimant, if there was one). The prime serjeant and solicitor general were only paid upon the reference itself. All fees seem to have been paid to the law officers through the crown solicitor.

	attorney general			prime serjeant			solicitor general		
	£	s.	d.	£	s.	d.	£	s.	d.
Earl of Ormond's claim	228	17	6	79	12	6	79	12	6
Lord Trimlestown's claim	341	17	6	179	12	6	179	12	6
Lord Dillon's claim	179	12	6	79	12	6	79	12	6
Roscommon peerage case	115	10	0						

7 Fees were paid to the attorney general for fiants relating to a number of posts in the ordnance department, and on entry to, or promotion in, the peerage. Where there was a remainder attached to the peerage, the fee appropriate to that rank was also payable for each remainder.

Fees payable upon:	£	s.	d.
– fiants in the ordnance dept	5	4	$8^{1}/_{2}$
– fiant for the master general	5	10	$1^{1}/_{2}$
– appointments to escheatorships (to resign from the commons)	3	0	0
– baronetcies	9	0	0
– baron	15	0	0
– viscount	25	0	0
– earl	35	0	0
– marquis	45	0	0
Average over four years for fees payable under all of these heads	565	13	$3^{1}/_{2}$

8 Fees were paid for offices granted by patent, presumably for offices other than those at 7 above. As the same figure appears for a number of years, it would seem probable that the fees had been commuted for a fixed annual sum and were paid for some time after the Union. No record has been traced for the payment of these fees in later years and it may well be the case that they lapsed, at least in the prime serjeant's case, when that post was abolished after Browne's death in 1805. No evidence has been found to suggest that either the second or third serjeant received such fees and there is a statement at *Liber munerum publicorum Hiberniae*, part vii, p. 186 that Serjeant Moore did not receive such fees. Moore was third serjeant at the time.

		£	s.	d.
Stewart, attorney general	(n.d.)	265	18	2
Smith, solicitor general	(n.d.)	265	18	2
O'Grady, solicitor general	(1803)	265	18	2
Plunkett, solicitor general	(1803)	265	18	2
Stanley, prime serjeant	(July/Dec. 1801)	277	11	6
Browne, prime serjeant		277	11	6

CONCLUSION

These figures suggest that the minimum which the prime serjeant received for parliamentary business was £826 a year. If one adds to that patent fees at £277 11*s*. 6*d*., and one circuit a year at £150 net, the annual total was probably in the region of £1,250. There was also the prospect of substantially more in some years from fees for other parliamentary bills, peerage cases and a second circuit as an assize judge, bringing the total up to as much as £1,600 or £1,700 in a good year. In such an event, the monetary value of the office was worth about the same as that of solicitor general, but appreciably less than that of the attorney general who could easily make £2,000 in a good year. Taking one year with the next, the compensation awarded by the commissioners probably represents a fair average of the annual value of each of the offices given below to the holders of those offices.

		£	*s.*	*d.*
Compensation:	attorney general	2,086	5	9
	solicitor general	1,379	7	1
	prime serjeant	1,375	15	0

In each case, there would be further fees for purely legal, non-parliamentary, work such as opinions and court appearances, mostly in criminal trials.

APPENDIX TWO

Professional earnings of Thomas Langlois Lefroy, 1799–1831

THOMAS LANGLOIS LEFROY was one of the leading members of the Irish bar for the greater part of his career until he was appointed a baron of the exchequer in 1841. Following a distinguished under-graduate career, he graduated from Trinity College, Dublin, in 1795, but his health broke down and he was not called to the bar until 1797. In 1798 he joined the yeomanry and took part in the fighting during the 1798 rebellion.[1] He married and seems to have started practice in Hilary term of 1799 when the entries commence in his fee book.

With the exception of 1820–1822, all his fee books have survived for the entire period from 1799 until 1831. They are amongst the Lefroy papers at Carrigglas Manor, Co. Longford, which he built on an estate he leased, and then bought, from Trinity College. The fee books are probably a unique record of the earnings of a successful member of the Irish bar over the first three decades of the nineteenth century. In 1831, the entries become spasmodic, before petering out, with the last regular entries being made in his own hand at the beginning of Trinity term of 1832. Why this happened is a mystery. Either Lefroy stopped keeping a record, which seems surprising, given his business-like approach before then, or his later fee books have not survived. Whilst the latter is possible, given the missing book for the period 1820–1822, such an explanation is difficult to reconcile with the spasmodic entries of 1831 and 1832.

The books themselves follow a common format and appear to list every fee Lefroy received as counsel during the period covered by each book. No entries appear for fees or allowances paid for service as an assize judge, although we know Lefroy served in this capacity on several occasions in the 1820s. Each fee is entered, either by term

---

1   The Lefroy MSS have been calendared by Dr A.P.W. Malcomson of the Public Record Office of Northern Ireland. A detailed account of Lefroy's life, as well as his legal and political career, is to be found in Dr Malcomson's introduction to PRONI T. 3746.

or by date, followed by the names of the parties, a brief description of the nature of the case and the fee received.

Lefroy kept a meticulous record of his fees, and the value of these records to the legal historian is that not only do they provide a record of his growing success at the Irish bar at the beginning of the nineteenth century, but they also provide a detailed picture of the fees paid for the different types of work he did. Perhaps the most interesting detail to emerge is that Lefroy was almost always paid for each item of work that he did in a case at the time, rather than being paid for all work done at the end of the case. Even at the height of his success in 1829, almost all the fees are for amounts of less than five guineas, and are rarely more than ten guineas. As his income in that year, from the beginning of Hilary term to the end of the year, was £2,928, it is evident that he dealt with an enormous volume of work.

VOLUME 1: 1799–1806

The first nine entries cover the Hilary, Easter and Trinity terms and the Limerick summer assizes, and come to £18 4s. 0d. The first fee was a brief fee of £3 8s. 3d. Fees for interlocutory applications were £1 2s. 9d. A nisi prius brief at Limerick was £2 5s. 6d., and the same fee was marked in two other cases. Until 1806, most entries are for one of these three amounts, although there are some instances where larger fees were charged. £5 13s. 9d. appears on several occasions, opposite entries such as 'marriage settlement', or other types of drafting work. Nevertheless, there are signs that Lefroy was already making his mark as there are a small number of large fees. In two cases, fees of £113 15s. 0d. are shown, as is a fee of 100 guineas in a case involving the bishop of Limerick in the summer of 1803. Lefroy had been educated by Dean Burroughs in Limerick, and, like many a young junior, obviously got some work on circuit on the strength of his local connections, with most of his circuit appearances in Limerick. For example, at the spring assizes of 1802, there is an entry 'case of vicar's choral at Limrk £1 2s. 9d.' The picture is of a slow, but steady, start, with total earnings by the end 1799, his first year of practice, of £27 8s. 9d. By 13 June 1800, he had earned £70 10s. 0d., and at the end of that year he noted 'due £100 2s. 0d.'

VOLUME 2: 1806–1813

By now, Lefroy was very busy, and there are 105 entries between August and the end of December 1806, mostly for small fees. Two were for 10 guineas, together with one of 15 guineas on appeal, and the same fee on a case for the duke of Leinster. Lefroy was obviously making a name for himself. Most of his appearances were in Dublin, with occasional entries for nisi prius cases or arbitrations, but by this time he was a leading equity practitioner, and his income continued to grow. In 1808, he received just over 1,200 guineas.

VOLUME 3: 1813–1815

During this period, Lefroy was indisputably a very successful member of the bar, and this is shown by the volume of business recorded. This fee book contains 97 pages and, with a random sample giving an average of 20/25 entries per page, this would suggest 1,900/2,000 entries. On the fly leaf are two pencil notations, '2,900' and '3,351 1 6', which may well be the total income for two of these years.

VOLUME 4: 1815–1817

The entries show the same pattern as volume 3, and, although Lefroy took silk in 1816, there appears to have been no falling off in work.

VOLUME 5: TRINITY 1817–JULY 1819

The fees for what is incorrectly described as Hilary vacation of 1818, when it should be Hilary term and Hilary vacation (as in volume 7), amounted to £889 12s. 0d. This period covered a quarter of the legal year, and would suggest an annual income of £3,560 if maintained throughout the year.

VOLUME 6: 1819–1822

This volume is missing.

VOLUME 7: 1822–1824

This volume follows the same format as earlier years, save that at the rear of the book are four loose fee notes listing retainers at £2 5s. 6d., a standard fee that seems to have changed to £2 2s. 0d. by 1826.

VOLUME 8: 1824–1826

The entries in this volume follow a similar pattern to previous years. There are many retainers, indicating that clients were anxious to ensure that Lefroy would be available, if required, in a particular case.

VOLUME 9: TRINITY 1826–HILARY VACATION 1828

This volume follows the same pattern as volume 8.

VOLUME 10: HILARY TERM 1828 TO END OF 1829

The entries for 1829 show that Lefroy was still extremely successful, earning £2,928 in that year.

Patent appointing Thomas O'Hagan
second serjeant at law

Patent[1] granting unto Thomas O'Hagan Esq the
Office or Place of Second Serjeant at Law in
Ireland in the room of Walter Berwick Esq

VICTORIA BY THE GRACE OF GOD
of

the United Kingdom of Great Britain and Ireland Queen Defender
of the Faith and soforth to all unto whom these presents shall come
– Greeting. Know ye that we of Our Special Grace certain knowledge
and mere motion by and with the advice and consent of Our Lords
Justices General and General Governors of the part of Our said United
Kingdom called Ireland Have given and granted and by these presents
We do Give and Grant unto Thomas O'Hagan Esquire one of our
Counsel learned in the Law in that part of Our said United Kingdom
called Ireland the Office and place of our Second Serjeant at Law in
that part of Our said United Kingdom called Ireland in the room of
Walter Berwick Esquire now appointed one of the Judges of the
Court of Bankruptcy and Insolvency in Ireland aforesaid. And Him
the said Thomas O'Hagan Second Serjeant at Law in Ireland
aforesaid We have created made constituted and ordained and by
these presents we do create make constitute and ordain. And
Moreover of Our more abundant special Grace certain knowledge
and mere motion by and with the advice and consent aforesaid We
have given and granted and by these presents We do Give and Grant
unto the said Thomas O'Hagan for the Execution and exercise of the
said Office as many of the like and as great fees Salaries profits
perquisites and advantages to the said Office of Second Serjeant at
Law in Ireland aforesaid in any sort belonging or appertaining and in

1   13 July 1859. PRONI D 2777/11/1.

as full and ample manner to all intents and purposes as the said Walter Berwick or any other person or persons having or exercising the said Office or place of Our Second Serjeant at Law in Ireland aforesaid hath or have had received or enjoyed for the Execution of the said Office or by virtue of the said Office ought to have had received or enjoyed To have hold enjoy and Exercise the said office together with all and singular the fees Salaries Profits preeminences commodities emoluments and advantages whatsoever as well ordinary as extraordinary to the said Office or place belonging or appertaining by any means unto the said Thomas O'Hagan during Our pleasure. And Our further Will and Pleasure is and We do Grant that these Our Letters Patent or the Enrolment hereof shall be in all things firm good valid sufficient and effectual in the Law against Us as well in all Our Courts in Ireland aforesaid or elsewhere any ordinance provision or any other thing course or matter whatsoever in any way notwithstanding And Lastly Our further Will is by and by these presents We declare Our Royal Pleasure to be that Our Letters Patent granted unto the said Walter Berwick of Second Serjeant at Law in Ireland aforesaid may be revoked determined cancelled and of no effect and the same by these presents We do revoke determine Cancel and make of no effect Provided Always that these Our Letters Patent be enrolled in the Rolls of Our High Court of Chancery in Ireland aforesaid within the space of six Calendar months next ensuing the date of these presents. In Witness whereof we have caused these Our Letters to be made Patent. Witness George William Frederick Earl of Carlisle Our Lieutenant General and General Governor of Ireland at Dublin the thirteenth day of July in the twenty third year of Our Reign.

Bibliography

MANUSCRIPT SOURCES

House of Lords Record Office
  Bonar Law Papers. Folder 83/4/14

British Library
  Hardwicke Papers, Add. MS 35,372
  Hardwicke Papers, Add. MS 35,717
  Hardwicke Papers, Add. MS 35,718
  Hardwicke Papers, Add. MS 35,726
  Hardwicke Papers, Add. MS 35,732
  Hardwicke Papers, Add. MS 35,750
  Hardwicke Papers, Add. MS 35,751
  Hardwicke Papers, Add. MS 35,760
  Peel Papers, Add. MS. 40,426
  Peel Papers, Add. MS. 40,486
  Stowe MS, 208. f.364

Carrigglas Manor, Co Longford
  Lefroy MS H/14 and H/18

Dublin Corporation, Gilbert Collection
  Vols 29, 32 and 36 (Robinson papers)

National Library of Ireland
  MS 2055 (Archbishop King's letters, 1690–1715)

National Archives of Ireland
  Calendar of plea rolls, 13 vols
  R/C 7/1, 7/2 and 7/4
  Calendar of memoranda rolls, 43 vols
  R/C 8/5 and 8/10
  Ferguson MS, iv
  Chief Crown Solicitor 1865/51
  Official Papers /527/16
  Official Papers /792

Public Record Office of Northern Ireland
  T.755/1, Pelham papers (BL, Add. MS 33,100)
  T.2915/11/48, Bedford MS

T.3502/1, Buckinghamshire MS
T.3158, Chatsworth MS
T.3294, Glenbervie MS
T.2863, Pelham MS
T.3319, Pitt/Prettyman papers
T.3019, Wilmot papers
T.2855/1, Willes, Miscellaneous observations on Ireland 1750–60
Mic/236/1, 236/2, 236/3 (Willes MS)
D 2777, O'Hagan MS

Surrey Record Office, Guildford Muniment Room

Midleton MS 1248/1

The Honorable Society of King's Inns

Green Book (admission of benchers, 1712–41)
Admission of benchers, 1741–92
Entry of benchers, 1794–1864
The reminiscences of Lord Shandon, lord chancellor of Ireland

Trinity College Dublin

Donoughmore MS, /6/2

PRINTED SOURCES

A repertory of the inrolments of the patent rolls of chancery in Ireland; commencing with the reign of King James I. ed. J.C. Erck. Vol. 1, Dublin, 1846.

Alumni Dublinenses: a register of students, graduates, professors and provosts of Trinity College in the University of Dublin. ed. G.D. Burtchaell and T.U. Sadlier. 2nd ed. Dublin, 1935.

Analecta Hibernica, no. 2 (1931).

    no. 32 (1986).

A roll of the proceedings of the king's council in Ireland, 1392–93. ed. James Graves. Rolls Series, 1877.

British Parliamentary Papers. H.C. 1805, vii.

M. Bodkin (ed.). 'Notes on the Irish parliament in 1773', in *RIA Proc*, xlviii–xlix (1942–44), sect. C, 145.

Calendar of the Carew manuscripts preserved in the archiepiscopal library at Lambeth, 1575–1588. 6 vols. London, 1867–73.

'Calendar of Christ Church Deeds'. *P.R.I. rep. D.K.* 20.

Calendar of Ormond deeds. ed. Edmund Curtis. 6 vols. Dublin, 1932–43.

Calendar of the Orrery papers. ed. E. MacLysaght. Dublin, 1941.

Calendar of the patent rolls (Ireland).

Calendar of the state papers relating to Ireland.

Chartularies of St Mary's abbey, Dublin, with the register of its house at Dunbrody, and annals of Ireland. ed. J.T. Gilbert. Rolls Series, 1884.

Commons' journals, Ireland. 1796 ed.

Crede Mihi: the most ancient register book of the archbishops of Dublin before the Reformation. ed. J.T. Gilbert. Dublin, 1897.

Dublin Gazette.

Eighteenth century Irish official papers in Great Britain-private collections. vol. 2. Belfast, 1990.

Extents of Irish monastic possessions, 1540–1541. ed. N.B. White. Dublin, 1943.

Hayden's Book of Dignities. 3rd ed. London, 1894.

Hughes, J.L.J. *Patentee officers in Ireland, 1173–1826.* Dublin, 1960.

HMC. *12th. Rep.* App. ix.

Irish cartularies of Llanthony Prima and Secunda. ed. E. St J. Brooks. Dublin, 1955.

Irish historical documents 1172–1922. ed. T.C. Curtis and R.B. McDowell. London, 1943.

King's Inns admission papers 1607–1867. ed. Edward Keane, P. Beryl Phair and Thomas U. Sadlier. Dublin, 1982.

Letters and papers, foreign and domestic, Henry VIII. 21 vols. London, 1862–1932.

Letters of the earl of Essex, lord lieutenant of Ireland 1675. London, 1770.

Liber munerum publicorum Hiberniae. ed. Rowley Lascelles. 2 vols. London, 1852.

Lords' journals, Ireland.

New Annual Register for 1805. London, 1806.

Parliamentary election results in Ireland 1801–1922. ed. Brian M. Walker. Dublin, 1978.

Prince of printers, the letters of George Faulkner. ed. R.E. Ward. Lexington, Kentucky, 1972.

Return of members of parliament, part II. London, 1878.

Rotuli patentium et clausorum cancellariae Hiberniae calendarium. ed. Tresham. Dublin 1828.

Sayles, G.O. (ed.). 'Contemporary sketches of the Irish house of commons in 1782'. *RIA Proc*, lvi (1954), sect. C.

—— *Documents on the affairs of Ireland before the king's council.* Dublin, 1979.

—— *Select cases in the court of king's bench in the reign of Edward III, vol. 5.* (Selden Society, vol. 76.)

State papers Henry VIII, ii.

Statute rolls of the parliament of Ireland–reign of King Henry the Sixth (vol. 2 of the early Irish statutes). ed. H.F. Berry. Dublin, 1910.

Statute rolls of the parliament of Ireland–Edward IV (vol. 3 of the early Irish statutes). ed. H.F. Berry. Dublin, 1914.

The correspondence of Jonathan Swift. ed. Harold Williams. 5 vols. Oxford, 1963–65.

The earl of Strafford's letters and dispatches. ed. William Knowler. 2 vols. London, 1739.

The Irish parliament, 1775. ed. William Hunt. Dublin and London, 1907.

The state letters of Henry, earl of Clarendon. 2 vols. Oxford, 1765.

Thom's Irish almanac and official directory.

SECONDARY SOURCES: BOOKS

Baker, J.H. *The legal profession and the common law.* London, 1986.
—— *The order of the serjeants at law.* London, 1984.
Ball, F.E. *The judges in Ireland 1221–1921,* 2 vols. London, 1926.
Barnard, T.C. *Cromwellian Ireland: English government and reform in Ireland 1649–1660.* Oxford, 1975.
Blackburne, Edward. *Life of the rt hon Francis Blackburne, late lord chancellor of Ireland.* London, 1874.
Bolton, G.C. *The passing of the Irish Act of Union: a study in parliamentary politics.* Oxford, 1966.
Bradshaw, Brendan. *The dissolution of the religious orders in Ireland under Henry VIII.* Cambridge, 1974.
—— *The Irish constitutional revolution of the sixteenth century.* Cambridge, 1979.
Brand, Paul. *The origins of the English legal profession.* Oxford, 1992.
Burns, Robert E. *Irish parliamentary politics in the eighteenth century.* 2 vols. Washington DC, 1989–90.
Canny, N.P. *From reformation to restoration:Ireland, 1534–1660.* Dublin, 1987.
Carte, T. *A history of the life of James, duke of Ormonde from his birth in 1610 to his death in 1638.* 3 vols. London, 1735–36.
Casey, J.P. *The office of the attorney general in Ireland.* Dublin, 1980.
Delany, V.T.H. *Christopher Palles, lord chief baron of her majesty's court of exchequer in Ireland 1874–1914, his life and times.* Dublin, 1960.
Dictionary of national biography.
Dunlop, Robert. *Ireland under the commonwealth: being a selection of documents relating to the government of Ireland from 1651 to 1659.* 2 vols. Manchester, 1913.
Edwards, J.Ll.J. *The law officers of the crown.* London,1964.
Ellis, S.G. *Tudor Ireland: crown, community and the conflict of culture 1470–1603.* London, 1985.
—— *Reform and revival, English government in Ireland, 1470–1534.* Royal Historical Society studies in history, vol. 47, London, 1986.
Foster, R.F. *Modern Ireland 1600–1972.* London, 1989.
Hand, G.J. *English law in Ireland, 1290–1324.* Cambridge, 1967.
Kearney, H.F. *Strafford in Ireland, 1633–41.* Manchester, 1959.
Keeton, G.W. *Trial for treason.* London, 1959.
Kelly, James. *Prelude to Union: Anglo-Irish politics in the 1780s.* Cork, 1992.
Kenny Colum. *King's Inns and the kingdom of Ireland: the Irish 'inn of court', 1541–1800.* Dublin, 1992.
King, William. *The state of the protestants in Ireland under the late King James' government.* 3rd ed. London, 1692.
Lefroy, Thomas. *Memoir of Chief Justice Lefroy.* Dublin, 1871.
Lynch, William. *A view of the legal institutions, honorary hereditary offices, and feudal baronies established in Ireland during the reign of Henry II.* London, 1830.
Lodge, John. *The peerage of Ireland.* ed. Mervyn Archdall. 7 vols. Dublin, 1789.
McBride, Lawrence, *The greening of Dublin Castle: the transformation of bureaucratic and judicial personnel in Ireland 1892–1922.* Washington DC, 1991.

McDowell, R.B. *The Irish administration 1800–1914.* London, 1964.

McNeill, D.B. *Irish passenger steamship services.* Newton Abbot, 1971.

Mason, W.M. *The history and antiquities of the collegiate and cathedral church of St Patrick, near Dublin, from its foundation in 1190, to the year 1819.* Dublin, 1820.

Moody, T.W., Martin, F.X. and Byrne, F.J. (ed.). *A new history of Ireland: ix.* Oxford, 1984.

O'Brien, Gerard. *Anglo-Irish politics in the age of Grattan and Pitt.* Dublin, 1987.

O'Flanagan, J.R. *The Munster circuit, tales, trials and traditions.* London, 1880.

Otway-Ruthven, A.J. *A history of medieval Ireland.* 2nd ed. London, 1980.

Pawlisch, H.S. *Sir John Davies and the conquest of Ireland: a study in legal imperialism.* Cambridge, 1985.

Richardson, H.G. and Sayles, G.O. *The administration of Ireland, 1172–1377.* Dublin, 1963.

—— *Parliaments and councils of medieval Ireland.* Dublin, 1947.

—— *The Irish parliament in the middle ages.* Philadelphia, 1952.

Shiel, R.L. *Sketches of the Irish bar.* 2 vols. New York, 1854.

Simms, J.G. *Jacobite Ireland, 1685–91.* London, 1969.

Smyth, C.J. *Chronicle of the law officers of Ireland.* London and Dublin, 1839.

Sullivan, A.M. *Old Ireland: reminiscences of an Irish KC.* London, 1927.

—— *The last serjeant.* London, 1952.

Urwick, William. *The early history of Trinity College, Dublin 1591–1660.* Dublin, 1892.

SECONDARY SOURCES: ARTICLES AND
COMPOSITE WORKS

Ball, F.E. 'Some notes on the Irish judiciary in the reign of Charles II 1660–85', in *Journal of the Cork Historical and Archaeological Society, 2nd series,* ix (1903).

Bartlett, Thomas, and Hayton, D.W. (ed.). *Penal era and golden age: essays in Irish history, 1690–1800.* Belfast, 1979.

Brand, Paul. 'The birth and early development of a colonial judiciary: the judges of the lordship of Ireland, 1210–1377', in W.N. Osborough (ed.), *Explorations in law and history: Irish Legal History Society discourses 1988–1994.* Dublin, 1995.

—— 'The early history of the legal profession in Ireland, 1250–1350', in Daire Hogan and W.N. Osborough (ed.), *Brehons, serjeants and attorneys, studies in the history of the Irish legal profession.* Dublin, 1990.

Edwards, R.D. 'The Irish reformation parliament of Henry VIII', in *Historical Studies: VI,* ed. T.W. Moody. London, 1968.

Falkiner, C. Litton. 'Correspondence of Archbishop Stone and the Duke of Newcastle'. *EHR,* xx (1905).

Gillespie, Raymond. 'The end of an era: Ulster and the outbreak of the 1641 rising', in Ciaran Brady and Raymond Gillespie (ed.), *Natives and newcomers: the making of Irish colonial society, 1534–1641.* Dublin, 1986.

Hart, A.R. 'Sir Audley Mervyn, lawyer or politician?' in W.N. Osborough (ed.), *Explorations in law and history: Irish Legal History Society discourses 1989–1994*. Dublin, 1995.

Hayden, Mary. 'The origin and development of heads of bills in the Irish parliament'. *RSAI Jn*, lv (1925).

Heuston, R.F.V. 'Legal history and the author: some practical problems of authorship', in W.N. Osborough (ed.), *The Irish Legal History Society: inaugural addresses*. Dublin,1989.

Hill, Jacqueline. 'The legal profession and the defence of the *ancien régime* in Ireland, 1790–1840', in Daire Hogan and W.N. Osborough (ed.), *Brehons, serjeants and attorneys: studies in the history of the Irish legal profession*. Dublin, 1990.

Hogan, Daire. ' "Arrows too sharply pointed": the relations of Lord Justice Christian and Lord O'Hagan, 1868–1874', in J.F. McEldowney and Paul O'Higgins (ed.), *The common law tradition: essays in Irish legal history*. Dublin, 1990.

McCavitt, John ' "Good planets in their several spheares" – the establishment of the assize circuits in early seventeenth-century Ireland', in *Ir Jur*, xxiv (1989).

McEldowney, J.F. 'Lord O'Hagan (1812–1888): a study of his life and period as lord chancellor of Ireland (1868–1874)'. *Ir Jur*, xiv (1979).

McGuire, J.I. 'The Dublin convention, the protestant community and the emergence of an ecclesiastical settlement in 1660' in *Parliament and Community* (Historical Studies: XIV), ed. A. Cosgrove and J.I. McGuire. Belfast, 1983.

—— 'The Irish parliament of 1692', in Bartlett & Hayton (ed.), *Penal era and golden age*.

Malcomson, A.P.W. 'The parliamentary traffic of this country', in Bartlett & Hayton (ed.), *Penal era and golden age*.

O'Donovan, Declan. 'The money bill dispute of 1753', in Bartlett & Hayton (ed.), *Penal era and golden age*.

Quinn, D.B. in Art Cosgrove (ed.), *A new history of Ireland: ii*. Oxford, 1987.

THESIS

Ellis, S.G. 'The administration of the lordship of Ireland under the early tudors'. Ph.D. thesis. Queen's University, Belfast, 1979.

NEWSPAPERS AND LEGAL JOURNALS

Belfast Newsletter.
Dublin Evening Mail.
Freeman's Journal.
Gentleman's Magazine, 1835 and 1844.

Irish Times.
Irish Law Times and Solicitors' Journal.
Law Recorder.
Law Times.

Index

The Irish Legal History Society

Established in 1988 to encourage the study and advance the knowledge of the history of Irish law, especially by the publication of original documents and of works relating to the history of Irish law, including its institutions, doctrines and personalities, and the reprinting or editing of works of sufficient rarity or importance.